The
MARKET
GURUS

Stock Investing Strategies You Can Use
from Wall Street's Best

John Reese
Todd Glassman

Dearborn™
Trade Publishing

A **Kaplan Professional** Company

Vice President and Publisher: Cynthia A. Zigmund
Editorial Director: Donald J. Hull
Senior Managing Editor: Jack Kiburz
Interior Design: Lucy Jenkins
Cover Design: Design Solutions
Typesetting: the dotted i

© 2002 by John Reese and Todd Glassman

Published by Dearborn Trade Publishing, a Kaplan Professional Company

Printed in the United States of America

02 03 04 10 9 8 7 6 5 4 3 2 1

Library of Congress Cataloging-in-Publication Data

Reese, John, 1953-
   The market gurus : stock investing strategies you can use from Wall Street's best / John Reese, Todd Glassman.
      p.   cm.
   Includes index.
   ISBN 0-7931-4595-3 (6x9 hardcover)
   1. Investments—Case studies. 2. Capitalists and financiers—Case studies.
I. Glassman, Todd. II. Title.
HG4521 .R37 2001
332.63'22—dc21

                                                                2001002728

CONTENTS

ACKNOWLEDGMENTS

Thanks to: Cindy Zigmund, vice president and publisher at Dearborn Trade Publishing, for encouraging us to write this book; Alan Horowitz, a gifted writer whose assistance was invaluable in the creation of this book; the founding team of Validea.com, Keith Ferry, Justin Carbonneau, Keith Guerraz, Jack Forehand, Dean Coca, and Norman Eng for the many long and enjoyable nights in the basement; and all the other members and interns who contributed heart and soul to making the company successful.

We certainly wish to acknowledge the gurus that are the basis of this book. In the process of distilling their published wisdom into a sequence of instructions, we are sure to have made mistakes in some cases and intentional simplifications in others. We accept full responsibility for this and gladly will receive comments and criticisms for the next printing if you e-mail us at jreese@validea.com.

John: I acknowledge the many enthusiastic supporters of Validea's promise and mission who also backed their enthusiasm with investments and/or exceptionally wise advice—Henry Siegel, Mark Hernandez, Nenad Marovac, Robert Odell, Dan Bricklin, Marc Strausberg, Mark Torrington, Troy Anderson, Barney Pell, David Grossman, Alan Meckler, Jon Abbey, Jerry Bobruff, Brad Feld, Ian Warhaftig, Frank Lecce, Gregory Speer, Alex Crutchfield, Mark Rosenblatt, Mark Oldman, Tom Hodgman, Chris Alden, Frank Lallos, Bob Frankston, Matthew Shevach, Adam Anhang, and Pat Farrell; the support and understanding of Ellen, Michael, Daniel, and Heather Reese during intensive periods of writing and editing; my Harvard Business School professors, Michael Porter, Mitch Madique, Charles Kelso, Jim Cash, Myra Hart, and Bill Sahlman; my friends, Benjamin Ng, Ed Esber, Tetsuto Numata, Janet Lent, Jerry Horowitz, Richard Horowitz, Nicole Mills, and the memory of my elementary school friend Stanley Foss; and for my mother, Annette Reese, and in memory of my father, Michael Reese.

Todd: Thanks to my mother, Diane Glassman, and my father, Stephen Glassman, who always encouraged me to do more; my friends Jessica Wescott, Justin Carbonneau, Scott Duquette, Joe Bannon, Jason Byrnes, and Kelani Dione; and my family, all the Glassmans, Newmans, and Olivers.

INTRODUCTION

I'm John Reese and I'm writing this book with my partner, Todd Glassman. It was I who started our Web site, Validea.com, which eventually led to our writing *The Market Gurus*. Like our Web site, this book has both a practical and educational side.

The Market Gurus is a handy reference that provides a quick and thorough discussion of the strategies of nine of the most famous and successful stock market investors of all time, including Warren Buffett, Benjamin Graham, Peter Lynch, William O'Neil, Ken Fisher, David Dreman, and others. If you've ever wondered what these men thought and how they achieved their success, this book will give you valuable insights. In addition, this book will be of enormous help if you ever wanted to *use* the ideas of some of the great stock market thinkers to *make money yourself.* Here are simple, step-by-step instructions illustrating each guru's strategy. And if you don't want to search for the financial, market, and other information these strategies require, you can visit our Web site <www.Validea.com>, where with a few mouse clicks you get more information. The site provides an analysis of virtually all stocks employing each guru's strategy.

The journey to where we are now began several years ago, when I sold my first business, Micro Networks of America, which was a system integrator specializing in local area networks. We basically designed and installed computer networks for companies. I owned Micro Networks for nine years and, quite honestly, the company did very well.

I sold Micro Networks in 1993 to Ameridata, which was then acquired by GE Capital Information Technology Solutions. I stayed with the company for three years, through the purchase by GE, before I retired. Because of the sale of my business, I had cash to invest and began wondering where was the best place to stash it.

Fortunately, I had long been a voracious reader of a number of business journals—*Forbes, Fortune,* the *Wall Street Journal, Barron's, Business Week, Money, Smart Money.* But the breadth of my reading created a problem. Each source had really interesting stock investment ideas, ideas so compelling I would get excited and want to immediately call my broker. The articles in the publications were well reasoned and would almost always quote a few impressive-sounding experts.

It dawned on me that not all of these articles or all of these gurus could be right. Some probably were, but some were more adept at getting their names in print than in making investment recommendations that resulted in profitable investments. I wanted to know who I should listen to, whose advice paid off, and who should be ignored.

Validea.com started as a research project to determine which individuals and columnists I should listen to. I wanted to know what happened to their recommendations, how well their recommendations did. I not only read periodicals, but I also went to my local bookstore and found books by famous investors. These books bolstered the education I was getting from magazines.

The first guru's book I read was Peter Lynch's. I was dumbstruck. The book had amazing insights on how to pick stocks and what to look for. The advice sounded good, but I wanted to apply Lynch's principles to the stock recommendations I was getting in the magazines. I wanted to know if I could use Lynch's strategy to find out whether the stocks being recommended were worth investing in.

I started to methodically apply Lynch's writings but found it very time consuming to do. I needed many pieces of data to make it work. And when I did find data, it often wasn't clear which data I should use. Earnings per share (EPS) may sound straightforward, but which version of EPS should I look at: future earnings, trailing earnings, earnings before extraordinary items, fully diluted earnings, or others? The answer wasn't obvious.

I was frustrated because I have always tried to automate my work. If a computer can perform a task, it probably can do it faster and easier than I can, so I try to automate as many of my tasks as possible. This desire, coupled with my frustration at getting and identifying the right data, led me to the idea of putting Lynch's strategy into a computer program that could automatically retrieve from a variety of data sources the pieces of information I needed to use Lynch's ideas.

By this time it wasn't just Lynch who interested me. I had continued my reading and was intrigued by other gurus, such as Ken Fisher and Benjamin Graham. Several exceptionally well-written books had tremendous wisdom to offer. And I believed this wisdom could be reduced to a computer program. My goal was to push a button on any stock I was interested in, such as those I came across in periodicals or received as hot tips, and see how the stock fared when using the principles gleaned from the guru's writings. That was the start of Validea.com. And once it was up and going, it was natural that we would want to put down all we had learned in writing, which is how we came to write *The Market Gurus*.

I wasn't looking for stocks that all the gurus agree on—that's rare—but rather stocks that were of strong interest to at least one of the gurus' methodologies. And why—and if not, why not. This was important to me—the why nots. I wanted to learn about all the flaws these gurus found that I wasn't aware of.

I liked Lynch. He had a down-home approach and potentially six different categories of stocks to look at, which gave me a range of choices. He was particularly successful with his fast growers and gave compelling reasons for the rules of thumb he used. We both agreed on another variable: the desirability of a long-term investment horizon. Lynch wasn't trying to get rich quickly, so you could ride his fast growers for three to ten years. He also had strategies for shorter-term gains, such as his "stalwarts," which could produce gains of 30 to 50 percent in one to two years.

The next guru who got my attention was Ken Fisher. He made a compelling case for how to identify excellent stocks with an investment time horizon of three to five years. You can also use his approach for stocks whose earnings were negative, which isn't true for the approaches of most of the other gurus; and his strategy works for the stock of any size company—another unusual aspect of Fisher.

Benjamin Graham, generally considered the father of value investing, was the third guru I focused on. Armed with a deeply conservative bias, I figured if anyone could find a bargain, a quality that appealed to me, it would be Graham.

William O'Neil was a totally new revelation. Up to the time I read O'Neil, I was very conservative about the price I wanted to pay; like almost everyone else, I wanted to buy when prices were low. O'Neil says no, you want to buy when prices are at a new high. He taught me how to identify a leader and how to look at stocks relative to all the other stocks in the market and to buy only the best quality merchandise. I was intrigued that his strategy allowed you to make a substantial profit in as little as three months.

I attended O'Neil's seminar in New York City and was amazed at his large following. He really does have "followers," true believers. I also realized how closely his newspaper, *Investor's Business Daily (IBD),* was tied to his strategy and provided so much of the information needed to implement his strategy. For instance, it provides relative strength ratings—that is, how a stock is doing compared with the other stocks in the market. And *IBD* provides a company's earnings compared with earnings of other companies. O'Neil also highlights excessive volume in a stock on a given day, and he combines technical analysis with fundamental analysis. I found his work inspiring, and it opened up a whole new dimension to my understanding of how to invest.

In applying his methodologies, there were periods when it performed exceptionally well, identifying stocks that would explode upward. And there were other periods when almost every investment that met O'Neil's criteria would almost instantly peter out and the price would fall rather than go up. He does emphasize that you should use his strategy during good markets. And by being constantly vigilant, you will see that the market always turns around, allowing you to invest in leaders that will really shoot up. Or you could recover money you lost during down times. If I wanted to use a system to pick stocks for contests on the Internet, I would use O'Neil's strategy because it generates the fastest returns.

The Motley Fool by this time was making quite a reputation for itself. I paid attention because it adopted principles used by O'Neil and Lynch—relative strength from O'Neil and the PEG ratio (price-earnings growth, or the Fool ratio as The Motley Fool calls it) from

Lynch. The approach incorporated aspects of two of my favorite gurus.

The other gurus covered in this book and on our Web site were also compelling. Martin Zweig impressed me because, as an uncommonly astute observer of the market, he is very good at analyzing the overall market and what constitutes a good market. In addition, he had strong guidelines for picking growth stocks. His orientation was longer term—a growth stock should be held for several years, an idea I like. He had also done a tremendous amount of research in the market. I value that wisdom. Zweig had collaborated with Ned Davis, who went on to establish his own stellar reputation for researching and predicting the performance of the market as a whole. Zweig had uncanny insights into specific parts of the market, whether it be specific sectors, bonds, or other parts. He developed a whole set of forecasting tools that are respected by professionals too.

David Dreman provided amazing insights because of his contrarian attitude and extensive research into the market. Dreman, Zweig, O'Neil, Fisher—they were all researchers. By research, I mean going back and thoroughly testing strategies. Dreman made an extremely compelling case that the earnings forecast from analysts is highly unreliable. And he establishes a case for buying badly beaten-down stocks that are in the lowest one-fifth of the market, as well as concentrating on only the 1,500 biggest stocks. Many individuals advise buying stocks with low PE ratios, and I value Dreman's wisdom in selectively applying that advice.

James O'Shaughnessy did a seminal study of what works in the market and thoroughly analyzed many variables to show, over a 45-year period, which ones repeatedly worked and which the market valued. More significant, he was able to combine some of the variables to arrive at formulas that had a higher chance of success overall. Going with him, you wouldn't find the greatest possible returns, but over a long period, you would likely earn a return greater than the average for the market. He did manage some mutual funds that didn't do too well for the first few years. But you need to follow a strategy for a full market cycle, which is five to ten years; O'Shaughnessy got out of the fund business before the full cycle was completed. Also, O'Shaughnessy has a strategy for both the growth investor and the value investor, and Validea.com analyzes stocks using both strategies. O'Shaughnessy's holding period is one year, after which you apply his principles again to another portfolio of stocks.

As for Warren Buffett, of course, I had heard of him, but it was my wife, Ellen, who encouraged me to research Buffett on what he had to say about a particular stock. Buffett's primary strategy is buying a good company according to his definition but waiting until it is available at an attractive price. He, more than any of our gurus, is patient—very patient. He buys after much research and then basically holds forever, which appealed to Ellen, who likes to buy and hold.

My wife and I had seen the benefits overall of buy and hold from sitting on shares of drug-maker Schering-Plough, which had a steady profit margin of 15 percent and grew its earnings steadily at 15 percent a year. We let the shares sit and, sure enough, with all that compound growth, the company grew very big and its shares became very valuable. We didn't incur any taxes (because we held it), and we didn't try to time the market. And we held the stock through times when drug companies were out of favor—when everyone predicted the government would take away their profits. Fortunately, we also lived through the good times when these companies were the darlings of the market. But the key fact is that with a company growing at 15 percent a year, if you hold the stock and ignore quarterly earnings and various claims of doom-and-gloom and don't pay capital gains taxes, you can do very, very well. Buffett recognized the power of compounding over a long period and has capitalized on it. But you have to have some confidence that a company will produce reasonably steady earnings for the foreseeable future. You, too, need patience.

USING *THE MARKET GURUS*

Use *The Market Gurus* as a source of information—and inspiration—about some of the greatest stock market investors. Our book covers the backgrounds of these gurus, where they are from, and

how their careers unfolded. But it also discusses, with a broad vi-
sion, the investment philosophies of these gurus—how they look at
the stock market, the economy, and investing in general. Each chapter provides an overview and introduction to the thinking of a successful strategist in easy-to-understand terms.

Think of *The Market Gurus* as something of a cookbook, filled
with hands-on recipes that allow you to make wonderful meals—
or wonderful investment decisions—yourself. And our Web site,
Validea.com, is your support service. It provides the research and
information you need to implement the strategies of each of the
gurus. It's like a *sous* chef who does the preparation for the head
chef. With our Web site at your side, you can become your own head
chef and make more informed investment decisions than was ever
possible before.

Todd and I hope *The Market Gurus* will provide insights into investing that you can use to enhance your bank account, your lifestyle,
and your retirement. At the very least, we hope you enjoy reading
about these extraordinary people as much as we enjoyed learning
about them.

CHAPTER 1

PETER LYNCH

WHICH INVESTORS MIGHT USE **Peter Lynch?**

RISK: Those investors willing to take on a moderate amount of risk. Lynch isn't really low risk because he does focus to a degree on fast growers, but he also avoids the higher-risk areas of the market, such as technology stocks. He has a nice cross section of stocks he considers, including large companies, which makes him suitable for many investors in terms of risk. Also, Lynch suggests focusing on companies you know, which is reassuring to many investors and helps hold down the anxiety level.

TIME HORIZON: Just as with risk, Lynch is suitable for a variety of investors in terms of time horizon. You can ride his fast growers for anywhere from three to ten years, but he also has strategies for shorter-term gains, like his stalwarts, which can produce gains of 30 percent to 50 percent in one to two years.

EFFORT: Because Lynch has an uncommonly wide range of choices and focuses on a range of fundamentals—but holds onto his investments for at least a medium length of time, usually for years—his strategy requires a moderate amount of effort on the part of the investor.

WHO IS PETER LYNCH?

With a shock of white hair, Peter Lynch bears more than a passing resemblance to bad-boy artist Andy Warhol, who said we will all be famous for 15 minutes. Lynch has defied this prediction by being famous for far longer than his Warholian-allotted time, even though he's no longer doing what he did to make him famous in the first place, namely, managing Fidelity's Magellan Fund, now one of the world's largest mutual funds.

Barron's (10 Jan. 2000) had this comment about Lynch: "He hasn't managed any public money for the past decade, yet he remains the most revered and popular money manager on the planet." The *Washington Post* (10 Sept. 1998) called Lynch, "the world's most famous mutual fund manager."

How does a money manager stop managing the public's money and yet remain more highly thought of than money managers who presided during the roaring stock market of the 1990s (Lynch retired in 1990)? For starters, Lynch bowed out when he was at the top of his game. His record was nearly miraculous, and he didn't wait around long enough to tarnish it in any way. Second, he wrote a folksy, easy-to-understand investment guide, *One Up on Wall Street,* that became a runaway best-seller, with more than a million copies sold.

Finally, Lynch has a compelling approach to investing that is aimed at "everyman"—average Joes and Janes who are neither rich nor well schooled in finance and don't have access to the sophisticated information and technical resources available to professional investors yet can still do well on Wall Street.

When we began researching investments, Lynch's book was the first we focused on. John had had an account with Fidelity for 20 years at that point, so he was familiar with the company's approach and was, of course, aware of Lynch. What struck us about Lynch's book—and we think the basis of its popularity to this day—is that the book made a lot of common sense. No highly technical language, no graduate-level mathematics, no esoteric theories. Anyone, suggests Lynch, can gain an investment edge by paying attention to his surroundings and doing his homework. Focus on where you shop, what you buy, the industry in which you work, where you live, and you'll likely come up with a series of big stock market winners over time. That's a simplistic view of Lynch, but one that's still fairly accurate.

Lynch is fond of telling how he came across one of his better investments, Hanes, maker of L'eggs pantyhose. Quality pantyhose were typically sold in department stores or specialty shops, where women shopped about once every six weeks. Poorer-quality pantyhose were sold in grocery and drug stores, where women usually shopped weekly. Hanes saw an opportunity: Sell higher-quality pantyhose made of heavier fabric with a better fit, in the most convenient places—namely grocery and drug stores. It was convenience the company was really selling.

While Hanes test marketed the product in Boston, Lynch's wife, Carolyn, bought a pair, liked them, and the rest, as they say, is history. Lynch researched the company, bought its stock, and made six times what he paid—a "six bagger" in Lynch-speak. This is a simple, compelling story that most everyone can understand and picture themselves doing. It's one of the more important reasons for Lynch's appeal: his approach is direct, everydaylike, and simple enough for all of us seemingly to do if we want.

Lynch starts with the premise that if you personally know something positive about a company (because of your job, because of where you shop, or because of where you live), it can give you an edge over professional investors. There's a degree of common sense here. It's not just a random stock you are considering; it's a stock you have a reason to look at. It may be that you like the company's product or service, think its marketing approach is very effective, find its stores unusually well organized, see its parking lots full when you drive by, or work in an industry that shows the company has a strong market niche and is well regarded. Lynch is big on instilling confidence in the average person—anyone can do this—which also helps his popularity.

But there's more to Lynch than just a good story based on what seems like common sense. He doesn't offer a one-size-fits-all approach. You invest in what you personally know about. Lynch's track record (we'll discuss it shortly) is legendary, which is another reason he's so popular. And he's been through the cycles, such as the trough of the 1970s and the great thud of 1987, which means he's been in battle and knows how to win the war. His career wasn't spent entirely in a bull market.

We personally found Lynch's approach so appealing that we wanted to be able to just push a button and do a Peter Lynch–type analysis on any stock that caught our eye. This was one of the foundations of our guru analysis application at Validea.com.

Lynch was born January 19, 1944. His father, at one time a mathematics professor at Boston College and then an auditor at the John Hancock insurance company, died of cancer when Lynch was ten years old. To earn money, the next year he began caddying at a private golf club in the Boston area. The 1950s were a good time for the stock market, and many club members were investing. One of them was a honcho at Fidelity Investments, D. George Sullivan, a contact who was to shape Lynch's career. While walking the fairways and greens, young Lynch heard the talk about stocks and became intrigued. Eventually, he attended Boston College and, after graduation, went to the University of Pennsylvania's famed Wharton School, where he earned an MBA. By then he had been following stocks for years and knew investing was where he wanted to spend his professional life.

So consumed was Lynch with investing (at a time when that was fairly uncommon), that he reportedly on his first date with his future wife, Carolyn, talked only about investing. That evidently wasn't a turnoff for her, then or now, as they eventually married, had three children, and are still together.

Lynch's career has been spent at Boston-based Fidelity Investments, starting with a summer job in 1966. Lynch recounts that even though there were 75 applicants for three jobs at Fidelity, he got the job in a "rigged deal," meaning he had "pull" in the company. He sure did; he caddied for the president of Fidelity for eight years.

In 1969, Lynch joined Fidelity full-time as an analyst, at times following textiles and then the metals industry. In 1974, he became Fidelity's research director, while continuing as an analyst. He never managed a fund until taking over the Magellan Fund on May 31, 1977, which by then had been around for 14 years. It began in 1963 as an international fund (hence, the name), but shortly after its start, a heavy tax on foreign investing was put in place, and the fund did little international investing. It focused on domestic stocks and still does. By the time Lynch took over the fund's reins, it had $20 million under management.

Through the 1950s and much of the 1960s, the stock market did well, but then it turned down and suffered during the 1970s. In an interview on the Public Broadcasting System program *Frontline,* whose transcript is on PBS's Web site, Lynch said: "The first three years I ran Magellan, I think one-third of the shares were redeemed. I mean there was very little interest. People didn't care." Not an auspicious beginning.

But Lynch was a performer. The fund did well and beginning in 1982, the stock market took a sharp turn up, and the press—and then the investing public—took increasing interest in the Magellan Fund based on its performance under Lynch. Lynch worked at least six days a week and sometimes part of Sunday, even though he is a devout Catholic. Eventually, the workload took a toll, he says, and he decided to retire, 13 years to the day from when he took over Magellan—May 31, 1990. Though only 46 (the same age at which his father died), he quit to spend time with his wife and three children, and do other things.

It is a testament to Lynch's investing prowess that when he announced his retirement, it was greeted with the kind of press interest usually reserved for the retirement of a Hollywood star. His leaving Magellan was reported around the world.

Why? Quite simply, it was his track record. Consider:

- Magellan had, during Lynch's tenure, a cumulative return of 2,703.0 percent and an average annualized return of 29.2 percent.
- He outperformed the market during his 13 years at Magellan's helm by an average of more than 13 percentage points a year— 15.8 percent for the S&P 500 versus 29.2 percent for Magellan. This record may never be repeated.
- In the last five years that he ran Magellan, according to *Barron's* (10 January 2000), the fund beat 99.5 percent of all other funds.
- The fund grew from $20 million in assets, when Lynch took over in 1977, to $14 billion, when he left in 1990. (It now has over $90 billion and is closed to new investors.)

- If someone had invested $10,000 in Magellan on the day Lynch took it over and left it there, that investor would have had $280,000 on the day Lynch retired 13 years later.

That's a nice track record. Very nice. It's no wonder a lot of people pay attention to Lynch, even today when he hasn't managed the public's money in over a decade.

Since his retirement, Lynch has kept busy. He wrote his book and is involved with the Catholic Church. He gave $10 million in 1999 to his alma mater, Boston College, where he serves on its board of trustees, and its education college is now the Lynch School of Education. He's given money to Wharton and others, and has a charitable foundation.

In addition, Lynch is a vice chairman of Fidelity and serves as a spokesman, including appearing in commercials.

OUR INTERPRETATION OF
THE LYNCH METHODOLOGY

In general, Lynch takes a long-term view of investing, believing one holds on to a stock as long as the fundamental story of the company hasn't changed.

As a general approach to investing, Lynch advises:

- Take advantage of what you already know.
- Look for opportunities that haven't yet been discovered and certified by Wall Street—companies that are off the radar screen of professional investors.
- Invest in companies, not the stock market.
- Ignore short-term fluctuations.
- The average person is exposed to interesting local companies and products years before the professionals.
- In the stock market, one in the hand is worth ten in the bush. The average person comes across a likely investment prospect two or three times a year—sometimes more.

- All other things being equal, it is better to buy smaller companies because their stocks can move much more. However, that said, Lynch has still invested in many big companies.

Lynch wrote his best-seller *One Up on Wall Street* in 1989 and wrote a new introduction when the book was reissued in 2000. In the intervening years, much had been written about Lynch's investment strategies, and he seems to think he was somewhat misrepresented. In his new introduction, he penned what he calls a "disclaimer":

> Peter Lynch doesn't advise you to buy stock in your favorite store just because you like shopping in the store, nor should you buy stock in a manufacturer because it makes your favorite product or a restaurant because you like the food. Liking a store, a product, or a restaurant is a good reason to get interested in a company and put it on your research list, but it's not enough of a reason to own the stock! Never invest in any company before you've done the homework on the company's earnings prospects, financial condition, competitive position, plans for expansion, and so forth.

You are warned. Though Lynch's approach may seem very straightforward and easy to understand, it involves work, research, and understanding. Remember, he retired, in part, because he spent at least six days a week studying companies. If he could have sat back and looked around his neighborhood for little-known businesses that were doing well, he might still be managing Magellan today.

These Are Some Characteristics Lynch Favors

Lynch lists favorable qualitative attributes of the best companies. In point of fact, most of the companies Lynch invested in didn't meet many, or even any, of these criteria. These were ideal characteristics that could get him initially interested when he discovered them in a company and would get him excited about doing further research. But they weren't turnoffs to him, even though most run contrary to the public's perception of characteristics needed for a successful investment. In fact, many investors and professional analysts find these characteristics to be turnoffs, though Lynch thinks they are just the opposite. Paraphrasing his book's words, these are the characteristics many investors and analysts, but not Lynch, consider turnoffs:

- The company has a boring name. Lynch says if you get in early enough with a company that has a boring name, you will probably get a few bucks off the stock's price just because of the name.
- The company does something dull. Like another of our gurus, Warren Buffett, Lynch downplays tech stocks. He believes if a company with terrific earnings and a strong balance sheet also does dull things, it gives you a lot of time to purchase the stock at a discount.
- The company does something disagreeable, such as making intestinal by-products or manufacturing a machine that washes greasy auto parts.
- It's a spin-off. Lynch's reasoning is that large companies don't want spin-offs to get into trouble because that would reflect poorly on the parent company, so the parent sends the spin-off into the world with strong balance sheets and preparation to succeed on its own.
- Institutions don't own it, and analysts don't follow it.
- Rumors abound about the company, such as its supposed involvement with toxic waste and/or the Mafia. Or better yet, toxic waste *and* the Mafia.
- The company is in a depressing (not depressed) industry, such as mortuaries. Lynch claims Wall Street tends to ignore companies that deal with mortality.
- It is in a no-growth or slow-growth industry—a situation that doesn't thrill professional investors, which is exactly why Lynch likes such companies.
- It has a niche, which appeals to Lynch because such companies have little if any competition.
- People have to keep buying the company's products—drugs, soft drinks, razor blades, and cigarettes, for example.

- It's a user (not a maker) of technology. His thinking: Technology helps companies that are heavy technology users to cut costs, while at the same time the companies benefit from falling technology prices.
- Insiders are buyers. Lynch believes there's no better tip-off to the probable success of a stock than that people in a company are putting their own money into it. Even though insider buying excites him, he considers insider selling usually meaningless because there are many reasons why insiders sell (to buy a house, pay for a child's college tuition, buy a toy such as a sailboat) but only one why insiders buy; namely, they think the stock is undervalued and will eventually go up.
- The company is buying back shares. By buying back shares and decreasing total shares outstanding, earnings can be affected magically, which can in turn affect the stock price significantly.
- Moderately fast growers (20 to 25 percent) in nongrowth industries; these are ideal investments.

Lynch has a further characteristic of the perfect stock: it's idiot proof. According to him, it's good if any idiot can run the business because sooner or later an idiot *will be* running it.

Additional advice:

- Don't be in a rush. It's better to miss the first move in a stock by waiting to see if a company's plans are working out than to jump in only to find the company is a flash in the pan.
- Sit tight. Lynch's stocks typically take three to ten years to play out.

HOW LYNCH DETERMINES A COMPANY'S CLASSIFICATION

Lynch has a company classification scheme consisting of six categories. All have value, but Lynch focuses in his book primarily on three—fast growers, stalwarts, and slow growers (he doesn't explain in sufficient detail for us to automate how to evaluate the others—

cyclicals, turnarounds, and asset plays). Because of our ability to automate the analysis in these three primary categories, we focus only on them, but keep in mind there are good reasons to hold the other types (in particular, Lynch was successful with turnarounds and held a good number of them in his portfolio), although they require special sophistication and finding evaluative data is difficult.

Lynch's overall philosophy addresses the long term. He says there's a good chance that a solid growth company is probably in the third inning of a nine-inning game. This comment doesn't just reveal his love of baseball images (he's an ardent baseball fan), but it illustrates his view that even though a company isn't new (just as the third inning isn't the start of the game), there's still plenty of time left for the score to go up a lot—and a lot of money to be made with a stock. Unfortunately, he doesn't tell us how we know which inning a company is in. Our own interpretation is that when a company can first show a three-year track record of strong growth of positive earnings, it is in the third inning. With less than that, you don't know the company has a proven business model.

The first step in Lynch's methodology is to classify the stock you are looking at into one of his three main categories—fast growers, stalwarts, or slow growers—based on its earnings per share (EPS) growth rate. The method for selecting these three types of companies will be discussed in more detail below. But first let's touch on the three types of companies Lynch mentions but doesn't emphasize.

Cyclicals.   Cyclicals include auto manufacturers, airlines, tire companies, steel and aluminum companies, chemical companies, large semiconductor companies, and defense companies. They are cyclical in that they tend to do well when the economy is doing well and falter when the economy heads south. For Lynch, timing is everything with cyclicals. You want to get in when they are on the upswing and get out before they go down. Lynch strongly suggests that you need to work in some profession connected to the industry if you are going to have a successful edge in detecting early signs that the business is picking up or falling off. And cyclicals are notoriously counterintuitive—when the PE is high or nonexistent, that might actually be a good time to buy; when it is very low (which can be seductive), a cyclical stock has probably peaked, and it is a bad time to buy.

Turnarounds.   Turnarounds are companies in trouble that are attempting to turn their situation around and become winners. Turnaround candidates make up lost ground very quickly. Lynch lists five types of turnarounds:

1. Bail-us-out-or-else: This turnaround is a play on hopes that the government will help bail out the company, as demonstrated by Chrysler (a Lynch winner) in the early 1980s.
2. Who-would-have-thunk-it: A company that surprises the market by being able to successfully turn around.
3. Little-problem-we-didn't-anticipate: A minor problem in a company that is perceived by the market to be worse than it really is.
4. Perfectly-good-company-inside-a-bankrupt-company: A quite healthy part of a sick company.
5. Restructuring-to-maximize-shareholder-values: This refers to the way companies rid themselves of unprofitable subsidiaries so what's left is the good stuff.

When Lynch evaluates turnarounds, he pays particular attention to the cash on hand and the long-term debt. He likes to see more cash than debt, and he likes to see that the type of debt is not bank debt or corporate paper (which are due on demand) but are funded debt like corporate bonds.

Asset plays.   An asset play is any company sitting on something valuable that you know about but the Wall Street crowd has overlooked. The local edge can be used to great advantage here. A supermarket chain might have stores it has owned for decades. The stores' value is on the books at original cost, which is a fraction of their present value. That represents a potential hoard of cash, which is not seen on the balance sheet if the company were to sell these stores. As a result, the company's price-book ratio might be much more favorable than depicted on its financials. In fact, the stock might be trading for less than the value of these hidden, undervalued assets. Lynch's two-minute drill:

- What are the assets and how much are they worth?
- How much debt is there to detract from these assets? Keep in mind, creditors are first in line in front of shareholders.
- Is there someone waiting on the sidelines to buy the assets?

The following are the categories that Lynch places the greatest emphasis on.

Fast growers.   These are companies whose annual EPS growth is equal to or greater than 20 percent for the past three years. This is very straightforward, but there are limitations to Lynch's stated methodology as applied to this category as well as to the others: What if the company hasn't been around three years or has had a year of losses? How would you then calculate three years of EPS? Is the EPS he looks at before or after extraordinary items? Lynch doesn't say. These are shortcomings in Lynch's explanation, but they apply to only a limited number of companies and do not negate the overall benefit of using Lynch's strategy.

■ To show how to use Lynch's methodology, we use for our examples of fast growers Dynacq International Inc. (stock symbol: DYII) (see Figure 1.1) and Genlyte Group Inc. (stock symbol: GLYT) (see Figure 1.2). Dynacq is a Houston-based operator of outpatient surgery, X-ray, and laboratory facilities; a medical office complex; and an acute care hospital in addition to providing home infusion services, such as parenteral nutrition. Sales for fiscal 2000 (ended August) were $26.0 million, and net income was $5.9 million. Genlyte, headquartered in Louisville, Kentucky, is a leading maker of lighting fixtures. It produces all of its lighting systems through a joint venture with Thomas Industries, which is called Genlyte Thomas Group LLC. The company's product line includes incandescent, fluorescent, and other types of lighting products. Sales for fiscal year 2000 (ended December 31) were $1,007,700,000, and net earnings were $36.3 million. The company has over 3,300 employees.

| **FIGURE 1.1** | DYNACQ INTERNATIONAL INC (DYII) | $16.65 as of 4/18/2001 |

	Year 1	Year 2
Total Net Income (mil.)	$5.9	$2.7
EPS	$0.41	$0.20
Sales (mil.)	$26.0	$20.3
Avg. PE	11.5	6.9
ROE	40.4%	32.1%
Long-Term Debt-Equity	3%	8%
Dividend	–	–
Payout	0%	0%
Shares Outstanding (mil.)	15.3	12.9

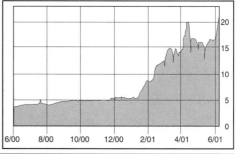

	Year 3	Year 4	Year 5	Year 6	Year 7	Year 8	Year 9	Year 10
Total Net Income (mil.)	$0.9	$(1.1)	$0.6	$0.9	$0.5	$0.9		
EPS	$0.07	$(0.07)	$0.04	$0.07	$0.03	$0.07		
Sales (mil.)	$10.9	$9.8	$7.4	$6.9	$2.6	$3.4		
Avg. PE	8.7	n/a	30.5	25	89.6	n/a		
ROE	15.5%	n/a	9.4%	15.5%	10.4%	29%		
Long-Term Debt-Equity	17%	15%	16%	21%	35%	26%		
Dividend	–	–	–					
Payout	0%	0%	0%					
Shares Outstanding (mil.)	13.1	14.2	14.2	14.2	14.2	13.5		

	Q1	Q2	Q3	Q4	Q5	Q6	Q7	Q8
EPS	$0.17	$0.17	$0.12	$0.13	$0.11	$0.07	$0.21	$0.08
Revenue (mil.)	$9.8	$8.9	$7.5	$7.5	$5.8	$5.2	$6.2	$4.3

	Market Cap (mil.)	TTM Sales (mil.)	Relative Strength	EPS Growth (4-yr. avg.)	Revenue Growth (TTM)	Current Ratio	Insider Buy-Sells (3 months)
DYII	$230.0	$33.7	99	79.0%	69.0%	2.7	0/0
Hospitals Industry	$4,580.0	$3,673.3	81	28.0%	24.0%	2.1	

	PEG	PE	Projected PE	PS	Price-Book	Price-Cash Flow	Free Cash Flow/Share
DYII	0.36	28.2	12.8	6.82	13.5	7.4	0.27
Hospitals Industry	1.15	56.9	34.4	1.99	3.9	15.7	

	Yield	Profit Margin (TTM)	ROE (TTM)	Total Debt-Equity	Long-Term Debt-Equity	Insider Ownership	Institutional Ownership
DYII	0.00%	25.0%	50.0%	47%	2.36%	70.0%	2.1%
Hospitals Industry	0.00%	6.0%	15.0%	117%	n/a		

Recent Balance Sheet Items ($ millions)		**Financial Statement Trends**			
Cash	6.2		Recent 12 mo.	FY1	FY2
Current Assets	16.7	Inventory/Sales	1%	1%	1%
Total Assets	26.7	AR to Sales	34%	32%	41%
Current Liabilities	6.3	R&D to Sales	–	–	–
Long-Term Debt	0.4				
Total Debt	7.95				
Equity	16.92				

FIGURE 1.2	GENLYTE GROUP INC (GLYT)	$27.56 as of 3/30/2001

	Year 1	Year 2
Total Net Income (mil.)	$36.3	$32.8
EPS	$2.65	$2.37
Sales (mil.)	$1,007.7	$978.3
Avg. PE	8.7	8.9
ROE	16.0%	16.2%
Long-Term Debt-Equity	0.29%	0.27%
Dividend	0	0
Payout	0%	0%
Shares Outstanding (mil.)	13.3	13.7

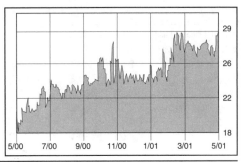

	Year 3	Year 4	Year 5	Year 6	Year 7	Year 8	Year 9	Year 10
Total Net Income (mil.)	$26.8	$19.1	$13.0	$8.3	$5.1	$3.3	$–2.2	$2.0
EPS	$1.95	$1.42	$1.00	$0.62	$0.40	$0.26	$–0.17	$0.16
Sales (mil.)	$664.1	$488.0	$456.9	$445.7	$432.7	$429.1	$425.4	$428.5
Avg. PE	11.3	11.0	10.0	9.7	11.3	18.0	NE	35.2
ROE	16.1%	18.4%	15.5%	11.2%	7.9%	5.4%	NE	3.4%
Long-Term Debt-Equity	0.37%	0.32%	0.5%	0.89%	1.37%	1.54%	2.01%	2.22%
Dividend	0	0	0	0	0	0	0	0
Payout	0%	0%	0%	0%	0%	0%	0%	0%
Shares Outstanding (mil.)	13.5	13.4	13.0	12.8	12.7	12.7	12.7	12.7

	Q1	Q2	Q3	Q4	Q5	Q6	Q7	Q8
EPS	$0.74	$0.73	$0.63	$0.55	$0.64	$0.66	$0.57	$0.50
Revenue (mil.)	$254.4	$257.3	$251.3	$244.7	$239.4	$257.8	$243.6	$237.5

	Market Cap (mil.)	TTM Sales (mil.)	Relative Strength	EPS Growth (3-yr. avg.)	Revenue Growth (TTM)	Current Ratio	Insider Buy-Sells (3 months)
GLYT	$367.0	$1,007.7	86	22.9%	6.3%	2.0	1/0
Business Equip. Industry	$2,125	$3,478	55	20.1%	–4.8%	1.37	

	PEG	PE	Projected PE	PS	Price-Book	Price-Cash Flow	Free Cash Flow/Share
GLYT	0.45	10.4	10.3	0.36	1.61	5.1	0.07
Business Equip. Industry	1.6	17.1	16.3	0.9	2.70	8.9	

	Yield	Profit Margin (TTM)	ROE (TTM)	Total Debt-Equity	Long-Term Debt-Equity	Insider Ownership	Institutional Ownership
GLYT	0.0%	3.6%	16.0%	0.31%	0.29%	6%	61.5%
Business Equip. Industry	1.5%	5.6%	22.5%	2.60%	0.78%		

Recent Balance Sheet Items ($ millions)		Financial Statement Trends			
Cash	23.8		Recent 12 mo.	FY1	FY2
Current Assets	347.7	Inventory/Sales	15.0%	15.0%	13.9%
Total Assets	635.9	AR to Sales	14.2%	14.2%	15.9%
Current Liabilities	175.6	R&D to Sales	–	–	–
Long-Term Debt	66.7				
Total Debt	69.4				
Equity	227.2				

Stalwarts.   Stalwarts are companies whose annual EPS growth is in the 10 percent to 19 percent range. Lynch talks a lot about fast growers, but stalwarts are what he focuses on most in his writings because, in part, fast growers, like Wal-Mart and Home Depot, eventually become stalwarts. Think of stalwarts as well-established companies that still have good growth potential.

■ For our stalwart examples, we use Oxford Health Plans Inc. (stock symbol: OHP), shown in Figure 1.3, and Outback Steakhouse Inc. (stock symbol: OSI) in Figure 1.4. Oxford was a high flyer until it crashed and nearly burned as a result of computer and regulatory problems but is now making a comeback. It is a managed health care company, or HMO, which operates in the tristate New York City area from its headquarters in Trumbull, Connecticut. It has 3,400 employees. Outback is a restaurant chain with an Australian theme that has more than 600 restaurants in the United States and 13 other countries. It also owns the Carrabba's Italian Grill restaurant chain as well as some smaller restaurant concepts. Its employee count is over 40,000.

Slow growers.   Slow growers have an annual EPS growth rate of less than 10 percent.

■ TXU Corporation (stock symbol: TXU) is our example of a slow grower. Based in Dallas, TXU is a utility holding company that sells gas and electricity (see Figure 1.5). It used to be known as Texas Utilities and is the Lone Star State's largest utility. It also has operations in Europe and Australia and an employee count of more than 16,000.

Determining the Classification

1. EPS growth < 10%   Slow grower
2. EPS growth ≧ 10% and < 20%   Stalwart
3. EPS growth ≧ 20%   Fast grower

FIGURE 1.3   OXFORD HEALTH PLANS INC (OHP) $26.75 as of 3/30/2001

	Year 1	Year 2
Total Net Income (mil.)	$285.4	$319.9
EPS	$2.24	$3.26
Sales (mil.)	$4,111.8	$4,197.8
Avg. PE	12.2	5.2
ROE	62.2%	323.8%
Long-Term Debt-Equity	6%	8%
Dividend	0	0
Payout	0%	0%
Shares Outstanding (mil.)	98.3	82.0

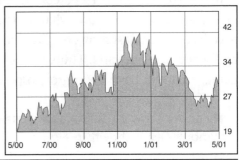

	Year 3	Year 4	Year 5	Year 6	Year 7	Year 8	Year 9	Year 10
Total Net Income (mil.)	$−596.8	$−291.3	$99.6	$52.4	$27.9	$14.9	$8.0	$3.6
EPS	$−7.79	$−3.70	$1.25	$0.71	$0.40	$0.18	$0.14	$0.08
Sales (mil.)	$4,719.4	$4,420.1	$3,075.0	$1,765.0	$720.7	$311.9	$155.7	$94.9
Avg. PE	NE	NE	36.0	43.0	38.4	49.7	33.0	29.9
ROE	NE	NE	16.6%	23.8%	22.0%	16.4%	12.1%	8.4%
Long-Term Debt-Equity	3.13%	0%	0%	0%	0%	0%	0%	0.01%
Dividend	0	0	0	0	0	0	0	0
Payout	0%	0%	0%	0%	0%	0%	0%	0%
Shares Outstanding (mil.)	80.5	79.5	77.4	68.8	63.7	62.4	60.3	54.7

	Q1	Q2	Q3	Q4	Q5	Q6	Q7	Q8
EPS	$0.58	$0.81	$0.45	$0.34	$3.04	$0.34	$−0.16	$0.04
Revenue (mil.)	$1,038.6	$1,038.1	$1,012.8	$1,022.4	$1,034.3	$1,052.4	$1,050.8	$1,060.3

	Market Cap (mil.)	TTM Sales (mil.)	Relative Strength	EPS Growth (3-yr. avg.)	Revenue Growth (TTM)	Current Ratio	Insider Buy-Sells (3 months)
OHP	$2,630	$4,112	94	15.7%	0.42%	1.3	1/3
Health Care Plans Industry	$5,735	$10,540	90	5.7%	7.0%	1.4	

	PEG	PE	Projected PE	PS	Price-Book	Price-Cash Flow	Free Cash Flow/Share
OHP	0.76	11.9	10.2	0.64	5.73	15.8	3.85
Health Care Plans Industry	1.3	23.8	19.7	0.73	1.90	16.0	

	Yield	Profit Margin (TTM)	ROE (TTM)	Total Debt-Equity	Long-Term Debt-Equity	Insider Ownership	Institutional Ownership
OHP	0.0%	6.9%	62.2%	0.40%	0.06%	10%	83.6%
Health Care Plans Industry	0.35%	3.1%	21.3%	0.45%	0.43%		

Recent Balance Sheet Items ($ millions)		Financial Statement Trends			
Cash	1,067.0		Recent 12 mo.	FY1	FY2
Current Assets	1,255.6	Inventory/Sales	−	−	−
Total Assets	1,444.6	AR to Sales	3.4%	2.4%	3.5%
Current Liabilities	957.4	R&D to Sales	−	−	−
Long-Term Debt	28.0				
Total Debt	180.7				
Equity	459.2				

FIGURE 1.4	**OUTBACK STEAKHOUSE INC (OSI)**	$25.46 as of 3/30/2001

	Year 1	Year 2
Total Net Income (mil.)	$141.1	$124.3
EPS	$1.78	$1.57
Sales (mil.)	$1,906.0	$1,646.0
Avg. PE	15.7	19.1
ROE	17.5%	17.9%
Long-Term Debt-Equity	1.0%	0.0%
Dividend	0	0
Payout	0%	0%
Shares Outstanding (mil.)	76.6	77.4

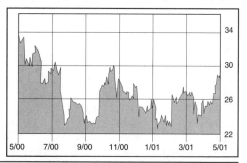

	Year 3	Year 4	Year 5	Year 6	Year 7	Year 8	Year 9	Year 10
Total Net Income (mil.)	$97.2	$61.5	$71.6	$53.7	$39.3	$23.7	$12.5	$5.8
EPS	$1.29	$0.85	$0.97	$0.79	$0.57	$0.35	$0.23	$0.13
Sales (mil.)	$1,358.9	$1,151.6	$937.4	$664.0	$451.9	$271.2	$124.0	$55.2
Avg. PE	16.9	19.4	21.4	25.6	32.0	39.7	41.8	36.7
ROE	17.8%	14.1%	20.9%	21.1%	22.8%	19.4%	13.5%	21.8%
Long-Term Debt-Equity	7.0%	16%	14%	11%	7%	1%	0.0%	3%
Dividend	0	0	0	0	0	0	0	0
Payout	0%	0%	0%	0%	0%	0%	0%	0%
Shares Outstanding (mil.)	74.0	73.6	72.0	67.7	64.4	59.7	56.5	47.2

	Q1	Q2	Q3	Q4	Q5	Q6	Q7	Q8
EPS	$0.41	$0.45	$0.48	$0.45	$0.41	$0.40	$0.37	$0.34
Revenue (mil.)	$485.1	$481.8	$464.8	$472.2	$393.8	$401.8	$379.3	$350.8

	Market Cap (mil.)	TTM Sales (mil.)	Relative Strength	EPS Growth (3-yr. avg.)	Revenue Growth (TTM)	Current Ratio	Insider Buy-Sells (3 months)
OSI	$1,953	$1,906	50	17.2%	20.1%	1.30	0/1
Restaurant Industry	$5,583	$3,828	77	21.9%	8.2%	0.91	

	PEG	PE	Projected PE	PS	Price-Book	Price-Cash Flow	Free Cash Flow/Share
OSI	0.83	14.3	12.4	1.02	2.5	10.1	0.48
Restaurant Industry	1.05	21.4	18.3	1.43	3.5	11.9	

	Yield	Profit Margin (TTM)	ROE (TTM)	Total Debt-Equity	Long-Term Debt-Equity	Insider Ownership	Institutional Ownership
OSI	0.0%	7.4%	18.0%	0.01%	0.01%	17%	70.2%
Restaurant Industry	0.24%	7.0%	17.6%	0.89%	0.25%		

Recent Balance Sheet Items ($ millions)		**Financial Statement Trends**		
Cash	131.6	**Recent 12 mo.**	**FY1**	**FY2**
Current Assets	134.9	Inventory/Sales	(minimal inventory—service company)	
Total Assets	931.3	AR to Sales	(no AR—restaurant)	
Current Liabilities	106.3	R&D to Sales	(no R&D—service)	
Long-Term Debt	11.7			
Total Debt	16.7			
Equity	807.6			

FIGURE 1.5   **TXU CORP (TXU)** $41.32 as of 3/30/2001

	Year 1	Year 2
Total Net Income (mil.)	$916.0	$985.0
EPS	$3.43	$3.53
Sales (mil.)	$22,009	$17,118
Avg. PE	10.40	11.30
ROE	11.8%	11.8%
Long-Term Debt-Equity	197%	196%
Dividend	$2.40	$2.30
Payout	70.0%	65.2%
Shares Outstanding (mil.)	258.1	276.4

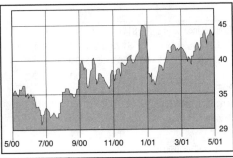

	Year 3	Year 4	Year 5	Year 6	Year 7	Year 8	Year 9	Year 10
Total Net Income (mil.)	$740.0	$660.5	$753.6	$−138.6	$542.8	$368.7	$619.2	$−410.0
EPS	$2.79	$2.85	$3.35	$−0.61	$2.40	$1.66	$2.88	$−1.98
Sales (mil.)	$14,736	$7,945	$6,550	$5,638	$5,663	$5,434	$4,907	$4,893
Avg. PE	15.50	12.90	12.30	NE	15.0	27.5	14.0	NE
ROE	9.0%	9.7%	12.5%	NE	8.4%	5.6%	9.4%	NE
Long-Term Debt-Equity	184%	128%	144%	160%	122%	128%	120%	17%
Dividend	$2.20	$2.10	$2.00	$3.08	$3.08	$3.07	$3.03	$2.99
Payout	78.8%	73.7%	59.7%	−505%	128%	185%	105%	−151%
Shares Outstanding (mil.)	282.3	245.2	224.6	225.8	225.8	224.3	217.3	210.7

	Q1	Q2	Q3	Q4	Q5	Q6	Q7	Q8
EPS	$0.62	$1.25	$0.87	$0.71	$1.23	$1.31	$0.35	$0.65
Revenue (mil.)	$6,807.0	$5,834.0	$4,592.0	$4,776.0	$4,486.0	$4,435.0	$3,729.0	$4,468.0

	Market Cap (mil.)	TTM Sales (mil.)	Relative Strength	EPS Growth (3-yr. avg.)	Revenue Growth (TTM)	Current Ratio	Insider Buy-Sells (3 months)
TXU	$10,666	$22,009	85	6.3%	51.7%	0.6	1/2
Electric Utilities	$17,346	$15,338	81	−3.7%	138%	0.8	

	PEG	PE	Projected PE	PS	Price-Book	Price-Cash Flow	Free Cash Flow/Share
TXU	0.99	12.0	11.2	0.48	1.37	5.4	−4.45
Electric Utilities	1.8	24.9	18.9	2.0		12.8	

	Yield	Profit Margin (TTM)	ROE (TTM)	Total Debt-Equity	Long-Term Debt-Equity	Insider Ownership	Institutional Ownership
TXU	5.8%	4.2%	11.8%	334%	197%	<1%	51.8%
Electric Utilities	2.8%	6.7%	10.8%	210%	148%		

Recent Balance Sheet Items ($ millions)		Financial Statement Trends			
Cash	1,039		Recent 12 mo.	FY1	FY2
Current Assets	7,288	Inventory/Sales	2.2%	2.2%	3.6%
Total Assets	44,990	AR to Sales	12.8%	12.8%	8.7%
Current Liabilities	12,838	R&D to Sales	−	−	−
Long-Term Debt	15,281				
Total Debt	21,300				
Equity	7,776				

Fast Growers

Fast growers are Lynch's favorite investment: small, aggressive, newer enterprises that grow at 20 to 25 percent a year. Lynch favors companies with 20 to 25 percent growth. He starts to be wary of companies growing in excess of 25 percent because a high growth rate is tough for companies to maintain. Companies growing 50 percent or more a year are usually in "hot industries," a Lynch no-no because everyone already knows about them, and they could be overpriced.

Some additional things to consider with fast growers:

- Look to see if the company has duplicated its successes in more than one city or town to prove that expansion will work.
- Make sure the company still has room to grow.
- Notice whether expansion is speeding up or slowing down and if sales are "one-shot" deals (like a Sony PlayStation), as opposed to products customers buy continuously (such as Coke or Gillette razor blades).
- It is a big plus if few institutions own it and only a handful of analysts have ever heard of it. The less people know about it, the better.

■ Dynacq is a fast grower because it has grown at an annual rate of 79 percent over the last four years. Genlyte is a fast grower because it has grown 22.9 percent annually over the past three years.

Dynacq Annual Earnings (most recent to oldest)

EPS_Y1	EPS_Y2	EPS_Y3	EPS_Y4	EPS_Y5	EPS_Y6	EPS_Y7
$0.41	$0.20	$0.07	($0.07)	$0.04	$0.07	$0.03

Note: EPS_Y1 is fully diluted earnings per share (after taxes) from continuing operations (and before extraordinary items) for the last reported fiscal year. Y2 indicates two years ago; Y3, three fiscal years ago. Note that the Validea.com site, which would ordinarily use the three-year growth rate, used the four-year growth rate instead as the three-year growth rate is not officially calculable because earnings per share in Year 4 were negative.

PE growth ratio.   This ratio is what Lynch is most famous for. The PEG ratio (pronounced "peg" or alternatively "price-earnings growth ratio") lets you know if a stock is fairly priced. He assumes a company has a PE ratio (meaning it is profitable), and he divides it by the business's historical growth rate. Others have used a similar formula but projected forward using the company's estimated long-term growth rate. Lynch looks at historical data because he feels that using the estimated future growth rate is just guessing.

What Lynch is basically looking for is a PE equal to the growth rate, which he considers a fairly priced stock. For the PE to equal the growth rate, it means it must move in sync with the growth rate—as growth increases, so does the PE. For Lynch, this is perfectly reasonable.

Of course, Lynch likes bargains, so if the PE is half or less than the growth rate (say growth is 40 percent a year while the PE is 18), that's even better. This situation makes Lynch a very happy man, but such a low ratio is rare.

Lynch finds PE to growth ratios up to 1.5 acceptable (growth of 20 percent and PE of 30, for instance). If a company has a PE to growth ratio of 1.5 to 1.8, it's unattractive but not ruled out altogether. If, however, the company's PE to growth ratio is above 1.8, that is explicitly unattractive.

PE Growth Ratio (PEG) for Fast Growers

1.	> 0 and ≤ 0.5	Pass—Best case
2.	> 0.5 and ≤ 1	Pass—Better
3.	> 1 and ≤ 1.5	Pass
4.	> 1.5 and ≤ 1.8	Pass
5.	> 1.8	Fail

■ At the time of this example, Dynacq's price was $13.81 and its trailing 12-month earnings per share were $0.53 (which you get by adding up the EPS from each of the last four quarters), giving the stock a multiple of 26.1. When Dynacq's PE multiple (28.2) is divided by its growth rate (78.9 percent annually), the PEG comes to 0.36. Note: This falls within Lynch's best-case scenario, which is where the PEG falls between 0 and 0.5. By this standard, Dynacq's stock price is very fair. Test results: Pass.

At the time of this example, Genlyte's price was $27.56 and its trailing 12-month earnings per share were $2.65. Its PE multiple is 10.4. When Genlyte's multiple is divided by its growth rate (22.9 percent), the PEG comes to 0.45, which fits Lynch's definition of very favorable, best case. Test results: Pass.

PE ratio.   If annual sales are greater than $1 billion and the PE ratio is less than 40, the stock passes muster. It's the right-sized company and the stock is reasonably priced, with its PE not too high. If annual sales exceed $1 billion and the PE is 40 or above, the stock is too expensive and should be rejected. Growth companies with annual sales of less than $1 billion are too small for applying a maximum PE (their PE can be quite large during their growth years).

PE for Fast Growers

1. Sales > $1 billion and PE < 40   Pass
2. Sales > $1 billion and PE ≥ 40   Fail
3. Sales < $1 billion   N/A

■ Dynacq's sales were $26.0 million, which were too small to apply the PE ratio analysis. However, you can still analyze the company using the PE ratio relative to the EPS growth rate, as we did above. Because the company is so small, it neither passes nor fails this PE test. Test results: Neutral.

Genlyte's sales were right at $1 billion and its PE ratio was 28.2, which less than 40. Test results: Pass.

EPS growth.   Lynch likes to see growth of between 20 and 50 percent, with 20 to 25 percent optimal. His thinking: These growth rates can be maintained.

EPS Growth for Fast Growers

1. ≥ 20% and ≤ 25%   Pass—Best case
2. > 25% ≤ 50%   Pass
3. > 50%   Fail

■ Dynacq's EPS growth rate of 79.0 percent actually fails Lynch's criteria as it is growing too fast. Lynch doesn't believe this kind of growth rate can be maintained in most companies year after year.

Bottom line interest in Dynacq: Some interest. Interest would become strong if other conditions stayed the way they are and the growth rate were under 50 percent per year.

Genlyte, on the other hand, passes all of Lynch's tests. Its EPS growth rate is 22.9 percent, which fits right into Lynch's ideal—EPS growth of between 20 and 25 percent. Lynch's fast grower methodology has a strong interest in Genlyte.

Stalwarts

Stalwarts experience 10 to 19 percent in annual earnings growth. Lynch likes these stocks and holds on to them for a 30 to 50 percent gain before selling and repeating the process with other stalwarts that have yet to appreciate. He always has stalwarts in his portfolio because they offer moderately good protection during recessions and hard times.

Sales.   A stock is considered a true stalwart if its earnings growth rate is in the teens and its annual sales are $2 billion or more. (Note: We actually interpret this criterion's threshold as $1.9 billion because a 5 percent difference in this rule of thumb just isn't meaningful.) If sales are less than $1.9 billion, it doesn't qualify as a stalwart and is ignored.

■ Oxford Health is considered a true stalwart because both its earnings growth rate of 15.7 percent and its annual sales of $4.1 billion meet Lynch's criteria. Test results: Pass.

Outback is also a true stalwart. Its earnings growth of 17.2 percent is within Lynch's boundaries of 10 to 19 percent, and its sales of slightly over $1.9 billion just meets Lynch's minimum size criterion. Test results: Pass.

Sales for Stalwarts
1. ≧ $1.9 billion   Pass
2. < $1.9 billion   Fail

Yield-adjusted PEG ratio.   With stalwarts, where yield is important, Lynch adjusts PEG for yield. He prefers PE to be ½ or less the growth rate plus the yield, though more than ½ but not greater than 1 is acceptable. If, however, it is more than 1, it fails. An example of a company that passes this test is one with a PE of 12, a growth rate of 22 percent, and a yield of 4 percent. If this same company had a PE of 27, it would fail this test because the PE (27) is more than the sum of the growth rate and yield (26).

■ Oxford Health's yield-adjusted PEG ratio is 0.76, which is okay. Test results: Pass.
   Outback's yield-adjusted PEG ratio is 0.83. Test results: Pass.

Yield-Adjusted PE Growth Ratio (PEG) for Stalwarts

1. > 0 and $\leqq 0.5$ Pass—Best case
2. > 0.5 and $\leqq 1$ Pass
3. > 1 Fail

Earnings per share.   Lynch wants the company to be profitable, which means its earnings per share over the trailing 12 months will be positive. If it makes no money or loses money, it fails the test.

■ Oxford Health earned $2.24 per share. Test results: Pass.
   Outback earned $1.78 per share. Test results: Pass.

EPS for Stalwarts

1. EPS > 0 Pass
2. EPS $\leqq 0$ Fail

Slow Growers

These are large and aging companies that pay dividends and are expected to grow slightly faster than the GNP. You won't find a lot of slow growers in Lynch's portfolio because if companies aren't going anywhere fast, neither will the price of their stocks. If growth in earnings is what enriches a company, then what's the sense of wasting time on these sluggards?

If such stocks appeal to you, invest in them primarily for their dividends.

Sales.   Lynch likes slow growers to be larger companies. If a company's annual sales are equal to or greater than $1 billion, it passes muster. If smaller than $1 billion, it fails.

■ TXU has annual sales of $22 billion, easily surpassing Lynch's minimum of $1 billion. Test results: Pass.

Sales for Slow Growers

1.	Sales ≧ $1 billion	Pass
2.	< $1 billion	Fail

Yield-adjusted PEG ratio.   With slow growers, where yield is important, Lynch adjusts PEG for yield. If PE is $\frac{1}{2}$ or less growth plus yield, Lynch is very happy, though if the PE to growth plus yield is more than $\frac{1}{2}$ and less than 1, he's still pretty content. However, if it equals or is greater than 1, it fails.

■ TXU's yield-adjusted PEG ratio is 0.99, just coming in under Lynch's maximum of less than 1. Test results: Pass.

Yield-adjusted PEG for Slow Growers

1.	> 0 and ≦ 0.5	Pass—Best case
2.	> 0.5 and ≦ 1	Pass
3.	> 1	Fail

Comparing yield with the S&P 500's yield.   A criterion Lynch uses with slow growers is to compare the stock's yield with the yield of the S&P 500; if it is higher than the S&P 500, it passes this test but if not, it fails. Note: Minimum acceptable yield is 3 percent. We interpret Lynch as putting this floor under the yield because a major reason for investing in slow growers is their yield. If they have too low a yield—irrespective of what the S&P 500's yield is—they aren't worth holding. Less than 3 percent just isn't worth it.

■ TXU's yield is 5.8 percent, while the S&P 500's yield is 1.6 percent. Because the company's yield is greater than both the S&P 500's and Lynch's 3 percent minimum, it's a winner. Test results: Pass.

Yield Compared with the S&P 500's Yield for Slow Growers

1. Yield ≧ S&P Yield and ≧ 3%   Pass
2. < 3%   Fail
3. Yield < S&P Yield and ≧ 3%   Fail

Other Criteria to Consider

The following apply to all six of Lynch's categories of companies.

Change in inventory to sales.   Lynch makes an important observation here. His view of inventory contains quite a bit of common sense, yet few other gurus mention it. Note: Inventory-to-sales criteria do not apply to nonmanufacturing companies, such as service and financial companies.

It's a red flag when inventories increase faster than sales. We interpret Lynch as giving an allowance of up to 5 percentage points (inventories can increase up to 5 percentage points faster than sales). Example: If sales go up 10 percent, inventory can rise no more than 15 percent.

The bottom line for Lynch: If inventories increase less than sales, are equal to sales, or are no more than 5 percentage points faster than sales, the company passes this test; but if inventories increase more than 5 percentage points faster than sales, the test fails.

Change in Inventory to Sales

1. If the business is a financial-oriented or service-oriented company, the ratio doesn't apply   n/a
2. Change in Inv./Sales is negative   Pass—Best case
3. Change in Inv./Sales = 0   Pass
4. Change in Inv./Sales is positive but ≦ 5%   Pass—Minimum
5. Change in Inv./Sales is positive and > 5%   Fail

■ Inventory to sales for Dynacq was 0 percent two years ago (Y2), whereas for the most recent year (Y1) it is 1.15 percent. Actually, these numbers are irrelevant because Dynacq is a service company and therefore has little or no inventory. Two years ago it, in fact, had no inventory. Last year's inventory was a relatively insignificant $300,000; but this criterion doesn't really apply to service companies.

Inventory to sales for Genlyte was 13.9 percent two years ago, whereas for last year (and on the most recent balance sheet) it is 15.01 percent. Because inventory has been rising, Lynch would not look entirely favorably at this stock, but its inventory increase, 1.11 percent, is below Lynch's 5 percent threshold. Therefore, it passes Lynch's test. Test results: Pass.

Oxford Health is a service company and doesn't have an inventory, so this criterion is not applicable to it.

TXU's inventory to sales was 3.6 percent two years ago, while this year it is 2.2 percent. Inventory to sales has decreased from last year, which is good. Test results: Pass.

Total debt-equity ratio.   Lynch likes companies with very low debt or no debt, companies that are in the minority (Microsoft is an example). Certain types of companies, such as financial institutions and utilities, generally carry large amounts of debt because of the nature of their business. Lynch has other criteria for dealing with these companies, which makes him unusual; other gurus also like low-debt companies but don't make explicit provisions for companies that naturally carry large amounts of debt.

If a company's debt is less than 80 percent of the company's equity, it passes this test. If more, with the exception of financial institutions and utilities, it fails. Keep in mind that there are some gradations here—the lower the debt-to-equity ratio, the better. Lynch especially likes companies whose debt is less than 50 percent of their equity.

■ Dynacq has an extremely favorable debt-equity ratio. Its long-term debt during its most recently reported quarter was $400,000 and its equity is $16,900,000, giving it a debt-equity ratio of 2.2 percent. This suggests the company is very strong financially. Test results: Pass.

Genlyte's debt-equity ratio works out to 29 percent, meaning the value of its equity is about three times the value of its debt. Lynch is looking for a debt-equity ratio of less than 80 percent, and Genlyte fits there comfortably. Test results: Pass.

Oxford Health's total debt-equity ratio is 6 percent, which is exceptionally low. Test results: Pass.

Outback's total DE is 1 percent, which is also exceptionally low. Test results: Pass.

TXU has a total DE of 197 percent. This is high, but remember we are dealing with a utility, which has high capital investments. As a result, this is an acceptable amount of debt for a company like TXU. Test results: Pass.

Special cases.   Lynch is the only guru to have specific criteria for banks, savings and loans, and other financial institutions. With financial institutions, he focuses on assets rather than debt. If the institution has an *equity-assets ratio* of 5 percent or more, it's okay; otherwise, it fails this test. The best case is when the equity-assets ratio is 13.5 percent or greater. If the financial institution's *return on assets* (ROA) is 1 percent or more, it passes this test, but fails if its ROA is below 1 percent.

Total Debt-Equity Ratio (DE)

1. If the business is a financial-oriented or service-oriented company, the ratio doesn't apply	n/a
2. If the company is a bank (including money center, regional, and S&L), then use the equity/assets and return on assets tests below	See tests below
3. DE = 0	Pass—Best case
4. DE ≥ 30 and < 50	Pass—Normal
5. DE ≥ 50 and < 80	Pass—Mediocre
6. DE ≥ 80, and a telecommunications or utility company	Pass
7. DE ≥ 80	Fail

Equity to Assets (EA) and Company Is a Bank or S&L

1. ≥ 5%	Pass
2. EA ≥ 13.5%	Pass—Best case
3. < 5%	Fail

Return on Assets (ROA) and Company Is a Bank or S&L

1. $\geqq$ 1%   Pass
2. < 1%   Fail

Free cash flow per share–current price ratio.   Lynch likes to see free cash flow, but most observers seem not to have picked up on this variable. We believe Lynch thinks it is important, and therefore we think it is important.

Cash flow, notes Lynch, is the amount of money a company takes in as a result of doing business. Every company takes in cash. That's no big deal. A distinguishing factor among companies is that some companies have to spend more money than others to bring in their cash flow. That's why Lynch emphasizes free cash flow, which he defines as "what's left over after the normal capital spending is taken out. It's the cash you've taken in that you don't have to spend." Technically, free cash flow is: Operating earnings + amortization + depreciation – the full amount paid for capital equipment.

The more free cash flow a company has, the better. Lynch looks at free cash flow per share compared to the stock's price. He gives the example of a company whose stock was $20 (and fairly priced according to his usual measures). But, in addition, it had $10 to $11 per share in total cash flow and $7 left over (free cash flow) after capital spending. If you divide the free cash flow (FCF) ($7) by the price ($20), you get 35 percent, which is Lynch's threshold for becoming excited about a high FCF. Though this criteron is not required for Lynch's analysis of his various categories of companies, it is considered a bonus if free cash flow meets or beats the minimum of 35 percent or more of the stock price.

■ Free cash flow per share for Dynacq for the last fiscal year was $0.55. Its stock price is $13.81, giving it a free cash flow–current price ratio of 4 percent, thus failing Lynch's bonus test. Test results: Does not receive a bonus.

Free Cash Flow per Share–Current Price (Bonus) Ratio

1. $\geqq$ 35%   Pass—Bonus

Net cash per share–current price.   Lynch likes to see a lot of net cash, which he defines as the cash and marketable securities found on the balance statement less long-term debt. If a company's stock is trading for $30, and it has net cash per share of $9 (30 percent), that's good. If it has $12 in net cash (40 percent), that's very attractive. And if it has $15 or more (50 percent +) and passes Lynch's other criteria, quick, mortgage the house and kids, your ship has come in. For Dynacq, net cash at the end of its last fiscal year was $6.2 million, long-term debt was $0.4 million, and the market cap of the company was $191 million equaling 3% net cash per share. Note that instead of trying to find the cash per share and the price per share, one is able to use the total cash less the total long-term debt in the company as of its most recent statement and divide by market cap.

Net Cash per Share–Current Price (Bonus) Ratio

1. ≥ 30% and < 40%   Pass—Good
2. ≥ 40% and < 50%   Pass—Better
3. ≥ 50%   Pass—Best

BOTTOM LINE

Dynacq is evaluated as a fast-growth company.

Tests passed: PEG ratio test
                 Total debt-equity ratio

Tests failed: EPS growth rate (too fast)

Tests neutral: PE ratio
                 Inventory to sales

Score: 80 percent

BOTTOM LINE: Dynacq is of SOME INTEREST but not strong interest.

Genlyte is evaluated as a fast-growth company.

Tests passed: PEG ratio test
                 Sales and PE ratio

Inventory to sales
EPS growth rate
Total debt-equity ratio

Tests failed: None

Score: 100 percent

BOTTOM LINE: There is STRONG INTEREST in Genlyte.

Oxford Health is evaluated as a stalwart.

Tests passed: Inventory to sales
Yield-adjusted PE growth ratio
Earnings per share
Total debt-equity ratio

Tests failed: None

Score: 100 percent

BOTTOM LINE: There is STRONG INTEREST in Oxford Health.

Outback Steakhouse is evaluated as a stalwart.

Tests passed: Yield-adjusted PEG ratio
Earnings per share
Total debt-equity ratio

Tests failed: None

Score: 100 percent

BOTTOM LINE: There is STRONG INTEREST in Outback Steakhouse.

TXU is evaluated as a slow grower.

Tests passed: Inventory to sales
Yield compared to the S&P 500
Yield-adjusted to PEG ratio
Total debt-equity ratio

Tests failed: None

Score: 100 percent

BOTTOM LINE: There is STRONG INTEREST in TXU.

LYNCH'S KEY INVESTING CRITERIA

- Peter Lynch is a guru with a real-world track record. First, he made a name for himself as a money manager, and only then did he become a best-selling author. This means his strategies have been proven in the real world.

- Lynch emphasizes taking advantage of what you already know. If you work in an industry and come across a company that's a star performer, for example, start researching it. Once you know it's a company that can perform in the marketplace, you now have to look at it more closely and study its financials, its future, and its stock price relative to its underlying value.

- Lynch is a fundamentalist. He's not into what the market is doing or is likely to do. Instead, he focuses on individual companies.

- Generally, Lynch invests in smaller companies, but he has, in fact, also invested in large ones.

- In general, he holds onto stocks for the medium to long term. He's not a trader nor a market timer.

- Lynch is best known for his PEG ratio, which is a company's price-earnings ratio divided by its growth rate.

CHAPTER 2

BENJAMIN GRAHAM

WHICH INVESTORS MIGHT USE **Benjamin Graham?**

RISK: Graham is suitable for investors seeking lower-risk stock plays. He looks for stocks that are deeply value priced in the belief they shield investors from losses, because, as a group, they are unlikely to drop much further (though there is no guarantee they won't drop significantly). Graham appeals to thrifty, discount-oriented investors.

TIME HORIZON: Long term.

EFFORT: Low. There's a bit of effort to choose stocks in the first place but very little effort required after that.

If there's a grand ol' man of investing, it's Benjamin Graham. This is the man generally credited with founding the field of security analysis. His disciples are many, including Mario Gabelli, John Neff, John Templeton, and, perhaps the most famous, Warren Buffett, who was at times Graham's student and employee.

In his introduction to the fourth revised edition of Graham's classic, *The Intelligent Investor,* Buffett wrote: "To me, Ben Graham was far more than an author or a teacher. More than any other man except my father, he influenced my life." That's quite an accolade from a man many consider to be the most successful stock market investor of the twentieth century. That someone like Buffett would say this about Graham suggests that Graham, even though dead for a quarter of a century, still has something to offer today's investor. We agree.

Although neither of us ever met Graham, he has always loomed large in our thinking about the stock market. In fact, coauthor John has been aware of Graham since he was seven or eight years old. A brother-in-law, who was considerably older than John, worked for Graham and talked about him endlessly. But you don't need a brother-in-law to introduce you to arguably the most influential investment strategist of all time. Read almost anything about security analysis, and you'll see Graham's name mentioned.

That's not to say Graham is totally modern. Some of his thinking, shaped of course by the stock market of his time, seems outdated today. He greatly valued dividends, for example, though today many companies pay historically low dividends, and, even more significant, many do not pay dividends at all. Rather than giving their shareholders a piece of the profits, these companies would rather reinvest their profits in expanding their businesses. Or if their stock prices are low, they prefer to buy back their stocks.

Nor was Graham a fan of technology stocks, finding them too risky. They are still risky, but technology has become such a large and vital part of our economy (which was not true when Graham was writing), the technology industry should not be ignored. Graham's approach, nonetheless, still makes a lot of sense. His strategy has come to be called "value investing," though that's a term others—not he—placed on it.

Graham was a believer in studying a company's fundamentals— its financial statements, performance, the basics. Then he looked at the company's price, and if it was a bargain compared with the value underlying the stock, he would buy.

In her book *Lessons from the Legends of Wall Street* (Dearborn, 2000), Nikki Ross writes: "Generally, value investors buy stocks at low prices relative to per share earnings, sales, or book value and apply other criteria as well. Often, stocks that value investors buy have higher dividend yields than the average stock."

Janet Lowe writes in *Value Investing Made Easy* (McGraw-Hill, 1996): "A value investor buys shares in a company as though he were buying the whole company, paying little attention to stock market temperament, the political climate or other exterior conditions." She goes on to note: "The value investor buys a stock as if he were buying the corner store. In the process, he might ask himself a series of questions. Is the business on a sound financial footing? Will I be assuming large debt? Does the price include the building and the land? Will it generate a steady, strong income stream? What kind of return on my investment will it produce? Is there the potential for sales and income growth?"

Lowe's approach to investing views buying a share of stock similar to buying a company, only you're not buying the whole company, just a tiny piece of it. Because you buy just a small piece doesn't mean you should approach the purchase of shares any differently than if you were buying the entire company.

This point was made by Warren Buffett in a talk at Columbia University in 1984 entitled "The Superinvestors of Graham and Doddsville." The talk was given in honor of the 50th anniversary of the publication of Graham's seminal work, *Security Analysis,* which he coauthored with David L. Dodd. *(The Intelligent Investor* is a popularized version of *Security Analysis.)* You can find an edited transcript of Buffett's speech in the appendix of *The Intelligent Investor.*

In his speech at Columbia, Buffett takes aim at technical analysts who consider the timing of buying a stock, such as in which day or month to make a purchase, or covariance in returns among securities or whatever. Buffett notes that when a businessperson buys a company, he or she doesn't factor into the decision the variables that technical analysts use. Buffett says: "Can you imagine buying an entire business simply because the price of the business had been marked *up* substantially last week and the week before?" In a sense, technical analysts do just that, and Buffett and Graham (as well as others) find this approach mysterious, even irrational. Instead, Buffett notes, followers of Graham and Dodd focus primarily on only two variables: price and value. In today's vernacular, Graham conducts a "reality check" on securities analysis rather than relying on fads or poorly thought-out strategies.

This is an important point that distinguishes Graham from many other security analysts. Graham was looking at neither trading volume nor the market's direction. In a lecture Graham gave in 1946, he said: "The correct attitude of the security analyst toward the stock market might well be that of a man toward his wife. He shouldn't pay too much attention to what the lady says, but he can't afford to ignore it entirely. That is pretty much the position that most of us find ourselves in vis-à-vis the stock market." That may not be a politically correct statement today, more than half a century after it was uttered, but the notion that you shouldn't put too much trust or emphasis on the market itself is an important tenet of Graham's approach. (The lecture, which was part of a series of ten lectures featured in Janet Lowe's *The Rediscovered Benjamin Graham: Selected Writings of the Wall Street Legend,* can be found on the Web site: <www.wiley.com>. When you get to the site, go to "search" and type in "Benjamin Graham," and one or more of the selections will be Graham's lectures.)

Graham was interested in the individual company and its value. He was not oblivious to what was happening around the stock—the market in general, the company's industry—but he thought that in the long run what will produce value for the investor is the stock of a solid company with good prospects that is selling below its worth.

In his introduction to *The Intelligent Investor,* Graham wrote: "Experience has taught us that, while there are many good growth companies worth several times net assets, the buyer of such shares will be too dependent on the vagaries and fluctuations of the stock market. By contrast, the investor in shares, say, of public utility companies at about their net-asset value can always consider himself the owner of an interest in sound and expanding businesses, acquired at a rational price—regardless of what the stock market might say to the contrary. The ultimate result of such a conservative policy is likely to work out better than exciting adventures into the glamorous and dangerous fields of anticipated growth."

Graham talked about the "defensive investor" and the "enterprising investor." Although mentioning these two, in reality he focused on the defensive investor. In his introduction, Graham wrote: "The defensive (or passive) investor will place his chief emphasis on the avoidance of serious mistakes or losses. His second aim will be freedom from effort, annoyance, and the need for making frequent decisions. The determining trait of the enterprising (or active, or aggressive) investor is his willingness to devote time and care to the selection of securities that are both sound and more attractive than the average."

Graham noted that the active investor, over time, expects a reward for his skill and efforts over the passive investor, but Graham had doubts this necessarily happens. He was not convinced that the enterprising investor (or most anyone) can consistently beat the market, though an underlying assumption of active, enterprising investors is, in fact, that they *can* beat the market.

In fact, Graham didn't provide much detail in explaining the differences between the two types. He implied that the defensive investor is passive (doesn't actively manage his or her portfolio) and conservative. The enterprising investor is viewed as more interested in actively managing his or her investments, and Graham loosened his criteria for this investor, such as allowing small companies to be in one's portfolio and permitting higher price-earnings ratios.

Most of Graham's strategy, however, seems aimed at the defensive investor. He was, after all, skeptical that most investors can beat the market and that most have an interest in spending much time studying and analyzing companies on an ongoing basis. For these reasons, we aim our analysis of Graham solely toward the defensive investor, who is conservative and fairly passive. If you want to take a more active, more risk-taking approach to your investments, there are better choices than Graham, such as O'Neil, which we discuss in other chapters.

An important issue for Graham was his margin of safety—that is, the difference between a stock's price and the company's underlying value. Diversification of your portfolio was another Graham technique for limiting your chances of a disaster. Disaster can strike because you miscalculated or the company has a run of plain old bad luck. If you have a margin of safety and there's a problem (the company doesn't perform as expected, the market goes a bit nutty), you, the investor, are protected because you bought the stock at so low a price, the stock—and you—should still be able to do okay.

Graham believed that to make money in the stock market, you don't just try to make money on your investments; you have to try to minimize your exposure to losses. After all, if you pay $20 for a stock that's really worth $40 (a margin of safety of 50 percent), the stock could get into trouble and you could still make money or at least break even. The larger the margin of safety, the more comfortable was Graham.

Graham wrote: "The buyer of bargain issues places particular emphasis on the ability of the investment to withstand adverse developments. . . . If these [undervalued issues] are bought on a bargain basis, even a moderate decline in the earning power need not prevent the investment from showing satisfactory results. The margin of safety will then have served its proper purpose." *(The Intelligent Investor)* Think of the margin of safety as being like a cellular phone you take on a trip. You don't expect to have trouble, but if you do, using the phone to call for help can get you out of a jam. So can the margin of safety.

Note that while Graham discussed the margin of safety, and his reputation is in part built on this concept, he didn't give clear-cut rules for determining what constitutes the margin of safety. He seemed to imply that he wanted to see stocks whose prices are 30 to 50 percent below their value, but he never made this a hard-and-fast rule. The most one can say is that if you follow his guidelines, there's an implicit margin of safety—you'll be buying stocks at a sufficiently low price that you will get a desired margin of safety.

Lacking a proper study of a company's assets and comparing this value to its stock's price, the investor is just speculating, not investing, Graham believed. In an article in *Fortune* entitled "Do You Believe? How Yahoo! Became a Blue Chip" (6 June 1999), author Joseph Nocera writes about a T. Rowe Price securities analyst named Lise Buyer. Buyer, it seems, tried "to make the math work" when analyzing a company like Yahoo! but couldn't. Internet companies and their valuations just didn't make sense based on traditional valuations— they lacked tangible assets, track records, profits, dividends, and even sales.

"I went back to Graham and Dodd," Buyer is quoted as saying. This is what she found: "Unseasoned companies in new fields of activity . . . provide no sound basis for the determination of intrinsic value. . . . Analysts serve their discipline best by identifying such companies as highly speculative and not attempting to value them. . . . The buyer of such securities is not making an investment, but a bet on a new technology, a new market, a new service. . . . Winning bets on such situations can produce very rich rewards, but they are in an odds-setting rather than a valuation process." We think Graham would completely agree with Buyer's analysis of Internet stocks and young, developing companies with little in the way of assets in general. Note, however, that despite her insights, at the time the article appeared, she had "buy" recommendations on 11 of the 13 Internet companies she followed, including Yahoo!

This reminds us of a comment Graham made in the 1946 lecture series we mentioned before (from Lecture Number 10):

> We all know that if we follow the speculative crowd we are going to lose money in the long run. Yet, somehow or other, we find ourselves very often doing just that. It is extraordinary how frequently security analysts and the crowd are doing the same thing. In fact, I must say I can't remember any case in which they weren't.
>
> It reminds me of the story you all know of the oil man who went to Heaven and asked St. Peter to let him in. St. Peter said, "Sorry, the oil men's area here is all filled up, as you can see by looking through the gate." The man said, "That's too bad, but do you mind if I just say four words to them?" And St. Peter said, "Sure." So the man shouts good and loud, "Oil discovered in hell!" Whereupon all the oil men begin trooping out of Heaven and making a beeline for the nether regions. Then St. Peter said, "That was an awfully good stunt. Now there's plenty of room, come right in." The oil man scratches his head and says, "I think I'll go with the rest of the boys. There may be some truth in that rumor after all."

GRAHAM: HIS STORY

Who was this man, Benjamin Graham? His life, as discussed by both Lowe's and Ross's books as well as other sources, reveals a very bright, capable individual who made his mark, not just through his ideas, but through his willingness to share those ideas with others and help others become successful themselves, such as Warren Buffett.

Graham was born in London in 1894 and, when a year old, came to New York with his parents. His father died when Graham was nine, and his mother, Dora, raised him and his two brothers. She must have been a risk taker, because it's reported that she tried several business ventures, all of which failed, and even invested in the stock market in 1907, just before the famous financial panic of that year, which wiped out her investment.

The family was often in financial straits and Graham, as a result, worked during both high school and college. A gifted student, he went to Columbia University on a scholarship. On graduation, he was asked to teach math, English, and philosophy at Columbia but instead opted for a job on Wall Street because the income potential was better there than in academia.

Initially, he worked in 1914 in the bond department of a brokerage firm, Newburger, Henderson and Loeb. Shortly after, World War I began and the financial markets panicked. The New York Stock Exchange closed for several months that year, and restrictions on prices and the trading of some stocks continued into the following year. When trading resumed, Graham's employer was understaffed, giving Graham an opportunity to work at—and learn from—a variety of jobs at the firm. Among the things he learned was that many investors had limited knowledge of investing.

It's probably a good thing Graham was not a technical analyst because these folks rely a great deal on timing, and Graham's timing in some of his life decisions was not always great. As noted, he went to work on Wall Street just before it shut down as the result of war. And he decided to go off on his own and start an investment firm with a partner, Jerome Newman, an accountant, in 1926, a mere three years before the stock market crash of 1929 and the long-term trough the stock market fell into at that time (it took the Dow Jones Industrial Average 25 years to climb back to the high it hit in 1929).

Despite these setbacks, Graham managed to make the best of the situation. According to Lowe: "The Crash of 1929 ravaged not only Graham's investment portfolio but also his plan to write a book on his investment principles. Despite his skills and dedication, Graham's clients lost money along with everyone else. Graham and his partner, Jerome Newman, worked 5 years without compensation until their clients' fortunes were fully restored. Though the experience was dreadful, it earned Graham widespread respect for his integrity as a money manager. . . . Once the Graham Newman Co. recouped its portfolio of 1929–30, Graham never again lost money for his clients."

Graham was a lecturer at Columbia University from 1928 to 1956, when he retired. There he taught a popular course on investing. It was at Columbia that Graham and Buffett met, Buffett being Graham's star student. Graham's course at Columbia was the basis for his and Dodd's (also a Columbia faculty member) classic, *Security Analysis,* which was published in 1934. The first edition of *The Intelligent Investor* came out in 1949. Both books were subsequently updated during Graham's lifetime. Graham died in 1976 at Aix in the south of France, where he had a second home.

Lowe writes:

> Value investing as taught by Graham slips in and out of vogue over the years, invariably gaining in popularity when markets are down or uncertainty runs rampant. Investors are just as likely to suffer memory lapses when markets are rising and making money seems easy. Despite the long-term success of value-investing practitioners, business schools across the nation have devoted greater attention to such concepts as the efficient market hypothesis, the capital asset pricing model, market timing, and asset allocation. . . . Yet as the business schools, the media, and fad investors chase one new rainbow after another, Buffett and other Graham disciples plod along, piling up profits.

USING GRAHAM FOR YOUR OWN INVESTMENTS: STEP-BY-STEP

■ General Motors Corporation (stock symbol: GM) is among the world's best-known companies (see Figure 2.1). Detroit-based, General Motors is the world's largest automaker. Its car lines include Buick, Cadillac, Chevrolet, Pontiac, Saab, Saturn, Opel, and Vauxhall as well as Oldsmobile (which is being discontinued). It also makes GMC trucks and has a variety of nonautomotive businesses in addition to minority holdings in other carmakers, including Fuji Heavy Industries (Subaru) and Fiat Auto (Alfa Romeo, Fiat).

The second company we use as an example is Oxford Industries Inc. (stock symbol: OXM) (see Figure 2.2). Headquartered in Atlanta,

FIGURE 2.1	GENERAL MOTORS CORP (GM)	$51.85 as of 3/30/2001

	Year 1	Year 2
Total Net Income (mil.)	$4,452	$5,576
EPS	$6.68	$7.12
Sales (mil.)	$184,632	$176,558
Avg. PE	10.7	9.6
ROE	14.8%	29.1%
Long-Term Debt-Equity	472%	628%
Dividend Yield	$2.00	$1.68
Payout	29.9%	23.6%
Shares Outstanding (mil.)	548.2	619.4

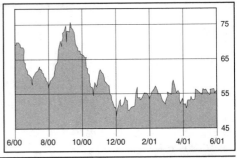

	Year 3	Year 4	Year 5	Year 6	Year 7	Year 8	Year 9	Year 10
Total Net Income (mil.)	$2,956	$6,698	$4,953	$6,932	$5,658	$2,466	$−2,621	$−4,992
EPS	$3.48	$7.18	$5.02	$5.89	$3.90	$1.41	$−4.05	$−7.39
Sales (mil.)	$161,315	$166,445	$158,015	$163,861	$150,591	$133,622	$128,533	$119,753
Avg. PE	14.8	7.2	8.7	6.4	10.9	26.4	NE	NE
ROE	19.7%	38.3%	21.2%	29.7%	44.1%	44.1%	NE	NE
Long-Term Debt-Equity	351%	24%	163%	157%	292%	611%	667%	284%
Dividend	$1.26	$1.68	$1.32	$0.93	$0.66	$0.66	$1.17	$1.32
Payout	36.2%	23.4%	26.3%	15.8%	16.9%	46.8%	NE	NE
Shares Outstanding (mil.)	785.4	831.5	907.2	902.9	904.5	863.4	847.5	744.6

	Q1	Q2	Q3	Q4	Q5	Q6	Q7	Q8
EPS	$−0.69	$1.55	$2.93	$2.79	$1.56	$1.11	$2.46	$2.55
Revenue (mil.)	$46,431	$42,690	$48,743	$44,471	$53,124	$40,473	$42,832	$40,129

	Market Cap (mil.)	TTM Sales (mil.)	Relative Strength	EPS Growth (3-yr. avg.)	Revenue Growth (TTM)	Current Ratio	Insider Buy-Sells (3 months)
GM	$28,441	$184,632	41	−2.25%	−12.8%	3.3	0/5
Major Auto Mfgs.	$41,805	$100,376	54	−7.3%	−3.2%	2.1	

	PEG	PE	Projected PE	PS	Price-Book	Price-Cash Flow	Free Cash Flow/Share
GM	NE	7.8	15.8	0.4	2.45	4.1	$6.14
Major Auto Mfgs.	2.0	19.7	17.0	0.48	1.65	4.6	

	Yield	Profit Margin (TTM)	ROE (TTM)	Total Debt-Equity	Long-Term Debt-Equity	Insider Ownership	Institutional Ownership
GM	3.9%	2.4%	14.8%	472%	472%	1%	57.1%
Major Auto Mfgs.	3.1%	0.7%	9.3%	233%	233%		

Recent Balance Sheet Items ($ millions)		Financial Statement Trends		
Cash	10,284		Recent 12 mo.	FY1	FY2
Current Assets	208,920	Inventory/Sales	5.9%	5.9%	6.0%
Total Assets	303,100	AR to Sales	73.1%	73.1%	69.2%
Current Liabilities	63,156	R&D to Sales	−	−	−
Long-Term Debt	142,447			
Total Debt	144,655			
Equity	30,175			

FIGURE 2.2	OXFORD INDUSTRIES INC (OXM)	$18.10 as of 3/30/2001

	Year 1	Year 2
Total Net Income (mil.)	$23.4	$26.4
EPS	$3.02	$3.11
Sales (mil.)	$839.5	$862.4
Avg. PE	7.4	9.4
ROE	14.2%	17.1%
Long-Term Debt-Equity	25%	26%
Dividend	$0.63	$0.82
Payout	20.9%	26.4%
Shares Outstanding (mil.)	7.6	7.9

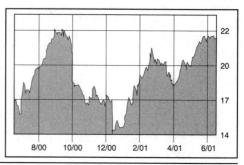

	Year 3	Year 4	Year 5	Year 6	Year 7	Year 8	Year 9	Year 10
Total Net Income (mil.)	$24.6	$19.6	$2.2	$10.6	$19.2	$14.8	$12.5	$5.5
EPS	$2.75	$2.23	$0.25	$1.20	$2.18	$1.70	$1.42	$0.62
Sales (mil.)	$774.5	$703.2	$664.4	$657.0	$624.6	$572.9	$527.7	$505.8
Avg. PE	11.3	9.6	70.5	21.7	11.4	12.20	13.70	15.70
ROE	15.4%	13.9%	1.7%	8.0%	15.0%	12.8%	11.6%	5.4%
Long-Term Debt-Equity	26%	30%	35%	35%	10%	15%	21%	27%
Dividend	$0.80	$1.00	$0.80	$0.74	$0.51	$0.63	$0.68	$0.50
Payout	29.1%	44.8%	320%	61.7%	23.4%	37.1%	47.9%	80.6%
Shares Outstanding (mil.)	8.8	8.8	8.8	8.7	8.6	8.7	8.8	9.0

	Q1	Q2	Q3	Q4	Q5	Q6	Q7	Q8
EPS	$0.53	$0.36	$0.45	$0.94	$0.6	$0.6	$0.74	$0.76
Revenue (mil.)	$194.9	$204.4	$246.4	$187.5	$219.9	$185.7	$225.2	$206.0

	Market Cap (mil.)	TTM Sales (mil.)	Relative Strength	EPS Growth (3-yr. avg.)	Revenue Growth (TTM)	Current Ratio	Insider Buy-Sells (3 months)
OXM	$134	$843.1	62	11.4%	5.3%	2.4	0/1
Apparel Clothing Industry	$2,111	$2,224	74	11.1%	8.0%	2.5	

	PEG	PE	Projected PE	PS	Price-Book	Price-Cash Flow	Free Cash Flow/Share
OXM	0.52	7.9	5.9	0.16	0.82	4.4	$2.52
Apparel Clothing Industry	2.5	20.3	13.9	1.06	2.3	11.3	

	Yield	Profit Margin (TTM)	ROE (TTM)	Total Debt-Equity	Long-Term Debt-Equity	Insider Ownership	Institutional Ownership
OXM	4.6%	2.1%	5.3%	39%	25%	<1%	51.8%
Apparel Clothing Industry	1.6%	6.4%	15.1%	79%	31%		

Recent Balance Sheet Items ($ millions)		Financial Statement Trends			
Cash	8.5		Recent 12 mo.	FY1	FY2
Current Assets	283.9	Inventory/Sales	18.8%	18.2%	19.0%
Total Assets	330.1	AR to Sales	12.2%	13.5%	14.8%
Current Liabilities	120.6	R&D to Sales	–	–	–
Long-Term Debt	40.4				
Total Debt	64.1				
Equity	162.4				

Oxford is a large maker of private-label clothing and produces clothing lines under licenses from a variety of big-name designers and design companies, including DKNY, Tommy Hilfiger, Geoffrey Beene, and Oscar de la Renta.

Sectors.   Graham lived in another era, at least as far as technology stocks are concerned. They remain risky, but these stocks are a major driving force not only in the stock market today but in the nation's overall economy.

The problem Graham had with technology companies was that they were generally too small and too new and lacking in certifiable tangible assets to provide the wherewithal for the analyst to analyze them and provide the margin of safety Graham liked for comfort. There's no dependable way to analyze these stocks and identify the most promising companies, thought Graham.

"Graham did not own technology stocks, which frequently have erratic earnings and can be difficult to value," writes Ross in her book.

■ Neither GM nor Oxford is a technology company. Test results: Pass.

Sectors

1. Technology	Fail
2. All others (including public utilities)	Pass

Company sales.   According to Graham, "Each company selected should be large, prominent and conservatively financed." What's a large, prominent company? Even Graham admitted the difficulty in defining such a company: "The words 'large' and 'prominent' carry the notion of substantial size combined with a leading position in the industry. . . . To supply an element of concreteness here, let us suggest that to be 'large' in present-day terms a company should have $50 million of assets or do $50 million of business. Again, to be 'prominent' a company should rank among the first quarter or first third in size within its industry group. It would be foolish, however, to insist upon such arbitrary criteria. They are offered merely as guides to those who may ask for guidance."

For our purposes, we extrapolate Graham's definition of size for inflation and define the minimum-sized company as having annual sales equal to or greater than $340 million.

The reason Graham emphasized size is that larger companies, with a leading position in their industries, tend to have stocks less volatile than those of smaller companies; have assets larger and less prone to negative surprises than those of smaller companies; have more of a track record and therefore lend themselves to better financial analysis; and are in a better competitive position than their industry counterparts.

Company Sales

1. $< 340 million   Fail
2. $\geq 340 million   Pass

■ GM, among the world's largest companies, has sales of almost $185 billion, easily surpassing Graham's minimum of $340 million. Test results: Pass.

Oxford's annual sales in the most recent year were $839.5 million. Test results: Pass.

Current ratio.   The current ratio (current assets divided by current liabilities) must be equal to or greater than 2, which means that the company has no more than $1 of current liabilities for every $2 of current assets it owns. This criterion evaluates (looks at) a company's liquidity. It compares those liabilities closest to maturity and thus the ones that must be paid back first (current liabilities) to the company's most liquid assets (current assets), such as cash and cash equivalents, accounts receivable, and so forth.

A high current ratio indicates the company's finances are highly liquid and that, in turn, suggests a lower risk for the company's getting into financial trouble. Keep in mind that certain circumstances may create a high current ratio when, in fact, that company is facing problems. Receivables are current assets, and a company with an uncommonly large amount of receivables may be having trouble collecting them. Inventory, another current asset, may be high because the company can't sell it rather than as a result of high customer demand.

JOHN STEINBECK LIBRARY

Date: 1/10/2020

Time: 2:13:30 PM

Name: Luis Guillermo Gonzalez

Fines/Fees Owed: $0.00

Total Checked Out: 1

Checked Out

Title: The market gurus :
Barcode: 33550087156S3
Due Date: 20200131 235900

CALL (831) 758-7311

or visit catalog salinaspubliclibrary.org to
renew items and avoid late fees

On the other hand, a low current ratio suggests the company is relatively illiquid and could have trouble paying off its current liabilities. This criterion is not required for public utilities and major telecoms because, according to Graham, this working capital factor takes care of itself in these industries as part of the continuous financing of their growth through sales of bonds and shares that these types of companies typically engage in.

■ GM's current ratio of 3.3 is above Graham's minimum of 2. Test results: Pass.
   Oxford's current ratio is 2.4. Test results: Pass.

Current Ratio

1. < 2 Fail
2. $\geqq 2$ Pass

Long-term debt in relation to net current assets.   For industrial companies, long-term debt must not exceed net current assets, also called working capital (current assets minus current liabilities). This, too, is a liquidity measurement. When long-term debt does not exceed net current assets, the company is in a strong financial position to meet its long-term obligations. Companies that meet this criterion are displaying one of the attributes of a financially secure organization.

■ For industrial companies, long-term debt must not exceed net current assets. Net current assets are calculated by taking the current assets of $208,920 and subtracting the current liabilities of $63,156. GM's long-term debt is $142,447 million, which doesn't exceed its net current assets of $145,764 million. Test results: Pass.
   Oxford's long-term debt is $40.4 million, which is easily surpassed by its net current assets of $163.3 million (current assets of $283.9 million less current liabilities of $120.6 million). Test results: Pass.

Long-Term Debt in Relation to Net Current Assets

1. LTD $>$ Net current assets   Fail
2. LTD $\leq$ Net current assets   Pass

Long-term EPS growth.   Companies must increase their EPS by at least 30 percent over a ten-year period. This is not an annual compound rate but is an amount EPS must grow over ten years. If earnings per share are $1.50 in Year 1, then they must reach at least $1.95 in ten years to pass this test. That's not much of a growth rate by today's standard, but remember that Graham was really looking here for growth—at almost any rate—which is sustained over a long period. Companies with this growth rate have proven themselves over time.

To calculate, Graham did not use just the earnings of a single year for the beginning and ending earnings. He *averaged* the earnings of the first three years of the ten-year period and then the last three years of that same ten-year period.

Also, no negative earnings in the past ten years are allowed. That's right. Even one year of losses in the past ten means the company fails this test.

■ GM's EPS growth rate fits the bill for Graham over the past eight years but not for Years 9 and 10, when GM had negative earnings. The average EPS for the first three years, when GM had positive earnings (Years 6, 7, 8) was $3.73. Its average for the three most recent years was $5.76, which is an increase of 54 percent. This meets Graham's goal of growth of at least 30 percent, but because GM had negative earnings during the past decade, it nonetheless fails this test.

Oxford's EPS averaged $1.25 for Years 8, 9, and 10. And for the three most recent years, EPS averaged $2.96. That's a 137 percent gain, easily outpacing Graham's minimum of 30 percent. Test results: Pass.

Long-Term EPS Growth (Ten Years)

1. $< 30\%$ Fail
2. $\geq 30\%$ Pass

Price-earnings ratio (PE).   The PE ratio must be "moderate," which this methodology states is not greater than 15, meaning the stock price cannot exceed 15 times the amount the company earned per share. Stocks with moderate PEs are more defensive by nature. The higher the PE, the more speculative the stock because there is less profit per share supporting the price.

Graham looked at earnings that are the average earnings for the last three years and not the last years' earnings or trailing 12-month earnings, which are more typically used as the earnings part of the PE ratio.

■ GM's PE of 9 falls easily within Graham's maximum of 15. Notice that 9 is different from the PE found on GM's data sheet (7.8), as the data sheet PE is based on the trailing 12-month (TTM) earnings. Here is how Graham's PE for GM was calculated for this example:

The EPS for the three most recent fiscal years was $6.68, $7.12, and $3.48. Average these together and you get an average earnings of $5.76. Take the price of GM, which was $51.85 and divide that by $5.76 and you get a PE of 9. Test results: Pass.

Oxford's PE of 6.1 is easily below Graham's maximum. Here is how the PE was calculated: The EPS for the three most recent years was $3.02, $3.11, and $2.75, and the average of these is $2.96. The current price is $18.10, which yields a PE of 6.1. Test results: Pass.

Price-Earnings (PE)

1.	> 15	Fail
2.	≦ 15	Pass

Price-book ratio (PB).   The price-book value ratio (PB) is the price of the stock compared with the book value per share. Book value is total assets minus intangible assets minus liabilities. Put another way, it is tangible assets less the money the company owes. Keep in mind that Graham was into "reality," real things, like tangible assets, not intangibles, such as so-called goodwill. He wanted the PB ratio to be reasonable. That is, the PB multiplied by PE cannot be greater than 22. If the stock price is $30, book value per share is $20, and earnings per share is $2, then the PB is 30:20 or 1.5:1, and the PE is 30:2 or 15:1. Multiplying PB by PE in this case, 1.5:1 × 15:1, gives us a number of 22.5:1. That just about matches Grahams target of PB × PE not being greater than 22:1.

■ PB multiplied by PE cannot exceed 22, while GM's PB is 2.45 and PE is 9, which, when multiplied, comes to 22.05. This is just barely over the threshold of 22, so we treat it as if it came to 22 even. Test results: Pass.

Oxford's PB is only 0.82, and with its PE of 6.1, this calculation comes to a very low 5. Test results: Pass.

Price-Book Ratio (PB)

1. $PB \times PE > 22$	Fail	
2. $PB > 1.5$	Fail	
3. $PB \times PE \leq 22$	Pass—Best case	
4. $PB \leq 1.5$	Pass	

Dividends. Uninterrupted dividends for the last 20 years was suggested as another conservative criterion by Graham. That is, during the past 20 years, the company had to pay a dividend every year (although there is no requirement that the dividend stay the same or increase every year). We are aware of only one place on the Web that has dividend data going back more than ten years. The site is MSN Money Central. The chart page with dividends can be found at: <http://moneycentral.msn.com/investor/charts/charting.asp?Symbol=gm>.

To see the dividend history, you need to click on the word "Period" on the top of the chart, and from the dropdown list that is displayed select "All." If dividends are not displayed at all on the chart, you first need to click on the word "Chart" on the top of the chart, then select "Display Options" and make sure there is a check in the event check box labeled "Dividends."

■ GM has had uninterrupted dividends for over 30 years, even though it has had years where it lost money. Test results: Pass.

We have data on Oxford going back only 13 years, but it has paid dividends each of those years. In the absence of additional data, we make our decision as a practical matter, based on just 13 years. Test results: Pass.

Dividends

1. Continuous dividend payment for last 20 years	Pass
2. If interrupted	Fail

Total debt-equity ratio (DE).   For industrial companies, total debt (both long-term and short-term debt but not other liabilities) must not exceed total equity. That is, total DE ≦ 100%.

For utilities (including regulated phone companies and railroads) the company can safely have a much larger long-term debt compared to equity. LTD/E ≦ 230%.

■ GM's total debt was $144,655,000,000 and equity was $30,175,000,000. Because total debt exceeds equity, GM fails this test. Test results: Fail.

Oxford's total debt was $64,100,000, which was easily exceeded by its equity, which totaled $162,400,000. Test results: Pass.

The utility TXU Corporation's long-term debt was $15,281,000,000, and equity was $7,776,000,000. The LTD/E is 200%, which is under 230%. Test results: Pass.

Total Debt-Equity Ratio

1. Industrial companies—DE > 100%	Fail
2. Industrial companies—DE ≦ 100%	Pass
3. Utilities, phone companies, railroads—LTD/E > 230%	Fail
4. Utilities, phone companies, railroads—LTD/E ≦ 230%	Pass

Diversification.   You should diversify your portfolio to minimize your risk. According to Graham:

There is a close logical connection between the concept for a safety margin and the principle of diversification. . . . Even with a margin in the investor's favor, an individual security may work out badly. For the margin guarantees only that he [the investor] has a better chance for profit than for loss—not that loss is impossible. But as the number of such commitments is increased, the more certain does it become that the aggregate of the profits will exceed the aggregate of the losses.

Graham has recommended holding, as a minimum, 10 value stocks and to consider holding as many as 30.

BOTTOM LINE

General Motors

Tests passed: Sectors
Company sales
Current ratio
Long-term debt in relation to net current assets
Price-earnings ratio
Price-book ratio
Dividends

Tests failed: Long-term EPS growth
Total debt-equity ratio

Score: 78 percent (7 of 9 pass)

BOTTOM LINE: There is NO INTEREST in General Motors.

Oxford Industries

Tests passed: Sectors
Company sales
Current ratio
Long-term debt in relation to net current assets
Long-term EPS growth
Price-earnings ratio
Price-book value ratio
Total debt-equity ratio
Dividends

Tests failed: None

Score: 100 percent (9 of 9 pass)

BOTTOM LINE: There is STRONG INTEREST in Oxford Industries.

GRAHAM'S KEY INVESTING CRITERIA

■ Look at the sector or industry the company is in. Be sure it is promising and that the company has a good position in it.

■ Look for the sales to be a substantial size.

- Look at the current ratio.

- Look at long-term debt in relation to net current assets.

- Look at long-term EPS growth.

- Look at the price-earnings ratio.

- Look at the price-book ratio.

- Look for continuous dividend payments.

CHAPTER 3

WILLIAM O'NEIL

WHICH INVESTORS MIGHT USE **William O'Neil?**

RISK: O'Neil's strategy involves a fair amount of risk, which is controlled by required disciplined buying and selling. This is a complex strategy best suited for experienced investors.

TIME HORIZON: Short. O'Neil can move very quickly in and out of stocks. O'Neil's is a strategy suited for someone who wants to make the most money in the shortest period of time.

EFFORT: A lot. Following O'Neil's strategy probably requires more ongoing effort than the strategy of any other guru we cover in *The Market Gurus*. It is also necessary to have the discipline to cut losses at 7 to 8 percent of your purchase price.

NOTE: O'Neil's techniques require you to monitor the stock almost continuously when you are looking to make a purchase. Sometimes he makes moves based on what a stock is doing during a day, which means you have to be up-to-date with the stock all the time, when you're looking to make a purchase. And you must be disciplined. He requires you to base your buys and sells on price movements and other factors, and you have to do so according to his rules. Emotion doesn't play any part in his approach. For example, because he tries to capitalize on volatility, he says you must sell when you have a loss of 7 or 8 percent. You can't argue about it. If you are unwilling to make a big commitment in time and effort or aren't highly disciplined, O'Neil is not the guru for you.

Nobody can accuse William J. O'Neil of being a bottom feeder. The adage "Buy low, sell high" doesn't make much sense to him as an investment strategy. If you want the best merchandise, you have to pay for it, whether it's a Rolex, a meal, or a stock. The very best companies command top dollar and rightfully so, he says. His philosophy can be summed up in one of his favorite phrases: "Buy high, sell even higher."

O'Neil, the founder of *Investor's Business Daily,* which has a devoted following, makes a compelling case that "values" and "bargains" are low priced because they are usually inferior merchandise, and investing in them is unlikely to bring long-term investment success. Success comes to those using a strategy that focuses on the very best companies, because they are the most likely to have dramatic increases in their stock prices. "The hard-to-accept great paradox in the stock market is that what seems too high and risky to the majority usually goes higher and what seems low and cheap usually goes lower," writes O'Neil in his book *How to Make Money in Stocks.* (Unless otherwise noted, all quotes from O'Neil are from that book.)

We've been to a couple of O'Neil's advanced seminars and have seen him in action in person. Well dressed, with a corporate, CEO look and demeanor, it's easy to understand O'Neil's appeal. We, too, were struck by his insight that you should buy quality, and when you buy quality, be prepared to pay for it. So-called bargains are discounted because they usually are inferior. This goes against what we had been thinking up to then—when a stock went down, we, like many others, ran after it thinking it might be a bargain— and goes against what most investors think. O'Neil's view of buying the best was an eye-opener for us, and we think it will be a revelation to many of our readers as well.

Look at it this way: If you visit a store and buy only its discounted merchandise, will you get the best the store has to offer—the most stylish, the best-made, the most desirable clothing? Not likely. Why? Because the really good stuff has already been sold and at higher prices. What can't be gotten rid of at retail prices, the store tries to sell at a discount. The market—in this case, clothing shoppers—has picked out the most desirable merchandise and left the remainder for the bottom feeders.

And the longer the bottom feeders wait—until the store takes a second or third discount—the fewer the pickings and the less desirable the merchandise. The same with stocks. If you wait to buy until a stock drops and drops and drops, chances are good what you'll buy won't be the best investment. You'll have a wardrobe or stock portfolio filled with leftovers, damaged goods, and merchandise whose time is past.

O'Neil didn't come to his strategy by being a shopping maven at Saks Fifth Avenue or Neiman Marcus. His strategy developed over time and was based on his penchant for numbers and analysis. He loves charts and graphs and statistics, and he has compiled one of the best databases around. O'Neil and his company track over 200 data items for over 10,000 companies.

WHO IS WILLIAM O'NEIL?

Born in Oklahoma on March 25, 1933, O'Neil grew up in Texas in modest circumstances. A graduate of Southern Methodist University in Dallas, where he was a business major, he lives in Los Angeles and is married with three daughters and a son.

Always a hard worker, he's held a variety of jobs in his life, including newspaper boy and vacuum cleaner salesman, but when he needed a job after college, he found himself working as a broker at Hayden Stone & Co., then a major brokerage firm. From this beginning came a life-long interest in the stock market.

It didn't take O'Neil long to prove himself on Wall Street. In 1963, at the tender age of 30, he founded William O'Neil & Company, the same year he bought himself a seat on the New York Stock Exchange, the youngest person to do so. In 1973, he founded O'Neil Data Systems Inc., a pioneer in the use of database publishing. Nine years later, believing that the average investor lacked the data needed to successfully invest in the stock market, he launched the newspaper *Investor's Daily,* now *Investor's Business Daily (IBD),* a cheeky gamble considering his competition was the ever formidable *Wall Street Journal. IBD*'s circulation is now over 310,000, and it calls itself the fastest-growing business publication in the country.

O'Neil's spokesperson, Kathleen K. Sherman, says O'Neil has a favorite saying: "Average people are average for a reason—they all think alike." In today's parlance, O'Neil likes to think "outside the box." Take price-earnings ratios (PEs), as an example. A PE is the result of dividing the price of a stock by its earnings per share. The ratio tells you how many times the stock's earnings is the stock price. If a company earns $1.50 per share and its stock sells for $24, its PE ratio is 16:1; it sells for 16 times what it earns per share.

PEs are a Wall Street staple. In fact, they may be the single most widely used and studied statistic in the entire field of stock market analysis. O'Neil is not impressed. Here's what he has to say about PE ratios: "Factual analysis of . . . winning stocks shows that P/E ratios have very little to do with whether a stock should be bought or not. A stock's P/E ratio is not normally an important cause of the most successful stock moves."

O'Neil is something of a contrarian—he likes to snub his nose at conventional wisdom. He's a sophisticated investor with an "attitude"; he knows how to make money in the stock market, and most others don't. He makes his claims based on what he says is a thorough study of stock market statistics, which includes looking for patterns found in successful stocks dating from 1953. The purpose of the exercise is to identify the common characteristics of the stocks that did best from 1953 on.

This approach is, in fact, representative of O'Neil's strategy: Look at what has happened in the past, identify the central characteristics of those stocks that have done best, and then look for those same characteristics in today's market. He's identified 500 stocks he calls the best-performing and found patterns that characterized these high flyers. He continues to study the market in the same way and annually updates his findings in what he calls "Model Study of the Greatest Stock Market Winners." An underlying assumption of his strategy is that what's worked well before will work well again—and again and again.

In O'Neil's words, "The first step in learning to pick stock market winners is for you to examine leading winners of the past to learn all the characteristics of the most successful stocks." And: "There's very little that's really new in the stock market. History just keeps repeating itself."

We've identified several factors we think O'Neil favors. He likes the new, something that catches his attention. New management or new products may qualify if they can boost the company onto the next level. Also favored are leaders in their fields (not unlike Warren Buffett, who also likes companies at or near the top of their particular industry).

Institutional interest, which often follows industry leaders, is also desirable. He figures institutions are great buyers of stocks, so it is a good thing when a number of institutions invest in a particular company.

Statistically, O'Neil seeks stocks with annual compound earnings growth of at least 18 percent annually for the last five years and also looks for quarterly earnings that increase 18 percent for the current quarter versus the same quarter last year. Plus, the recent market overall should be moving upward. You want your stocks to go up, which means you don't want to be in an acquisition mode when the market is going down.

Buying when the market is correct is an important part of O'Neil's strategy and is one of his secrets for controlling risk. Obviously, most of the gurus would like to buy when the market is going up and stop buying and possibly sell when they know the market is going down. Neither O'Neil nor anyone else knows how to predict accurately what the market is going to do in the upcoming days and months. So, he looks to see what the market, as defined by the common market indexes such as the Dow, the S&P, and the Nasdaq, have done in the past several days. Buying is permitted when the market has "bottomed" and there is a confirmation with a "follow-through signal." When the market shows a topping pattern over the last several days, you should not be buying and possibly should be selling until the market shows the next bottoming pattern.

A simple view of the topping pattern is when one or more indexes close down on above-average volume for at least four or five days in a row. After you have the topping signal, you start looking for a valid bottoming signal, which may be weeks or months later. You should see a rally in the market followed four through ten days later by another rally in the market that has at least a 1 percent rise in one or more indexes on higher volume than the prior day. Note, there can be false signals, which is when the market doesn't perform as expected. There is no simple way to predict which signals will prove false, but false signals should only occur about one in five times (20 percent). The rest of the time, the market should perform as you expect.

For the best interpretation of what the market is doing according to O'Neil's rules, read the daily column "The Big Picture" in O'Neil's publication *Investor's Business Daily.* Quoting O'Neil: "We're buying companies with strong fundamentals, large sales, and earnings increases resulting from unique new products or services and trying to time the purchases at a correct point as the company emerges from consolidation periods and before the stock runs up dramatically in price."

OUR INTERPRETATION OF O'NEIL'S METHODOLOGY: STEP-BY-STEP

■ Dynacq International Inc. (stock symbol: DYII), used previously to illustrate Peter Lynch's strategy, is a Houston-based operator of outpatient surgery, X-ray and laboratory facilities, a medical office complex, and an acute care hospital. It also provides home infusion services, such as parenteral nutrition. See Figure 3.1.

A second company we use to illustrate O'Neil's methodology is Hot Topic Inc. (stock symbol: HOTT), which is based in City of Industry, California, and has almost 300 retail stores. Hot Topic sells a variety of merchandise—clothing, jewelry, posters, cosmetics—all of which have a music orientation. The company's target market is 12 to 22 year olds. See Figure 3.2.

Current quarterly earnings per share (growth from Q5 to Q1). O'Neil says that three-quarters of the best-performing stocks had earnings increases averaging more than 70 percent in the latest publicly reported quarter. And this was before the stocks began their big price increase. Where many investors look for sequential growth—

FIGURE 3.1   **DYNACQ INTERNATIONAL INC (DYII)** $16.65 as of 4/18/2001

	Year 1	Year 2
Total Net Income (mil.)	$5.9	$2.7
EPS	$0.41	$0.20
Sales (mil.)	$26.0	$20.3
Avg. PE	11.5	6.9
ROE	40.4%	32.1%
Long-Term Debt-Equity	3%	8%
Dividend	–	–
Payout	0%	0%
Shares Outstanding (mil.)	15.3	12.9

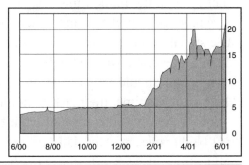

	Year 3	Year 4	Year 5	Year 6	Year 7	Year 8	Year 9	Year 10
Total Net Income (mil.)	$0.9	$(1.1)	$0.6	$0.9	$0.5	$0.9		
EPS	$0.07	$(0.07)	$0.04	$0.07	$0.03	$0.07		
Sales (mil.)	$10.9	$9.8	$7.4	$6.9	$2.6	$3.4		
Avg. PE	8.7	n/a	30.5	25	89.6	n/a		
ROE	15.5%	n/a	9.4%	15.5%	10.4%	29%		
Long-Term Debt-Equity	17%	15%	16%	21%	35%	26%		
Dividend	–	–	–					
Payout	0%	0%	0%					
Shares Outstanding (mil.)	13.1	14.2	14.2	14.2	14.2	13.5		

	Q1	Q2	Q3	Q4	Q5	Q6	Q7	Q8
EPS	$0.17	$0.17	$0.12	$0.13	$0.11	$0.07	$0.21	$0.08
Revenue (mil.)	$9.8	$8.9	$7.5	$7.5	$5.8	$5.2	$6.2	$4.3

	Market Cap (mil.)	TTM Sales (mil.)	Relative Strength	EPS Growth (4-yr. avg.)	Revenue Growth (TTM)	Current Ratio	Insider Buy-Sells (3 months)
DYII	$230.0	$33.7	99	79.0%	69.0%	2.7	0/0
Hospitals Industry	$4,580.0	$3,673.3	81	28.0%	24.0%	2.1	

	PEG	PE	Projected PE	PS	Price-Book	Price-Cash Flow	Free Cash Flow/Share
DYII	0.36	28.2	12.8	6.82	13.5	7.4	0.27
Hospitals Industry	1.15	56.9	34.4	1.99	3.9	15.7	

	Yield	Profit Margin (TTM)	ROE (TTM)	Total Debt-Equity	Long-Term Debt-Equity	Insider Ownership	Institutional Ownership
DYII	0.00%	25.0%	50.0%	47%	2.36%	70.0%	2.1%
Hospitals Industry	0.00%	6.0%	15.0%	117%	n/a		

Recent Balance Sheet Items ($ millions)		Financial Statement Trends			
Cash	6.2		Recent 12 mo.	FY1	FY2
Current Assets	16.7	Inventory/Sales	1%	1%	1%
Total Assets	26.7	AR to Sales	34%	32%	41%
Current Liabilities	6.3	R&D to Sales	–	–	–
Long-Term Debt	0.4				
Total Debt	7.95				
Equity	16.92				

FIGURE 3.2   **HOT TOPIC INC (HOTT)** $28.00 as of 3/30/2001

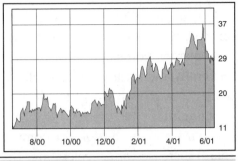

Year 1 = FY 2000	Year 1	Year 2
Total Net Income (mil.)	$23.2	$13.5
EPS	$1.09	$0.69
Sales (mil.)	$257.2	$168.9
Avg. PE	15.7	12.1
ROE	23.3%	20.1%
Long-Term Debt-Equity	0%	0%
Dividend	0	0
Payout	0%	0%
Shares Outstanding (mil.)	20.1	19.3

	Year 3	Year 4	Year 5	Year 6	Year 7	Year 8	Year 9	Year 10
Total Net Income (mil.)	$6.0	$4.5	$2.6	$0.4				
EPS	$0.31	$0.23	$0.17	$0.04				
Sales (mil.)	$103.4	$70.5	$43.6	$23.6				
Avg. PE	16.3	24.9	32.4	nc				
ROE	12.3%	10.1%	6.6%	50.0%				
Long-Term Debt-Equity	0%	0%	0%	0				
Dividend	0	0	0	0				
Payout	0%	0%	0%	0%				
Shares Outstanding (mil.)	18.6	19.0	18.4	3.1				

	Q1	Q2	Q3	Q4	Q5	Q6	Q7	Q8
EPS	$0.48	$0.34	$0.145	$0.115	$0.36	$0.22	$0.06	$0.035
Revenue (mil.)	$88,428	$72,203	$51,717	$44,839	$59,920	$47,964	$32,779	$28,286

	Market Cap (mil.)	TTM Sales (mil.)	Relative Strength	EPS Growth (3-yr. avg.)	Revenue Growth (TTM)	Current Ratio	Insider Buy-Sells (3 months)
HOTT	$564	$257.2	91	58%	47.8%	2.6	0/1
Specialty Retail Industry	$2,112	$2,224.9	74	11.1%	8.0%	2.5	

	PEG	PE	Projected PE	PS	Price-Book	Price-Cash Flow	Free Cash Flow/Share
HOTT	0.44	25.7	25.9	2.19	6.8	12.4	0.52
Specialty Retail Industry	2.47	20.3	13.9	1.1	2.3	11.2	

	Yield	Profit Margin (TTM)	ROE (TTM)	Total Debt-Equity	Long-Term Debt-Equity	Insider Ownership	Institutional Ownership
HOTT	0%	9.0%	28.2%	0%	0%	28%	89.5%
Specialty Retail Industry	1.6%	6.4%	15.1%	31.3%	31.3%		

Recent Balance Sheet Items ($ millions)		Financial Statement Trends			
Cash	41.4		Recent 12 mo.	FY1	FY2
Current Assets	73.4	Inventory/Sales	8.2%	9.1%	10.1%
Total Assets	112.4	AR to Sales	0%	0%	0%
Current Liabilities	27.9	R&D to Sales	–	–	–
Long-Term Debt	0.1				
Total Debt	0.2				
Equity	82.3				

quarter by quarter—he compares the most recent quarterly earnings (Q1) with those of the previous year's same quarter (Q5).

In general, O'Neil advises against buying any stock whose quarterly earnings per share are not up at least 18 percent in the most recent quarter compared with the same quarter for the prior year. Generally, the greater the percentage increase, the better. O'Neil remarks that growth of 40 to 50 percent, even 70 percent, is most meaningful.

Even better is to look for companies whose EPS (earnings per share) increases are accelerating. But because we are dealing with accounting, which is more art than science, O'Neil has certain caveats you must heed. Be sure the earnings you are comparing are meaningful. If last year's earnings were a paltry 1 cent per share, getting to 10 cents per share is not as meaningful as if the growth were from $1 to $10 per share. Also, if current quarter EPS growth rate is equal to or greater than 18 percent *and* the current quarter EPS is greater than analysts' estimates by an additional 25 percent on top of the recent EPS growth, it's a plus.

■ The EPS growth for this quarter relative to the same quarter a year earlier for Dynacq is 142.9 percent (Q1/Q5) − 1 = (0.17/0.07) −1 = 142.9%), well above O'Neil's 18 percent minimum, and is, in fact, a best case. Test results: Pass.

Hot Topic's EPS growth for this quarter relative to the same quarter a year earlier is 33.3 percent (Q1/Q5) − 1 = (0.48/0.36) − 1 = 33.3%). Test results: Pass.

Current Quarterly Earnings (Growth for Q5 to Q1)

1. < 18%	Fail
2. ≧ 18%	Pass
3. ≧ Prior quarter's growth rate plus 25%	Pass—Best case

Annual compounded EPS growth.   Not only does O'Neil want to see quarterly EPS grow at a minimum of 18 percent (with 25 percent growth even better), but he wants to see the same growth rate for annual EPS because he found in his studies that among the best-performing stocks, annual EPS growth averages 21 percent.

■ Dynacq's annual earnings growth rate is a best case by O'Neil's standards—79 percent. Test results: Pass.

  Hot Topic's rate of 58.1 percent is also a best case. Test results: Pass.

Annual Compounded EPS Growth

1. $< 18\%$ Fail
2. $\geq 18\%$ Pass
3. $\geq 25\%$ Pass—Best Case

Earnings consistency.   O'Neil looks at the past five years for earnings consistency. Consistency is important. He wants to see earnings increase over the past five years year by year. Keep in mind that by looking at the past five years, four measurements are possible: between years 5 and 4, 4 and 3, 3 and 2, and 2 and 1. If earnings go up year by year over the past five years, the stock passes the test with the following exception.

A company is allowed one misstep (a one-year dip), but only if such a dip is followed by a new high the following year. Even well-run companies can hit a bad patch, says O'Neil. If the stock earned $5, $6, and $7 in consecutive years, followed by a dip to $4, it's not enough that the stock increase 25 percent to $5 the following year. It must break into a historic high, which would be above $7. A company is allowed one poor year. Anything more than that suggests instability, which makes O'Neil antsy.

There's a missing case in O'Neil's analysis. What if the dip comes in the most recent year? If you were looking at such a stock today, you would have no way to see if the dip persisted or if the company recovered to a new high. That's why, in our analysis, when a dip comes in the most recent year, we take the most recent quarters, annualize them, and use that figure to project the current year's earnings. Let's say a company over the past five years had an annual EPS of $3, $4, $6, $8, and $7. Everything was going along fine, meeting O'Neil's minimum requirement of 18 percent EPS growth until the last year. Let's assume the current year is half over and the company reported earnings for the first two quarters of $2 and $2.50. That's $4.50 for six months or—projected for the entire year—

$9. That's a new record high and we would give this stock a passing grade on this criterion.

■ Dynacq's annual EPS before extraordinary items for the last five years (from the earliest to the most recent fiscal year) were: 0.04, –0.07, 0.07, 0.20, and 0.41. One dip is acceptable. Test results: Pass.

Hot Topic's annual EPS before extraordinary items for the last five years (from the earliest to the most recent fiscal year) were: 0.17, 0.23, 0.31, 0.69, and 1.09. Test results: Pass.

Earnings Consistency

1. 0 Dips in earnings	Pass—Best case
2. 1 Dip in earnings, but following year a new high	Pass
3. > 1 Dip	Fail

EPS growth rate in most recent quarters compared with long-term EPS growth. There are a couple of special situations that O'Neil watches for in the EPS growth rate of the most recent quarters—one a major slowdown and the other a major acceleration.

If the growth rates of the EPS in the two most recent quarters compared to their same quarter a year earlier have slowed to less than half of the long-term EPS growth rate, you should probably stay away from the stock. Its days of exciting increases in stock price are likely to be over regardless of what the analysts on Wall Street may say. O'Neil prefers to see two quarters of major slowdown before turning negative on a company "since the best of organizations can periodically have one slow quarter."

The flip side: O'Neil looks favorably at companies whose earnings per share over the last three to five years were growing annually at more than 18 percent and then suddenly spurt at least 25 percentage points higher in the most recent quarter. Let's say a company's annual earnings were growing at 21 percent, but in the most recent quarter (Q1), EPS grew 46 percent compared to the same quarter a year earlier. This is the type of earnings acceleration that can ignite a spark and cause a major price surge, and it is treated as a nice bonus in our scoring.

■ Dynacq's EPS growth rate for the last quarter (Q5 to Q1) is 243%, which is well over the long-term growth rate of 79%. Test results: Bonus.

Neither condition applies to Hot Topic. Test results: Neutral.

EPS Growth Rate in Most Recent Quarters Compared with Long-Term EPS Growth

1. If EPS growth rate from Q5 to Q1 and Q6 to Q2 are both < 50% of long-term EPS growth rate	Fail
2. If EPS growth rate for the last quarter is ≧125% of long-term growth	Pass—Bonus
3. Neither condition applies	Neutral

Current price within 15 percent of 52-week high. This is a simplification of O'Neil's many rules for reading a chart. O'Neil considers chart reading essential to his analysis. Investors should avoid stocks that are not trading within 15 percent of their 52-week highs. You want a stock that dips down and comes back (it forms the shape of a "cup" when graphed) and has been below its high for at least six weeks, which gives the stock time to consolidate and build a base for a breakout. When O'Neil graphs such a stock, he looks for a "cup and handle," where there's a dip and recovery after the major consolidation period.

Ideally, your goal should be to purchase at the exact "pivot point"— loosely defined as when a stock in a basing pattern breaks through to a new high on volume at least 50 percent higher than normal. The price pattern in Dynacq between mid-April and early June shows a cup and a breakout. However, there is much more to recognizing the optimum pivot point than we could possibly convey in a chapter of a book. In fact, a major portion of O'Neil's advanced seminar is understanding basing patterns and pivot points and learning to recognize "faulty patterns."

If a stock doesn't trade within 15 percent of its 52-week high, ignore it. If a stock is making a new 52-week high or is within 15 percent of its 52-week high, take note: it may be poised for a breakout. Exception: A stock that has dropped more than 50 percent should be avoided even if it recovers.

■ Dynacq's current stock price of $13.81 is within 15 percent of its 52-week high of $15.97. Test results: Pass.

  Hot Topic's current stock price of $28 is within 15 percent of its 52-week high of $29.88. Test results: Pass.

Current Price within 15% of 52-Week High

1. Current price < 85% of high   Fail
2. Current price ≧ 85% of high and
    < 52-week high   Pass
3. Current price ≧ 52-week high   Pass—Better

Relative strength.   O'Neil writes: "Relative strength measures the cold, realistic auction marketplace's appraisal of a stock, in spite of the theoretical value of the company or its past popularity, name, and image. How did the stock's price behave in the market in the last year? Its running 12 months' performance is updated daily, compared to all other stocks, and then placed on the same easy-to-use 1 to 99 scale" [with 99 being the highest]. Relative strength is a key technical indicator that O'Neil relies on to tell him how the price of a stock has performed over the last year compared to all other stocks. He uses relative strength to find the leaders and to cut out the large number of laggard, mediocre-performing companies.

You don't have to calculate relative strength yourself. O'Neil supplies the figure for stocks on the New York Stock Exchange, the American Stock Exchange, and the Nasdaq in his *Investor's Business Daily,* and we provide the information free on our Web site, Validea.com. O'Neil uses a proprietary way of calculating relative strength that he won't completely publicly disclose, but he does say he double-counts the most recent quarter, thereby giving added weight to the most current performance. Microsoft Money Central also has relative strength ratings.

O'Neil defines a leader as a company whose relative strength is at least 70 (elsewhere he mentions 80), meaning its stock has outperformed 70 percent (or 80 percent) of the stocks in the comparison group during a given period. O'Neil's research found that the 500 best-performing stocks had an average relative price strength rating of 87 just before their big price increases began. O'Neil says not to buy or hold stocks with a relative strength below 70. Our interpretation of his analysis: Restrict your stock picks to securities whose relative strength is 80 or higher. Better yet, focus on stocks with a relative strength of 90 or higher. And sell when the relative strength drops below 70.

Note: If a company is close to the relative strength minimum of 80, namely, between 75 and 79, pay attention to it. It doesn't pass muster on this variable, but if all other factors are favorable, it can still be considered a winner.

■ Dynacq's relative strength is 99, fitting O'Neil's definition of a best case. Test results: Pass.

Hot Topic's relative strength is 91, also fitting O'Neil's best-case scenario. Test results: Pass.

Relative Strength

1.	< 80	Fail
2.	≥ 80 and < 90	Pass
3.	≥ 90	Pass—Best case

Four-month S&P relative strength trend line.   O'Neil requires an important confirmation that the stock is still acting strongly with respect to the market. Relative strength requires a more short-term confirmation than one year. He wants to see the stock performing more strongly than the S&P 500 index in the recent past. O'Neil uses the four-month trend of the stock's weekly performance relative to the S&P 500 index as this confirmation, which compares the stock to the top capitalization stocks reflected in the S&P 500. O'Neil says he checks for four months because this period includes the quarterly earnings cycle. A simple way to measure the four-month trend is to compare the stock's current week-ending price to the S&P 500 index with this same ratio four months ago. If it's less, then the trend is down and the stock fails this test. If the two ratios are the same or the current one is greater than the older ratio, it passes.

■ Dynacq's relative strength has been increasing over the last four months. Test results: Pass.

Hot Topic's relative strength has been increasing over the last four months. Test results: Pass.

Four-Month S&P Relative Strength Trend Line

1. Current price to S&P 500 $<$ Price to S&P 500 4 months ago	Fail
2. Current price to S&P 500 $\geqq$ Price to S&P 500 4 months ago	Pass

Confirmation by another stock in the same industry.   O'Neil likes to know that a stock is in good company. It's a positive confirmation of a company's performance if at least one other company in its specific industry has a relative strength of 80 or more.

Confirmation by Another Stock in the Same Industry

1. At least one other stock in the same industry has a relative strength $\geqq$ 80	Pass
2. No other stock in same industry has a rel. strength $\geqq$ 80	Fail

■ There are 9 companies in Dynacq's hospital and health care industry with a relative strength at or above 80. Test results: Pass.

Hot Topic's retail apparel industry has 14 companies with a relative strength at or above 80. Test results: Pass.

Leading industries.   O'Neil has observed that stocks tend to move in industry groups. For the biggest gains, you should seek stocks that are in the top-performing industries. O'Neil looks at 200 industries over the past *six* months and ranks them from 1 to 99 based on how much each industry (using the average of all the stock in each industry) has increased in price compared to the other industries; leading industries are in the top 30 percent or, put another way, have a rating of 70 or above. The second way of identifying a leading industry is by looking at the percentage of stocks in each industry making a new high that day. Those with the highest percentage of stocks making new highs are leading industries. In such cases, the top is defined as the top 15 percent of the 200 industries he looks at.

O'Neil offers yet a third way of identifying leading industries. He creates approximately 30 industry sectors (sectors are broader than industries; for example, there are 6 or 7 medical industries, including biotech and hospitals, in the medical sector). He takes the top 5 sectors that have the highest absolute number of stocks making new highs that day as the leaders. Due to the lower precision of this approach compared to the previous approach, we have chosen not to implement it at Validea.com at this time.

Stock Is in a Leading Industry

1. Industry relative strength ≥ 70 Pass
2. Top 15% of industries with the highest % of stocks making new 52-week highs   Pass
3. Both 1 and 2   Pass—Best case
4. Neither 1 nor 2   Fail

■ The hospital industry, of which Dynacq is a part, is not one of the top-performing industries at this time. Test results: Fail.

Retail apparel, Hot Topic's industry, is currently one of the top-performing industries. Test results: Pass.

Decreasing long-term debt-equity ratio.   This variable involves the relationship between a company's debt and its equity by creating a ratio between the two, where the amount of a company's long-term debt (LTD) is divided by the worth of its equity.

O'Neil doesn't like LTD. In fact, he heartily dislikes it. His most desirable scenario for this variable is absolutely no debt. Microsoft is an example of a company without LTD. If a company's LTD is 0 (or very, very close—no more than 1 to 2 percent), the company passes this test.

A company that has long-term debt, but the debt has been declining for each of the last three years is okay, and the company passes. If in one of the last three years the debt has gone up no more than 10 percent (for example, if one year's debt equaled 20 percent of equity and the next year it equaled 22 percent, the debt has gone up 10 percent), but in the next year the debt is below where it was the first year, that's okay and the company passes. Generally, less debt-equity is better, but there is no limit that O'Neil states is too much debt.

This variable cannot be applied to financial-type businesses such as banks, insurance companies, brokerage firms, and other financial institutions, like Fannie Mae, because such businesses typically have a great deal of LTD and require such debt to run their operations.

Also, O'Neil fails to address how to deal with companies that are hybrids—traditional businesses with a strong financial component, such as General Motors (General Motors Acceptance Corporation), General Electric (GE Capital), IBM (Global Financing), and Sears' credit operations.

■ Dynacq has consistently been cutting its long-term debt-equity over the last three years (from the earliest to the most recent fiscal year): 17 percent, 8 percent, and 3 percent. Test results: Pass.

Hot Topic's debt-equity ratio has been at 0 percent for the past three years. Test results: Pass—Best case.

Decreasing Long-Term Debt-Equity (DE)

1. If LTD to equity $\leq$ 2%	Pass—Best case
2. Year 1 $\leq$ Year 2 $\leq$ Year 3	Pass
3. Year 1 < Year 3 and Year 2 $\leq$ 110% of Year 3	Pass
4. Anything else	Fail

Return on equity.   O'Neil prefers companies that have a return on equity (ROE) for the trailing 12 months of 17 percent or more, meaning their net income over the last four quarters is 17 percent or more of the total value of their equity. (Equity is averaged between the beginning and ending value over the period.)

■ Dynacq's return on equity is 50 percent, well above O'Neil's 17 percent minimum. Test results: Pass.

Hot Topic's return on equity is also acceptable—28.3 percent. Test results: Pass.

Return on Equity (ROE)

1. < 17%	Fail
2. $\geq$ 17%	Pass

Shares outstanding. This variable addresses the total number of shares a company has outstanding. The fewer the shares, the more volatile a stock—that is, the more it will respond to buying and selling pressure. O'Neil favors this volatility. This variable is relatively unimportant to O'Neil compared to other criteria, a sort of bonus. O'Neil likes companies with 30 million or fewer shares; most desirable are companies having between 3 million and 7 million shares.

- Dynacq has 15.3 million shares outstanding. Test results: Pass.
  Hot Topic has 20.1 million shares outstanding. Test results: Pass.

Shares Outstanding (Bonus)

1. Between 3 and 7 million shares   Pass—Best case
2. ≦ 30 million shares   Pass
3. > 30 million shares   Neutral

Insider ownership. Companies with the best prospects, says O'Neil, are those with large amounts of stock owned by insiders, especially management. He likes to see insider ownership because he feels when insiders are at risk by having a large amount of money at stake (through their ownership of shares and/or through options), their interests are more likely to align with those of shareholders.

In our research into insider ownership, we found inconsistencies. Some define insiders as management and board members, whereas others include mutual funds (they have access to corporate management). Some observers include among insiders those with stock options, others do not. O'Neil does not address these differences. If insiders own 15 percent or more of the company's shares, the company passes O'Neil's muster. If they own less, the company fails.

- Insiders own 70 percent of Dynacq's stock. Test results: Pass.
  Insiders own 28 percent of Hot Topic's stock. Test results: Pass.

Insider (Management) Ownership

1. < 15%   Fail
2. ≧ 15%   Pass

Something new.   Look for companies where something new and exciting is happening, such as the release of new products or services that *currently* add to revenues, the arrival of a new CEO, president, or CFO from the outside ("new" is top management that has been with the company for less than two years), or changes that significantly improve the company's industry situation. It's important that what's new should *now* be adding to revenues. O'Neil stresses this because so many times companies promise a new product or service and never deliver or deliver much later than promised. He wants the product or service on the market before he'll consider it as part of his analysis.

O'Neil is not entirely consistent about another aspect of this variable: new stock highs. He doesn't always say it, but in a number of public speeches he includes a new high in a stock price as something that's an exciting new event.

Unlike the other variables, seeking "something new" (new products, management, etc.) is more qualitative than quantitative and therefore can't be filtered down into a set of equations. As a result, we don't include this variable in our computerized results. But O'Neil thinks it is important, and therefore we take it into consideration. To get a feel for what is happening of importance that's new, see the "Media Buzz" section of our Web site, Validea.com.

Institutional ownership.   Here is another variable where O'Neil goes against much of the Street's conventional wisdom. He likes ownership by institutions—insurance companies, mutual funds, pension funds, and other large, professional investors. Many analysts tell you that once the big boys have found a stock, it's over the hill. The thinking is that the stock is now well known and its major gains in price have already happened.

Not O'Neil. He thinks institutional ownership is good. His reasoning: Institutions have big budgets and have done lots of research. If they ignore a stock, there must be a good reason for it, but he gives credence only to the best-performing institutions based on their three-year performance. Web sites owned by unknown companies or analysts that are touting a stock don't count. O'Neil (rightly in our opinion) respects only the opinions of institutions with top-performing track records. O'Neil advises not investing in any stock lacking at least one institutional sponsor.

One caveat: Don't invest in stocks that are among the 50 most popular investments of institutions. O'Neil's reasoning is that once a stock has become so popular that it is among the top institutional investments—which means that most institutions own the stock—the ship has already sailed. The stock has had its run-up and there's not much, if any, room to move upward. As he so succinctly puts it, "The heart is already out of the watermelon."

Where do you find out the most popular investments among institutions? On his Web site, O'Neil says you can find this information in several places in *Investor's Business Daily.* There's the "New Buys of Top-Rated Mutual Funds," a monthly feature. And each day there is "Making Money in Mutuals," which lists the top ten holdings and the largest buys and sells of top-performing mutual funds. "Your Weekend Review," which appears every Friday, provides sponsorship data also. Every Tuesday, *IBD*'s stock tables show O'Neil's proprietary Institutional Sponsorship Rating, which compares the amount of buying in a stock by top-rated mutual funds.

■ Institutions own 2.1 percent of Dynacq's stock. Test results: Pass.

Institutions own 89.5 percent of Hot Topic's stock. Test results: Pass. (Notice that institutions own 89.5 percent while insiders are shown as holding 28 percent, which totals more than 100 percent. At first, we were troubled that the two could add to more than 100 percent. However, in certain circumstances some closely held investment corporations as well as institutions (typically those that hold more than 5 percent of the company's stock) are included in the Beneficial Ownership table in the SEC filings from which insider information is obtained by data vendors and are therefore counted as part of both.)

Institutional Ownership

1. Institutional ownership = 0   Fail
2. Institutional ownership > 0   Pass

BOTTOM LINE

Dynacq

Tests passed:	Current quarterly earnings growth
	Annual compounded EPS growth
	Earnings consistency
	Current price within 15 percent of 52-week high
	Relative strength
	Four-month S&P relative strength trend line
	Decreasing long-term debt-equity ratio
	Return on equity
	Shares outstanding
	Insider ownership
	Institutional ownership
Bonus:	EPS growth in most recent quarter compared with long-term EPS growth
Tests failed:	Leading industries
Score:	92 percent (11 of 12 passed) plus bonus

BOTTOM LINE: There is STRONG INTEREST in Dynacq.

Hot Topic

Tests passed:	Current quarterly earnings growth
	Annual compounded EPS growth
	Earnings consistency
	Current price within 15 percent of 52-week high
	Relative strength
	Four-month S&P relative strength trend line
	Leading industries
	Decreasing long-term debt-equity
	Return on equity
	Shares outstanding
	Insider ownership
	Institutional ownership
Score:	100 percent (12 of 12 passed)

BOTTOM LINE: There is STRONG INTEREST in Hot Topic.

O'NEIL'S KEY INVESTING CRITERIA

- Don't look for bargains; they are typically inferior merchandise.

- Buy high, sell much higher.

- Keep abreast of the market throughout the day, every day.

- Be disciplined. Be willing to cut your losses to 8 percent below purchase price. Don't try to ride out significant downturns.

- Be willing to view stocks in new ways. For example, don't focus on those things you've been told to focus on, such as PE ratios.

CHAPTER 4

WARREN BUFFETT

WHICH INVESTORS MIGHT USE **Warren Buffett?**

RISK: Warren Buffett is for those looking for relatively low-risk investments.

TIME HORIZON: Forever. Yes, Buffett believes you should spend a lot of time identifying the right companies to invest in, wait until their price is right, and then buy and hold . . . and hold and hold. He's held some of his investments for decades.

EFFORT: "Highly selective" best describes Buffett's approach to identifying companies he will invest in. He requires in-depth analysis of every company he looks at. On the front end, therefore, a considerable amount of effort is required to use Buffett's strategy. But on the back end—the time after you made the purchase and are holding it (usually for years)—there's very little effort.

NOTE: Buffett is not into diversification (owning stocks in several industries). He concentrates his investments in a few stocks. Such a strategy would usually be considered risky but not in his case because he does such a thorough analysis of his investments before he buys; he waits until the price is low; he looks for companies with superior market positions; and he holds for so long. All of these help lower his risk level.

Mildred Othmer died in April 1998, about three years after the death of her husband, Donald. These Brooklyn residents, both in their 90s when they passed away and both retired educators, were, by all accounts, an unassuming couple. They lived for years in the same house in Brooklyn Heights, a neighborhood known for its easy access to Manhattan via subway and stunning views of the New York harbor but no competition to the ritzy 'hoods of Fifth Avenue or Park Avenue. Appearances aside, the death of Mildred and the story of her and Donald's estate made the front page of the *New York Times* and newspapers around the country. And it wasn't because of anything nefarious but because of their incredible wealth.

After receiving a Ph.D. from the University of Michigan in 1927, Donald began working for Eastman Kodak. Not happy with the $10 bonus he received for each of his patents, he left the camera and filmmaker and tried to create a business on his own. It was during the depression and business was slow, so when Brooklyn Polytechnic University offered him a position in chemical engineering, he took it. There he remained until retirement, and he continued living in Brooklyn until his death. Mildred, who did volunteer work, was a former teacher and buyer for her mother's dress store.

Neither was born to wealth. Neither won the lottery. Neither was known to be a financial genius. But when it was made public how large was their estate, the world paid attention. Their estate's value at the time of Mildred's death was estimated at over $750 million. How could two teachers amass a fortune so large that few other fortunes in the world were its equal?

Here are their secrets:

- They were patient investors. They took a long-term view of investing.
- They were willing to invest in the stock market. They didn't put their money in such low risk—and low return—investment vehicles as savings bonds.
- They were lucky to live through much of the greatest bull market of all time. If they had died a decade earlier, for example, their estate would have been sizable but a fraction of what it was in 1998.
- Finally—and very important—they placed their money with a man who is arguably the greatest stock market investor of all time: Warren Buffett.

Of all our gurus, Buffett is perhaps closest to being legendary. Benjamin Graham is certainly revered, but Buffett, who is still with us, personifies great stock market investing. He is the only investor profiled in *The Market Gurus* who has not written a book, though a number of books have been written about him and his investment strategies. For our analysis, we use one of these books, *Buffettology,* written by Buffett's ex-daughter-in-law, Mary Buffett, and friend of the Buffett family David Clark.

But Buffett himself has not explained in any comprehensive detail how he has become, at last count (year 2000), the fourth wealthiest person in the country (he's been as high as number one on the *Forbes* list of the 400 wealthiest Americans). Interestingly, he does little in the way of self-promotion, yet he has an international following that has aspects of a cult. Back in August 1991, a writer for *Money* tried to get an interview with Buffett, only to be rejected even after flying to Omaha to try to meet the man some call the Oracle of Omaha. The writer called his article "Warren and Me: My assignment: Track down the elusive Warren Buffett, the world's greatest investor, and learn his trade secrets," which pretty much explains the writer's experience in interviewing Buffett: the two never met and Buffet revealed none of his trade secrets.

Lots has been written about the thousands of Buffett devotees (up to 14,000 or 15,000) who attend Berkshire Hathaway's (Buffett's investment company) annual meetings in Omaha. The faithful are reportedly called "Berkies" by local taxi drivers to describe these annual meeting attendees. Berkies know the man's favorite restaurant (Gorat's Steak House), candy (See's, which he owns), and soft drink (Cherry Coke—he's a big holder of Coke stock). He is to Wall Street what Michael Jordan is to basketball, Bill Gates to software, and Monica Lewinsky to interns: a superstar. In fact, no investment guru alive comes close to Buffett for shear celebrity wattage—nor does anyone come close to his track record of financial success.

Despite all the hoopla, Buffett's reputation is based on his performance. One of the interesting aspects of the Othmer's story is that it is real. Many investment mavens say, "If you had invested *x* amount of money for *y* years in my strategy, you'd now be a multimillionaire." That's hypothetical, because no one gave them that much money back then and let them invest it over time. Each of the Othmers really did give Warren Buffett $25,000 in the early 1960s, and when they died, thanks to his investing prowess, they really did have assets worth over $750 million. Buffett really is on the *Forbes* list of the 400 wealthiest Americans, usually in the top 5. According to Mary Buffett, Warren is the only one on the list who made his fortune solely by investing in the stock market.

Of course, Warren Buffett is not the only guru who has a track record of stellar performance. Peter Lynch, for example, made his name first as a mutual fund manager with long-term outstanding results, and only later as a guru who wrote down his strategies. But no other stock market investor has had quite the track record of Buffett, nor has any come close to accumulating the amount of his personal wealth ($28 billion, according to *Forbes* in October 2000).

WHO IS WARREN BUFFETT?

First, let's be honest. We don't know who Warren Buffett is, and neither does just about anyone who writes about the man. That said, we can certainly share some observations about him and his strategies. Buffett was born August 30, 1930, in Omaha. His father, Howard Buffett, came from a line of grocers but decided to become a stockbroker. Then, in 1942 he ran for Congress as a Republican and won. (Warren was first a Republican, including being president of the Young Republicans Club at the University of Pennsylvania but is now a registered Democrat, and he even cohosted fund-raisers for Hillary Clinton during her successful run for the Senate from New York in 2000.)

There are lots of tales about Warren Buffett's early entrepreneurialism. Supposedly, at age six he bought six-packs of Coke for 25 cents and resold them for 30 cents. At 11, he bought his first stock, three shares of Cities Service Preferred. He paid $38 a share, watched them drop to $27, held on until the stock rebounded and sold it for a $6 profit at $40. However, he learned that patience could be a virtue when the stock subsequently hit $200.

At 14, with savings from his two newspaper routes, he reportedly bought 40 acres of Nebraska farmland for $1,200, which he leased. While still in high school, he bought pinball machines that he installed in barbershops and, by graduation, had earned $10,000, which is the equivalent of more than $100,000 in today's dollars.

Buffett first attended college at the University of Pennsylvania's Wharton School but transferred to the University of Nebraska, graduating in 1950. In his last year there, he read Benjamin Graham's *The Intelligent Investor* and decided to become a stock market investor. Harvard reportedly turned him down for its MBA program, but Buffett also had a hankering to attend Columbia University, where Graham taught. Buffett went to Columbia and became Graham's star student. To this day, Buffett speaks with reverence about Graham.

After earning his master's degree, Buffett began working at his mentor's New York firm. In 1956, he returned to Omaha and started his own investment partnership. His partners each put in $25,000 (supposedly, Buffett invested $100), and he appointed himself general partner. With the money he raised, Buffett began to buy stocks. He did well, earning a 29.5 percent compounded annual rate of return between the start of the partnership and its dissolution in 1969 versus 7.4 percent for the Dow. One of his investments in the 1960s was in a struggling textile mill in Massachusetts called Berkshire Hathaway. As Berkshire's textile business faded in the face of foreign competition, Buffett used its assets to buy other businesses, eventually turning it into the investment vehicle it is today.

When Buffett dissolved his partnership in 1969, he offered his partners the choice of taking cash or holding stock in Berkshire Hathaway, which was a public company, and a few other companies. An article in the online magazine *Salon* (31 August 1999) has reported that a $10,000 investment in Berkshire Hathaway when Buffett took control of it in 1965 would be worth more than $50 million at the time the article was published versus $500,000 from investing in the Standard & Poor's 500 stock index. Keep in mind that the Othmers invested with Buffett early and kept their money with him until they died, so these numbers are not hypothetical; people really did turn $10,000 investments into $50 million ones.

Buffett sports an aw-shucks, average-guy demeanor combined with a bit of the cranky grandfather. He's lived in the same stucco house in Omaha that he bought for $31,500 in the late 1950s. His look is unabashedly rumpled. Steak and hamburgers are his meals of choice. As for his annual salary, it fits neatly into today's middle class: $100,000. He likes spouting homespun humor, calling Berkshire Hathaway's annual stockholder meetings "Woodstock for Capitalists."

Following are some of his comments—usually humble, witty, and at times self-critical—from the widely read (and copyrighted) letters he writes to Berkshire Hathaway shareholders in the company's annual reports.

In his letter in the 2000 Berkshire Hathaway annual report, after reporting that the previous year he had bought eight companies that had sales of $13 billion and 58,000 employees, he wrote: "I will tell you now that we have embraced the 21st century by entering such cutting-edge industries as brick, carpet, insulation, and paint. Try to control your excitement."

Also from the 2000 annual report: "Charlie Munger, Berkshire's Vice Chairman and my partner, and I are a year older than when we last reported to you. Mitigating this adverse development is the indisputable fact that the age of your top managers is increasing at a considerably lower rate—*percentage-wise*—than is the case at almost all other major corporations. Better yet, this differential will widen in the future."

From the 1999 annual report: "The numbers on the facing page show just how poor our 1999 record was. We had the worst absolute performance of my tenure and, compared to the S&P, the worst relative performance as well. Relative results are what concern us: Over time, bad relative numbers will produce unsatisfactory absolute results."

He continues: "Even Inspector Clouseau could find last year's guilty party: your Chairman. My performance reminds me of the quarterback whose report card showed four Fs and a D but who nonetheless had an understanding coach. 'Son,' he drawled, 'I think you're spending too much time on that one subject.'"

From that same annual report, a note of reassurance: "To repeat a fact you've heard before, well over 99% of my net worth resides in Berkshire. Neither my wife nor I have ever sold a share of Berkshire and—unless our checks stop clearing—we have no intention of doing so."

In the 1998 annual report, after a year when Berkshire Hathaway's stock did well, Buffett, who always likes to lower expectations, wrote: "But one thing is certain: Our future rates of gain will fall far short of those achieved in the past. Berkshire's capital base is now simply too large to allow us to earn truly outsized returns. If you believe otherwise, you should consider a career in sales but avoid one in mathematics (bearing in mind that there are really only three kinds of people in the world: those who can count and those who can't)."

Buffett's heartland America, salt-of-the-earth shtick is a bit at odds with some of his lifestyle choices, though admittedly he makes no claim to being a role model for family virtues, and his personal choices are his own business. But he is a public figure, and more than one report about Buffett has discussed his somewhat unusual living arrangements. His wife for decades, Susan T. Buffett, mother of his three children, accompanies him on most of his public appearances, but they haven't lived together since 1977. At that time, she moved to an apartment in San Francisco and has been described in *Salon* as "a sometime cabaret singer and passionate abortion-rights activist."

The story goes that Susan introduced Buffett to a Latvian-born waitress who worked at a restaurant in Omaha and now lives with the man. *Salon* reports: "Susan and Astrid remain friends, and the three send presents to relatives from 'Warren, Susie and Astrid.'"

Buffett is legendary for more than just his investing prowess; he is often looked at as a classic skinflint. Stories abound about how he kept his children on a tight financial leash, and to date he's given away little of his fortune. He's done nothing similar to what several other members of the superwealthy (almost all younger than Buffett) have done, such as the $150 million Jim Clark of Netscape fame gave to Stanford or the foundations with billions in them set up by David Packard, Bill Gates, and, of course, capitalists of yore like Rockefeller and Ford. Buffett has said he will eventually leave just about all of his wealth to charity.

BUFFETT AS INVESTOR

In her book, *Lessons from the Legends of Wall Street* (Dearborn, 2000), Nikki Ross lists Buffett's commonsense investment rules:

- Have an investment plan and follow it.
- Be flexible enough to change your investment strategies when needed.
- Study sales and earnings of a company and how they were derived.
- Know your company's products or services, its position in its industry, and how it compares with its competition.
- Know the company's management.
- When you find a great stock value, don't be swayed by predictions for the stock market or the economy.
- If you can't find any investments that meet your criteria, don't be afraid to sit on the sidelines with your cash and wait for an opportunity.
- Define what you don't know as well as what you do know and stick to what you know.

Now let's look at some of the more nitty-gritty aspects of Buffett's investment approach. He's interested in a company's intrinsic value and will buy only when a company's stock is selling at a price that makes sense, given the company's intrinsic value. Mary Buffett (we'll call her Mary from now on to distinguish her from Warren Buffett) in *Buffettology* says of this concept: "To Warren the intrinsic value of an investment is the projected annual compounding rate of return the investment will produce." Buffett is looking at what finance types call "future value"—in this case, what the company will be worth at some specified time in the future, say, ten years or more.

Let's say a stock is currently selling for $21 and you project that in ten years it will sell for $65. Is this a good, bad, or indifferent track record? Using a financial calculator, you can quickly calculate the stock's annual compound rate of return. Using a Hewlett-Packard 12C financial calculator (all financial calculators work similarly), you would punch in *−$21* and *PV* for present value (the stock's value today; we need to change the sign to a minus too), *65* and *FV* for future value (the stock's value in the future), *10* and *n* for the number of periods (the periods in this example are years and their number is ten), and *I* for the compound interest rate, which is 11.96 percent. This means we project the stock will earn for us 11.96 percent each year, compounded, over the next ten years. Buffett would then look at this and decide if this rate of return is worth the investment.

How does he know what the stock will be worth in the future? That's the tough part. Mary wrote: "Warren focuses on the predictability of future earnings; and he believes that without some predictability of future earnings, any calculation of a future value is mere speculation, and speculation is an invitation to folly. Warren will make long-term investments only in businesses whose future earnings are predictable to a high degree of certainty. The certainty of future earnings removes the elements of risk from the equation and allows for a sound determination of a business's future value." Buffett is interested in looking into the future and seeing where a company is likely to go and what it will be worth when it gets there. Then he looks at what it's selling for now. If it is selling for a price that will provide him with a good return over the long term, he'll buy.

Technology doesn't interest Buffett because, he claims, he doesn't understand it and because future earnings of tech companies tend to be highly unpredictable as a result of technical surprises and rapid product cycles, so he makes no attempt to calculate a tech stock's long-term future value. Buffett is, of course, a close student of Graham's methods, but Graham was interested in bargains, stocks selling for so much below their value that you were very unlikely to suffer a loss.

Another variable that Buffett views favorably is stock buybacks, or repurchases. These occur when a company thinks its stock is so low priced that it is a good investment, and it goes into the public markets and buys back shares of its own stock. By doing so, it decreases the number of shares in the market. Under the law of supply and demand, if demand is constant and supply decreases, prices should go up, which is what companies are counting on when they repurchase their shares. These programs are generally announced publicly.

As an example, in January 2001, AOL Time Warner announced it would buy back up to $5 billion of the company's common stock in the open market over the following two years. Gerald M. Levin, chief executive officer of AOL Time Warner, was quoted in a company press release as saying: "Thanks to the strong growth prospects for our company, we're able not only to continue to invest in our world-class businesses, but to use a portion of our growing financial capability to buy back stock at a time when we believe our shares are undervalued."

Some of the companies Buffett has invested in, including Coca-Cola and Gillette, have had stock buyback programs. Buffett is a fundamentalist at heart, always looking for value and trying to determine if a company has good prospects and is undervalued. One thing he likes to see in a company is a consumer monopoly, a market position that is virtually unassailable and gives the company power and leverage in the marketplace.

Note: Although Mary uses the word *monopoly,* we have found the word conjures up a much stricter requirement for companies—in particular that they have overwhelmingly dominant market share—than the requirement for companies that Buffett necessarily invests in. Many of Buffett's investments, including recent ones, aren't anywhere near classic monopolies. Virtually all have many competitors in the market, such as Dairy Queen restaurants, Shaw's Carpets, US Air, or even American Express. To us, Buffett places a lot of weight on what most people call brand image; he looks for a very strong, well-recognized brand, usually a consumer brand that may be regional (like See's or Dairy Queen). Occasionally, he does buy businesses that sell commodities—GEICO, Shaw's—but only if he believes they have the lowest production cost in their industry. And remember: banks are also a commodity industry!

Buffett recently invested in a business that combined commodity, brand, and regionality: a brick manufacturer with a brand name in a region. He also looks for businesses whose main product has not changed much over time nor is expected to change much in the foreseeable future, as this is a major, major component in being able to have predictable earnings in the future. Auto insurance doesn't change much; candy doesn't change much; and the same for burgers, Coke, carpet, and so on. A third theme, which Buffett also harps on in his current annual report, is that of buying companies with top-quality management—they have kept the business focused and out of trouble, they are thrifty, and they don't pay themselves egregiously. Plus, they are committed to their employees so that the employees can do well financially and will want to stay with the company for many years.

Mary describes how Buffett determines if a company has a consumer monopoly in this way: "Warren has developed a conceptual test to determine the presence of . . . a consumer monopoly. In testing for the presence of a consumer monopoly, he likes to ask this question: *If he had access to billions of dollars (which he does) and his pick of the top fifty managers in the country (which he does), could he start a business and successfully compete with the business in question?* . . . If the answer is a resounding no, then the company in question is protected by some kind of strong consumer monopoly." (Mary's emphasis)

To go further, Buffett looks at how much damage a competitor could inflict even if he didn't care about making money. Mary cites such companies and products as Coca-Cola, the *Wall Street Journal,* Wrigley's gum, and Hershey chocolate bars as examples of companies and products largely impervious to competition, even competition willing to fight the good fight without making any money.

These paragraphs are true to the book, but again they are the ideal and may not be all that helpful in identifying the full range of companies Buffett might consider. Buffett wants to invest in excellent companies, and this test of consumer monopoly is an important criterion for determining if a company is truly an excellent company.

Mary lists nine questions to help you determine if a business is truly excellent:

1. Does the business have an identifiable consumer monopoly, brand, or franchise?

2. Are the earnings of the company strong with an upward trend?
3. Is the company conservatively financed?
4. Does the company earn a high rate of return on shareholders' equity?
5. Is the business able to retain its earnings?
6. How much does the business have to spend on maintaining current operations?
7. Is the company free to reinvest in new business opportunities, business expansions, or stock buybacks? Does it do a good job at this?
8. Is the company free to adjust prices to inflation?
9. Will the value added by retained earnings increase the market value of the company?

How does one find businesses worth investing in? Mary mentions several things to look for when trying to identify investment opportunities. One telltale sign is a business that makes products that wear out fast or are used up quickly, that has brand-name appeal, and that merchants have to carry or use to stay in business. Examples include Coca-Cola, Marlboro cigarettes, Wrigley's chewing gum, Crest toothpaste, Gillette razor blades, and Doritos corn chips. Supermarkets, convenience stores, and drugstores have to carry some or all of these products, which means the makers of these products are good investment prospects.

Another example would be communications businesses providing a repetitive service that manufacturers must use to persuade the public to buy their products. When there were only three television networks, each made a bunch of money, which prompted Buffett to invest in Capital Cities and then ABC, says Mary. Strong local newspapers are another example (Buffett owns the *Buffalo Evening News*). Multinational advertising agencies, which can service consumer companies that sell products in many countries, are another example, and Buffett has invested in at least one of these: Interpublic.

A third characteristic to look for would be businesses providing repetitive consumer services that people and businesses are consistently in need of. Here we are dealing with services, not products. Buffett has invested in credit card companies, which fit the bill, including American Express and Discover Financial Services. A credit card company gets a fee every time one of its credit cards is used. H&R Block, the tax preparation service, is another example of a company that meets this criterion.

To find companies that meet all of these criteria, Buffett reads many publications, such as the *Wall Street Journal,* the *New York Times, Business Week,* and the like and keeps abreast of what is happening at companies, in industries, and in the economy in general.

BUFFETT'S INVESTMENT STRATEGY: STEP-BY-STEP

Buffett's companies, as referred to throughout this analysis, are firms in which Warren Buffett has invested in the past. We use, for our example, Gannett Company Inc. (stock symbol: GCI), which Mary Buffett uses in her book, and we use the figures she uses (see Figure 4.1). Buffett invested in this company in the summer of 1994. Gannett, based in Alexandria, Virginia, is a very large newspaper company that owns 95 newspapers around the country, its best known being the nationally distributed *USA Today.* The company also owns television stations.

We have also included in our analysis two technology companies—both software giants—that have very strong brands and dominant market share: Microsoft (stock symbol: MSFT) and Oracle (stock symbol: ORCL). Microsoft, based in Redmond, Washington, is the world's largest software company (see Figure 4.2); Oracle, whose headquarters are in Redwood City, California, is the world's second largest (see Figure 4.3). Buffett might consider these companies' future earnings to be unpredictable in the long run because they continually cannibalize and make obsolete their own products. Nonetheless, we feel comfortable in using these two companies as examples for two reasons: (1) They have now shown a long track record of steady earnings increases and (2) the nature of their newer products requires a level of historical compatibility with their older products that assures a steady supply of future customers. And while Buffett might feel that he doesn't understand the products these com-

FIGURE 4.1   GANNETT (GCI) $48.90 as of 7/10/1994

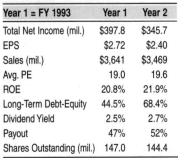

Year 1 = FY 1993	Year 1	Year 2
Total Net Income (mil.)	$397.8	$345.7
EPS	$2.72	$2.40
Sales (mil.)	$3,641	$3,469
Avg. PE	19.0	19.6
ROE	20.8%	21.9%
Long-Term Debt-Equity	44.5%	68.4%
Dividend Yield	2.5%	2.7%
Payout	47%	52%
Shares Outstanding (mil.)	147.0	144.4

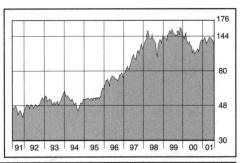

	Year 3	Year 4	Year 5	Year 6	Year 7	Year 8	Year 9	Year 10
Total Net Income (mil.)	$301.6	$377.0	$397.5	$364.5	$319.4	$276.4	$253.7	$224.4
EPS	$2.00	$2.36	$2.47	$2.26	$1.98	$1.71	$1.58	$1.40
Sales (mil.)	$3,382	$3,442	$3,518	$3,314	$3,079	$2,802	$2,210	$1,960
Avg. PE	20.7	15.7	17.0	14.9	23.0	21.5	18.3	14.8
ROE	19.6%	18.3%	19.9%	20.4%	19.8%	19.3%	19.9%	19.6%
Long-Term Debt-Equity	86.7%	41.1%	46.2%	63.5%	68.0%	83.7%	83%	83%
Dividend	3.0%	3.3%	2.6%	3.0%	2.1%	2.3%	2.6%	3.2%
Payout	64%	51%	44%	44%	47%	49%	49%	48%
Shares Outstanding (mil.)	143.8	159.0	161.0	161.1	162.0	161.6	160.6	160.3

Q1 = March 1994	Q1	Q2	Q3	Q4	Q5
EPS	$.54	$.87	$.61	$.78	$.46
Revenue (mil.)	$876.6	$982.6	$876.5	$937.8	$844.7

	Market Cap (mil.)	TTM Sales (mil.)	Relative Strength	EPS Growth (3-yr. avg.)	EPS Growth (10-yr. avg.)	Revenue Growth	Current Ratio
GCI	$7,188	$3,673.5	50	17%	8.6%	3.8%	1.7

	PEG	PE	Projected PE	PS	Price-Book	Price-Cash Flow	Free Cash Flow/Share
GCI	1.03	17.5	15.1	2.0	3.8	11.8	3.78

	Yield	Profit Margin (TTM)	ROE (TTM)	Total Debt-Equity	Long-Term Debt-Equity	Insider Ownership	Institutional Ownership
GCI	2.65%	10.9%	20.8%	44.6%	44.5%	1%	60%

1993 Balance Sheet Items ($ millions)		Financial Statement Trends		
Cash	75.5		Recent 12 mo.	FY1
Current Assets	758	Inventory/Sales	1.4%	1.5%
Total Assets	3,213.9	AR to Sales	12.8%	12.3%
Current Liabilities	455.1	R&D to Sales	–	–
Long-Term Debt	850.7			
Total Debt	850.9	FY0 (1994) Estimated EPS: $3.20		
Equity	1907.9	Estimated ROE: 24.5%		
		Estimated Payout: 40%		
		Estimated Long-Term Growth Rate: 8.6%/annum		

FIGURE 4.2	MICROSOFT CORP (MSFT)	$56.19 as of 4/6/2001

	Year 1	Year 2	
Total Net Income (mil.)	$9,421.0	$7,785.0	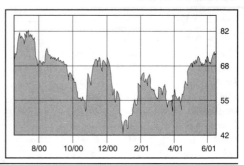
EPS	$1.70	$1.39	
Sales (mil.)	$22,956.0	$19,747.0	
Avg. PE	53	49.1	
ROE	22.8%	28.4%	
Long-Term Debt-Equity	0%	0%	
Dividend	–	–	
Payout	0%	0%	
Shares Outstanding (mil.)	5,283	5,109	

	Year 3	Year 4	Year 5	Year 6	Year 7	Year 8	Year 9	Year 10
Total Net Income (mil.)	$4,490.0	$3,454.0	$2,195.0	$1,453.0	$1,146.0	$953.0	$708.1	$462.7
EPS	$0.89	$0.66	$0.43	$0.29	$0.25	$0.20	$0.15	$0.07
Sales (mil.)	$14,484.0	$11,358.0	$8,671.0	$5,937.0	$4,649.0	$3,753.0	$2,758.7	$1,843.4
Avg. PE	49.9	35.7	29.9	30	23.4	25.5	25.2	21
ROE	28.7%	35.3%	31.8%	27.2%	25.8%	29.4%	32.3%	34.3%
Long-Term Debt-Equity	0%	0%	0%	0%	0%	0%	0%	0%
Dividend	–	–	–	–	–	–	–	–
Payout	0%	0%	0%	0%	0%	0%	0%	0%
Shares Outstanding (mil.)	4,969	4,850	4,770	4,720	4,520	4,512	4,354	4,180

	Q1	Q2	Q3	Q4	Q5	Q6	Q7	Q8
EPS	$0.47	$0.46	$0.44	$0.43	$0.44	$0.40	$0.40	$0.35
Revenue (mil.)	$6,585.0	$5,800.0	$5,804.0	$5,656.0	$6,112.0	$5,384.0	$6,525.0	$4,331.0

	Market Cap (mil.)	TTM Sales (mil.)	Relative Strength	EPS Growth (3-yr. avg.)	Revenue Growth (TTM)	Current Ratio	Insider Buy-Sells (3 months)
MSFT	$299,785.0	$23,845.0	49	36.6%	7.7%	3.6	0/19
Application Software	$52,920.1	$5,395.93	41	17.7%	30.9%	2.6	

	PEG	PE	Projected PE	PS	Price-Book	Price-Cash Flow	Free Cash Flow/Share
MSFT	0.9	31.2	31.0	12.6	6.5	22.1	$2.47
Application Software	4.0	56.8	38.2	8.4		124.8	

	Yield	Profit Margin (TTM)	ROE (TTM)	Total Debt-Equity	Long-Term Debt-Equity	Insider Ownership	Institutional Ownership
MSFT	0%	42%	21.5%	0%	0%	19%	42.2%
Application Software	0.04%	14.9%	33.5%	0.114%	0.1%		

Recent Balance Sheet Items ($ millions)		Financial Statement Trends			
Cash	4,149.0		Recent 12 mo.	FY1	FY2
Current Assets	37,789.0	Inventory/Sales	0%	0%	0%
Total Assets	59,605.0	AR to Sales	14%	14%	11%
Current Liabilities	9,740.0	R&D to Sales	16%	13%	13%
Long-Term Debt	–	FY0 (2001) Estimated EPS: $1.38			
Total Debt	–	Estimated ROE: 15.7%			
Equity	48,090.0	Estimated Payout: 0%			
		Estimated Long-Term Growth Rate: 16.9%/annum			

FIGURE 4.3	ORACLE CORPORATION (ORCL)	$14.97 as of 4/10/2001

Year 1 = FY 2000	Year 1	Year 2
Total Net Income (mil.)	$6,296.8	$1,289.8
EPS	$0.44	$0.22
Sales (mil.)	$10,130.1	$8,827.3
Avg. PE	24.4	30.3
ROE	97.5%	34.9%
Long-Term Debt-Equity	5%	8%
Dividend	–	–
Payout	0%	0%
Shares Outstanding (mil.)	5,615	5,725

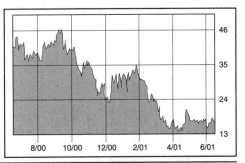

	Year 3	Year 4	Year 5	Year 6	Year 7	Year 8	Year 9	Year 10
Total Net Income (mil.)	$813.7	$821.5	$603.3	$441.5	$283.7	$141.7	$61.5	$(12.4)
EPS	$0.16	$0.14	$0.11	$0.07	$0.05	$0.03	$0.01	–
Sales (mil.)	$7,143.9	$5,684.3	$4,223.3	$2,966.9	$2,001.1	$1,502.8	$1,178.5	$1,027.9
Avg. PE	35.7	33	33	28.3	28.5	24.2	17.6	n/a
ROE	27.5%	34.7%	32.3%	36.4%	38.3%	26.8%	14.1%	n/a
Long-Term Debt-Equity	10%	13%	0%	7%	11%	16%	22%	5%
Dividend	–	–	–	–	–	–	–	–
Payout	0%	0%	0%	0%	0%	0%	0%	0%
Shares Outstanding (mil.)	5,837	5,862	5,897	5,842	5,787	5,749	5,655	5,509

	Q1	Q2	Q3	Q4	Q5	Q6	Q7	Q8
EPS	$0.10	$0.11	$0.08	$0.81	$0.12	$0.06	$0.04	$0.09
Revenue (mil.)	$2,674.4	$2,659.5	$2,261.9	$3,374.3	$2,449.4	$2,321.9	$1,984.5	$2,943.3

	Market Cap (mil.)	TTM Sales (mil.)	Relative Strength	EPS Growth (3-yr. avg.)	Revenue Growth (TTM)	Current Ratio	Insider Buy-Sells (3 months)
ORCL	$83,627.0	$10,970.1	23	46.5%	9.2%	2.2	0/7
Application Software	$52,920.1	$5,395.9	41	17.7%	30.9%	2.6	

	PEG	PE	Projected PE	PS	Price-Book	Price-Cash Flow	Free Cash Flow/Share
ORCL	0.1	13.4	29.4	7.6	17.0	20.7	$0.47
Application Software	4.0	56.8	38.2	8.4		124.8	

	Yield	Profit Margin (TTM)	ROE (TTM)	Total Debt-Equity	Long-Term Debt-Equity	Insider Ownership	Institutional Ownership
ORCL	0.0%	60.3%	134.3%	6%	6%	25%	43.2%
Application Software	0.04%	14.9%	33.5%	11%	11%		

Recent Balance Sheet Items ($ millions)		Financial Statement Trends		
			Recent 12 mo.	FY1	FY2
Cash	4,129.3				
Current Assets	7,459.0	Inventory/Sales	0%	0%	0%
Total Assets	9,450.7	AR to Sales	18%	28%	32%
Current Liabilities	3,305.7	R&D to Sales	9%	8%	8%
Long-Term Debt	300.9	FY0 (2001) Estimated EPS: $0.44			
Total Debt	303.7	Estimated ROE: 39.6%			
Equity	5,324.1	Estimated Payout: 0%			
		Estimated Long-Term Growth Rate: 22.9%/annum			

panies make, we feel that most people have a basic understanding of technology as today's widespread use of computers is transforming them into common, everyday appliances. The lack of knowledge and the complexity of technology are no longer reasons to ignore this very important segment of the market.

There are two major stages in making a Buffett investment decision. The first is determining whether a particular company is a Buffett-type company, that is, whether it fits within Buffett's "realm of confidence"—a company whose high returns can be predicted with a fair amount of certainty. The second stage is determining whether the stock price a company is currently selling for will allow a commensurate high return that is better than your other options.

First Stage—"Is This a Buffett-Type Company?"

Look at the nature of the company's business.   Buffett invests only in companies that have strong brand recognition, not quite correctly called consumer monopolies by Buffett, or companies that other firms must go through to conduct a major business project or campaign, which he calls tollbridge companies. Only a handful of companies have the size, depth, and reach that meet Buffett's requirements. Examples include Coca-Cola, Gillette, the *Washington Post*, McDonald's, and American Express.

■ Gannett has, in effect, monopolies or near monopolies, in that most of its newspapers are the only newspapers in their cities. Test results: Pass.

Microsoft essentially has a monopoly in the operating systems of personal computers, with a market share of about 85 percent. Test results: Pass.

Oracle is the dominant company in the database space, with a 60 percent market share. Test results: Pass.

Look to see if the company has the ability to pass on costs. See if the company has the ability to adjust prices to inflation, which helps companies make money no matter what type of economic climate exists at the time. This particular function cannot be automated.

It can be performed simply, though, by asking whether over the past decade or two or three the company has been able to substantially raise the price of its main product, such as newspapers that originally cost 25 cents per copy but now cost 75 cents. The companies mentioned above fit the bill.

■ Gannett: Mary writes in her book about Gannett: "Newspapers and TV stations make their real money by selling advertising. If you own the only newspaper in town, you can charge really high advertising rates, and there is not much in the way of alternatives for people to switch to." Test results: Pass.

Microsoft and Oracle are technology companies, and often technology prices decline over time without regard to inflation. However, both Microsoft and Oracle have dominant market positions, which allows them to charge more than others and raise prices. In fact, while the cost of microprocessors and PCs have come down, both Microsoft and Oracle have been able to hold the line and sometimes raise the average price of their software. Test results: Pass.

Look at the complexity of the product.   Buffett likes companies that are easy to understand. He wants to be able to comprehend the exact business of the company (Lynch and Graham take very similar approaches). Products that Buffett considers understandable include soft drinks, razors, diapers, and ice cream. We believe, however, that certain major technology products, such as personal computers, are at least fairly understandable in today's technologically advanced society.

■ Gannett is in the newspaper business, a business that virtually everyone is familiar with and able to understand. Test results: Pass.

Microsoft is a software company, which, in Buffett's eyes, is as understandable as a language you never heard before. Test results: Neutral.

Oracle is also a software company. Test results: Neutral.

Look at earnings predictability.   See if earnings are predictable. Earnings predictability is a cornerstone of Buffett's methodology. Check to see if any year's earnings per share (EPS) is negative. If so, with one exception, it fails Buffett's criterion. Again, he wants to see predictability. Buffett would not consider a company's earnings predictable if the earnings have been negative at some point, with the possible exception of the very last fiscal year. If earnings were otherwise predictable but there is a loss or a sharp drop in earnings in the last fiscal year that he thinks is "temporary," Buffett might see that as an opportunity. Bad news can substantially lower the price of the company temporarily to the "strike zone," where it is attractive to invest in or acquire. That temporary qualification, however, does call for a lot of contrarian business judgment because media articles about the company at the time are likely to paint a dismal outlook. However, the bad news may also be a recession in an industry or a dramatic drop in the popularity of an industry, whereby all stocks in the industry are well off their highs, in which case there is substantially less concern about permanent flaws in a specific company.

Buffett wants his companies to have solid, stable earnings that continually expand, which allows him to accurately predict future earnings. Buffett would consider a company's earnings predictable if in fact EPS has increased every year. Buffett would not consider a company's earnings predictable if earnings have declined any time in the past ten years. Note that Mary implies Buffett might accept a dip under certain circumstances, citing as an example his investment in Gannett.

■ Gannett, between 1983 and 1994, had strong and steady rising earnings per share, except for 1990 and 1991, when there was a 20 percent dip. Mary discounts the importance of this dip by noting that the entire publishing and media business was in a recession at the time. Test results: Pass.

Microsoft's earnings, for the past ten years, increased each year without exception. Test results: Pass.

Like Microsoft, Oracle's earnings, for the past ten years, went up each year without interruption. Test results: Pass.

Earnings Predictability

1. Y1 > Y2 > Y3 > Y4 > Y5 > Y6 > Y7 > Y8 > Y9 > Y10 (except for a one-time dip of up to 20 percent from the prior year's earnings). If the most recent year (Y1) is negative or a sharp loss, ignore it in the comparison.	Pass
2. All others	Fail

Note: To find the last ten years of EPS, go to: <www.moneycentral. msn.com/investor/>. In the lower left will be a box for searching; type in "Statements." You will then be asked which company you want statements for, and you'll type in the company's stock symbol.

Finally, there will be a pull-down menu with the following choices: "Income Statement, Balance Sheet, Cash Flow, 10 Year Summary." Click on "10 Year Summary," and you'll get all the information you need.

Look at the level of debt.   Buffett likes conservatively financed companies. Nonetheless, he has invested in companies with large financing divisions and in firms with rather high levels of debt. He seems to exempt financially oriented companies such as American Express, Salomon, and Wells Fargo as well as such insurance companies as Geico and Freddie Mac.

Buffett is different from other gurus in determining what level of debt is considered conservative. Whereas other gurus use a debt-equity ratio, Buffett wants to see that the long-term debt of a company can be paid off from net income in two years or less.

If a company is not in finance, banking, or insurance:

> Long-term DE $\leq$ 2 $\times$ Net income (use the prior year's
> net income if the most recent year is negative): Pass

■ Gannett's earned $465 million in 1994 (the last year of Mary's figures), when it had long-term debt of $767 million. Thus, long-term debt is less than two times earnings. Test results: Pass.

Microsoft has no debt and earnings of over $9.5 billion. Well, if any company could pay off its long-term debt, it's probably Microsoft. Test results: Pass.

Oracle's long-term debt is $301 million, and its earnings are over $6 billion. Test results: Pass.

Long-Term Debt

1. $>$ 2 times earnings   Fail
2. $\leq$ 2 times earnings   Pass

Note: If you looked at Mary's examples in terms of traditional LTD-equity, the highest level Buffett invested in for a nonfinancial company was Gannett at 46.2 percent.

Look at return on equity.   Buffett likes companies with an average return on equity (ROE) of at least 15 percent or better and, ideally, consistently above 15 percent each year, which is better than average. U.S. corporations have, on average, returned about 12 percent on equity over the last 30 years. Buffett looks at the average ROE over the last ten years.

If the ten-year average ROE is greater than or equal to 15 percent, Buffett would consider this high enough to pass. A high return on equity indicates management has done a great job allocating retained earnings, leaving shareholders with a solid, above-average return.

A ten-year average ROE lower than 15 percent is unacceptable and suggests that management is not doing a good job allocating retained earnings. This test, too, is a cornerstone of Buffett's methodology and cannot be compromised.

■ Gannet's average return on equity for the last ten years was 20.4 percent, nicely surpassing Buffett's 15 percent minimum. Test results: Pass.

  Microsoft earned an average of 29 percent on equity during the past seven years. Test results: Pass.

  Oracle earned an average 44 percent return on equity during the past seven years. Test results: Pass.

Return on Equity Averaged over the Last 10 Years

1. $< 15\%$ Fail
2. $\geq 15\%$ Pass

Look at capital expenditures.   Buffett likes companies that do not require major capital expenditures. That is, the company does not need to spend a ton of money on major upgrades of plant and equipment or on research and development to stay competitive. He looks for free cash flow to be a positive number.

Free cash flow greater than zero is wonderful, indicating that the company is generating more cash than it is consuming. On the other hand, free cash flow equal to zero or negative is a bad sign, indicating that the company is spending more money than it is taking in.

■ Gannett's business—newspapers and TV stations—requires large up-front capital expenditures but not much on an ongoing basis to stay competitive. Test results: Pass.

Microsoft's free cash flow per share is $2.47, which meets Buffett's desire for it to be positive. Test results: Pass.

Oracle's free cash flow per share is also positive: 47 cents. Test results: Pass.

Free Cash Flow

1. ≤ 0 Fail
2. > 0 Pass

Look at management's use of retained earnings. Mary Buffett writes in her book that we take "the per share earnings retained by a business for a certain period of time, then compare it to any increase in per share earnings that occurred during this same period." We're interested here in seeing if management is using retained earnings properly—that is, to increase shareholder wealth.

To figure this out, Buffett looks at the total amount of retained earnings for a specified period and compares it to any gain in EPS over the same period. Specifically, this variable looks at the additional earnings gain from seven years back to the present. That is, it takes the difference between last year's fiscal earnings and earnings for the fiscal year seven years ago, and divides that figure by the total amount of retained earnings over that same period. This then gives a rate of return.

It is more than acceptable to Buffett if use of retained earnings provides a return of 15 percent or better. Essentially, management is doing a great job putting the retained earnings to work. If use of retained earnings provides a return of less than 15 percent but greater or equal to 12 percent, management has proven it can earn shareholders a decent return on the earnings they kept. Buffett prefers 15 percent or better but nonetheless has invested in companies where the use of retained earnings is between 12 percent and 15 percent.

Buffett would consider unacceptable use of retained earnings that provides a return of less than 12 percent as management is not profitably allocating retained earnings. Essentially, investors would be better off if the company paid all earnings out to shareholders and let them invest the earnings on their own.

■ Mary writes of Gannett: "The company from 1984 to 1994 had retained earnings of $11.64 a share. Per share earnings grew by $1.80 a share from $1.40 a share at the end of 1984 to $3.20 by the end of 1994. Thus, we can argue that the retained earnings of $11.64 a share are projected to produce in 1994 an after-corporate-income-tax return of $1.80, which equates to a 15.5 percent rate of return." Test results: Pass.
   Microsoft earns a 25.8 percent return on the earnings it keeps. Test results: Pass.
   Oracle earns 55.6 percent on the earnings it keeps. Test results: Pass.

Utilization of Retained Earnings

1.	< 12%	Fail
2.	≥ 12% and < 15%	Pass
3.	≥ 15%	Pass—Best case

The preceding concludes Buffett's first-stage analysis. When he gets positive responses to all of the above criteria, which confirms that the company being looked at is a "Buffett-type company," only then does he proceed with the second stage, a price analysis. The price analysis will determine whether the stock is at an attractive enough price to be purchased.

Second Stage—"Is This Buffett-Type Company Attractively Priced?"

Once you have determined that the firm is a Buffett-type company, you need to let the market price determine whether to invest in the company, as your initial price heavily determines the returns you can make over the long run. There are always alternative options for investments (one of which is Treasury bonds) and a goal of Buffett's is determining that the current price of the company is more attractive than bonds.

There are three major parts to the second-stage analysis. First, you need to find out your expected return using something Buffett calls the ROE method. Second, you find your return using another tactic that Buffett calls the EPS growth method. The third and final step is to average both returns to create the final return.

We'll now describe how to find the expected rate of return using Buffett's ROE method. Several steps are needed to arrive at this number.

If you are following along doing the calculations yourself, you should note three adjustments that Mary Buffett made in her Gannett example. First, she included the 1994 EPS estimate of $3.20 to figure out her long-term EPS growth rate of 8.6 percent. Second, Mary assumed the average payout would decrease to 40 percent in the future. And last, Mary used the 1994 EPS estimate of $3.20 to come up with a 1994 estimated ROE of 24.5 percent. She averaged in this number to get a ten-year average ROE of 20.4 percent.

Step 1: Look at the initial rate of return. The first number we need to find is our initial rate of return: IRR. You'll look at the company's initial rate of return and see how it will expand relative to the static long-term Treasury bond yield. To calculate the initial rate of return, the EPS is divided into the current market price.

■ Gannett's initial rate of return, says Mary, is 6.5 percent.
  Microsoft's initial rate of return is 3.2 percent.
  Oracle's initial rate of return is 8.1 percent.

Step 2: Compare the initial rate of return with the long-term Treasury bond yield. With the initial rate of return determined, compare it with the long-term Treasury bond yield. Buffett favors companies in which the initial rate of return is as good as or better than the long-term Treasury bond yield, which at the time of this writing is a relatively low 5.5 percent. However, he has occasionally invested in companies with lower initial rates of return than the long-term T-bond yield as long as the company's yield is expected to expand rapidly.

If the IRR is greater than or equal to the long-term bond yield, the company is an obvious choice, as the expanding initial rate of return is greater than the Treasury yield. However, if the IRR is less than the long-term bond yield, Buffett prefers to avoid the stock.

■ Gannett's per share earnings growth rate for the last ten years has been 8.6 percent compounded. The long-term Treasury yield Mary cites is 7 percent. Test results: Pass.

Microsoft's rate of return will grow at 16.9 percent. At this time (year 2001), we estimate the long-term Treasury yield to be about 5.5 percent. Because Microsoft's initial rate of return of 3.2 percent is below this Treasury rate, it fails this test. Test results: Fail.

Oracle's initial rate of return is 8.1 percent, which surpasses the Treasury's yield of 5.5 percent. Also, earnings are expected to grow 22.9 percent. Test results: Pass.

Initial Rate of Return

1. < Long-term bond yield   Fail
2. ≥ Long-term bond yield   Pass

Step 3: Calculate the future EPS.   Now we need to find the future EPS, which involves several small calculations first. Let's start with the current equity per share. Find total equity on the balance sheet and divide by shares outstanding. This gives you equity per share. Next, we need the return on equity (ROE) for the last ten years, including the estimated ROE for the current year (if available), which we sum and divide by 10. This gives a ten-year average ROE. The next step is finding the average payout. Again, this is a simple average. Find the dividend payout ratio (the percent of earnings that the company pays out as a dividend) for each of the last ten years (including the estimated payout for the current year, if available), and average them.

Next we need to find the average retained earnings. To do so, perform the following calculation with the number you found just a minute ago.

$$\text{Percent ROE retained} = (\text{Avg. ROE} / 100) \times (1 - (\text{Avg. payout} / 100))$$

Now multiply the answer by 100 to get a percent. This is where it gets a little tricky. We need to do a time value of money calculation, so get your calculator ready. Our *PV,* or present value, is the per share equity that we calculated a minute ago. Our time period, or *n,* is ten years. We'll be solving for *FV,* or future value.

At this point, you may be thinking, "Well, what about *i,* the interest rate?" And yes, we did leave it out. This is the tricky part. To find the appropriate rate, we have to go back to our previous calculation; that is, the equation where we solved for the percent of ROE retained.

PV = Current equity per share
n = 10 (the time period, or ten years)
i = Percent ROE retained (from above)

Solve for FV = Future equity per share

And, finally, we are able to find future EPS. Take the future equity per share and multiply it by the ten-year average ROE to get the future EPS.

■ Future EPS of Gannett is $8.44.
   Future EPS of Microsoft is $111.62.
   Future EPS of Oracle is $33.54.

Step 4: Calculate the future stock price (with dividends).

Now you'll need to find the future expected stock price. To find this number, we can back into it using the average historical PE (just find the PE in each of the past ten years and average it) and the EPS. Because the stock price divided by EPS equals the PE, we can figure out the stock price as we have the two other variables. Take the expected future EPS you just found and multiply it by the average PE for the past ten years (*Note:* Sometimes it's hard to find ten years' data, so use seven years if available). This gives you a projected future stock price of $XXX.

Now that you've found the future stock price, you'll need to do another calculation to find the total dividend pool so you can add that to the stock price. To start, take the company's estimated EPS for the current year and multiply by the growth rate to figure out the projected EPS in each year for the next ten years. Then multiply each year's projected EPS by the (Average payout / 100). Then sum up all the years. Add this number to the stock price to get the future price with dividends.

■ Gannett's future stock price: $160.36 plus dividends of $23.85. Microsoft's future stock price: $1,111.58 (no dividends). Oracle's future stock price: $375.30 (no dividends).

Step 5: Calculate your expected rate of return based on the average ROE method.   Now we can move to the final part of the second step, which is to find our expected return. To do so, do a time value of money calculation with your financial calculator. This is pure plug-and-chug. Enter the following values in your calculator to solve for i, which is the expected return:

PV = Current stock price
FV = Future stock price + Total dividend pool
n = 10 (the time period, or ten years)

Solve for i (or your expected return using the ROE method).

If the expected return using the ROE method is greater than or equal to 22 percent, you have an exceptionally good return. Buffett would consider this absolutely fantastic. If the return is less than 22 percent but greater than or equal to 15 percent, Buffett would consider this a good return. If the return is less than 15 percent but greater than or equal to 12 percent, you have a return slightly below what Buffett prefers. However, he has invested in companies like this before, as it is still a solid return. For instance, he invested in McDonald's in 1996 when the return was expected to be 12.6 percent. Anything below 12 is unacceptable.

■ Gannett's expected rate of return surpasses Buffett's 12 percent minimum with an average of 14 percent. Test results: Pass.
    Microsoft's expected rate of return is 34.78 percent, well above Buffett's minimum of 12 percent. Test results: Pass.

Oracle's expected rate of return is 39.08 percent, also dramatically above Buffett's 12 percent minimum. Test results: Pass.

Expected Return (ROE Method)

1. < 12%   Fail
2. ≧ 12% and < 15%   Pass
3. ≧ 15%   Pass—Best case

Now we enter the second part of the second stage of this analysis. We'll find the expected rate of return using another tactic that Buffett calls the average EPS growth method. We need to take a couple of steps to get to this number.

Step 6: Calculate the expected future stock price (with dividends) based on average EPS growth.   First, we'll have to find our future stock price. If you take the historical EPS growth, you can project EPS in ten years. Basically take 1 + EPS growth and raise it to a factor of 10, then multiply by the current year (Y0) estimated EPS. The number you get is EPS in Year 10. Now multiply EPS in Year 10 by the ten-year average PE, which we found earlier. This equals the future stock price. Add in the total expected dividend pool, based on the EPS calculated using this growth rate, starting with the EPS the year after the current year, to get a total dollar amount. This is your stock price in Year 10.

■ Gannett's future stock price is expected to be: $142.12 plus dividends of $21.19.
Microsoft's future stock price is expected to be: $294.25.
Oracle's future stock price is expected to be: $224.53.

Step 7: Calculate your expected rate of return based on the average EPS growth method.   With the stock price in Year 10, you can figure out your expected return based on the current price and the future expected stock price, including the dividend pool. To do so, you'll need to break out your financial calculator again to do a time-value-of-money calculation.

Enter the following values into your calculator to solve for i, which will be your expected return using the EPS growth method:

PV = Current stock price
FV = Future stock price with total dividend pool (calculated above)
n =   10 (time period, or ten years)

Solve for i (or your expected return using the EPS growth method)

An expected return greater than or equal to 22 percent is an exceptionally good return. A return below 22 percent but greater than or equal to 15 is a good return. And below 15 percent but greater than or equal to 12 percent is acceptable. Buffett likes to see a 15 percent return or better but nonetheless would consider this a good, solid return. Anything below 12 percent is too low for Buffett to have interest.

■ Gannett: 12.64 percent is the expected return. Test results: Pass.
   Microsoft: 18.01 percent is the expected return. Test results: Pass.
   Oracle: 32.11 percent is the expected return. Test results: Pass.

Expected Return (EPS Growth Method)

1. < 12%	Fail
2. ≧ 12% and < 15%	Pass
3. ≧ 15%	Pass—Best case

Now we've come to the third and final step, where we average the two expected rates of return. This will give you a final expected rate of return, which determines whether you should invest in the stock.

Step 8: Look at the range of expected rates of return.   First, we compare and then average the range of returns that we found using both ROE and historical EPS growth methods.

Avg. final return = ((Expected return of ROE method + Expected return of EPS method) ÷ 2) × 100

A return of 22 percent or more is an exceptional return. A return less than 22 percent but greater than or equal to 15 percent is a good return. A return less than 15 percent but 12 percent or more is still acceptable. As mentioned, Buffett likes to see a 15 percent return but has nonetheless invested in companies with this expected return. Any return below 12 percent, however, is unacceptable to Buffett.

■ Gannett's expected range of returns: 12.64 percent and 14 percent. Test results: Pass.

Microsoft's expected range of returns: 18.01 percent and 34.78 percent. Test results: Pass.

Oracle's expected range of returns: 32.11 percent and 39.08 percent. Test results: Pass.

Range of Expected Returns

1. < 12%   Fail
2. ≧ 12% and <15%   Pass
3. ≧ 15%   Pass—Best case

BOTTOM LINE

Gannett

Tests passed:	Nature of the company's business
	Ability to pass on costs
	Complexity of the product
	Earnings predictability
	Level of debt
	Return on equity
	Capital expenditures
	Management's use of retained earnings
	Comparison of initial rate of return with long-term Treasury bond yield
	Expected rate of return based on average ROE method
	Expected rate of return based on EPS growth method
	Expected rates of return
Tests failed:	None
Score:	100 percent (12 passed, 0 failed)

BOTTOM LINE: There is STRONG INTEREST in Gannett.

Microsoft

Tests passed: Nature of the company's business
Earnings predictability
Level of debt
Return on equity
Capital expenditures
Management's use of retained earnings
Expected rate of return based on average ROE method
Expected rate of return based on EPS growth method
Expected rates of return

Tests neutral: Complexity of the product

Tests failed: Comparison of initial rate of return with long-term
Treasury bond yield

Score: 90 percent (9 passed; 1 neutral; 1 failed)

BOTTOM LINE: There is SOME INTEREST in Microsoft.

Oracle

Tests passed: Nature of the company's business
Earnings predictability
Level of debt
Return on equity
Capital expenditures
Management's use of retained earnings
Comparison of initial rate of return with long-term
Treasury bond yield
Expected rate of return based on average ROE method
Expected rate of return based on EPS growth method
Expected rates of return

Tests neutral: Complexity of the product

Tests failed: None

Score: 100 percent (10 passed; 1 neutral, 0 failed)

BOTTOM LINE: There is STRONG INTEREST in Oracle.

BUFFETT'S KEY INVESTING CRITERIA

- Look for companies with commanding market shares.

- Invest as though you were buying the entire company, not just buying shares.

- Look into the future. Estimate the stock's future value and then determine if it is a good buy today.

- Know management.

- Know the industry.

- Do your homework up front. Study and thoroughly analyze the companies in which you place your faith—and your money.

- Don't rush out to buy the stock of a good company. Be sure it is priced low enough that it is likely to provide you with a good return.

- After you buy, put the stock in the back of your mind. You are holding for the long term, and unless you have made a poor choice of investment or something totally unforeseen occurs, plan on keeping the stock through thick and thin. This is a stock you may well pass on to your children or grandchildren.

CHAPTER 5

THE MOTLEY FOOL

WHICH INVESTORS MIGHT BEST USE The Motley Fool?

RISK: The Fool likes small cap stocks, which are risky. However, the Fool is also very picky, which lowers risk somewhat. Overall, we'd say the Fool involves relatively high risk for a relatively higher return.

TIME HORIZON: Short term.

EFFORT: The Fool's strategy requires effort up front but very little later on.

NOTE: It's been our experience that very few stocks ever pass the Fool's test. Generally, if a company is that good, the market knows it and its stock price has gone up. The Fool likes extremely good companies at extremely low prices (who doesn't?). We've found that when a stock does meet the Fool's criteria, it tends to be a very good performer, often going up dramatically in a relatively short period of time.

WHO IS THE MOTLEY FOOL?

In the world of investing, there's probably no guru whose shtick remotely resembles that of The Motley Fool, two guys famously wearing foolscaps and proudly calling themselves "fools."

The Motley Fool is really a company headquartered in Alexandria, Virginia, and headed by two brothers—David and Tom Gardner. These are not business-trained folks, and they take every opportunity to let you know that they have no business—or investing—background. Both graduated as English majors: David from the University of

North Carolina in 1988 and Tom from Brown University in 1990. They use this nonfinancial background to their advantage by positioning themselves as an investment Everyman who is out to help the little guy compete with the Big Boys—the professionals and institutions that make the big bucks.

The organization's name is a sign of their attitude that not everything should be taken seriously. The (motley) fool in question is from Shakespeare's *As You Like It* (Act II, Scene 7). The fool refers to the court jester, who was the only one able to speak the truth to the king's face and not suffer beheading.

The Gardner boys would like you to think that they, alone among investment gurus, tell the truth, see the financial world as it really is, and have the answers to your financial conundrums. And never worry about beheading by the institutions of Wall Street.

The Gardners have several things going for them. They rely a lot on common sense, which is good because a lot of investing really should be based on common sense. Plus, such reasoning is easy to understand. In addition, they do investors a service by exposing the financial interests that are often behind stock recommendations.

What might at first seem a negative is really a positive: the Fool has the most restrictive methodology of any of our gurus. At any given time, few (and often no) stocks pass its rules, based on our interpretation of its strategy. As a result, we pay attention when a stock passes the Fool's rules on our Validea.com site. We often find the few stocks that do pass the Fool's criteria have a sharp price rise starting anytime within a few weeks of when it passes the test. If you do follow this strategy, be sure to lock in a portion of your profit when it occurs as the prices of these smaller-cap stocks tend to be very volatile.

As for the Fool's track record, it has had its ups and downs. According to *Forbes ASAP* (19 February 2001), the Fool's Rule Breaker Portfolio has averaged an annualized return of 44 percent since 1994 compared with 19 percent for the S&P 500.

However, a strategy the Fool promoted—the Foolish Four—was recently discarded by the Fool itself. *Money* (February 2001) describes the strategy this way: "A portfolio of stocks that only a mathematician could love, the Foolish Four were culled from the 30 names in the Dow by taking each company's dividend yield and dividing it by the square root of its share price. The stock with the highest ratio was then discarded and the runners up became the Foolish Four. For 2000 the stocks that made the grade were Caterpillar, Eastman Kodak, SBC Communications, and, alas, GM."

The Motley Fool reports on its Web site that for a while it thought the strategy was the greatest thing since online trading. But the strategy was questioned by a number of critics, prompting the Fool to do extensive research into the strategy. It didn't live up to its original billing, and the Fool has since dropped it.

The Gardners penned their first book in 1996, *The Motley Fool Investment Guide: How the Fool Beats Wall Street's Wise Men and How You Can Too* (the basis of our analysis of the Fool's investment strategy), which became a best seller. This was followed by three other hot-selling books, including: *The Motley Fool Investment Workbook* (1998), *The Motley Fool's Rule Breakers, Rule Makers: The Foolish Guide to Picking Stocks* (1999), and *You Have More Than You Think: The Foolish Guide to Personal Finance* (2001).

Originally found only on America Online, the Fool created its Internet Web site in 1997. Reportedly, AOL still has a small ownership interest in the company, which is privately held. The Gardners also have a syndicated newspaper column, which is carried by more than 190 papers, and host *The Motley Fool Radio Show,* which airs weekly on more than 145 stations.

With the sharp drop in the stock market starting in early 2000, interest in investment Web sites waned, including The Motley Fool's. With the loss of stock market value and investor interest came a loss of advertising revenue. In February 2001, the Fool announced it was laying off 115 people, or about a third of its workforce.

THE FOOL'S SHTICK

More than most gurus, the Gardners have a shtick—an attitude, a branding strategy, a look-and-feel, a "message"—that they rely on heavily. Elements of it include humor and irreverence. *Forbes ASAP* has made this observation: "The Gardner brothers may be the only grown men in America who can dispense financial advice on television while wearing fools' hats and be taken seriously."

The Gardners love poking their fingers in the face of authority. They call themselves and their followers fools, considered a good thing, and equate foolish with intelligent. Conversely, wise is a put-down. Just look at the subtitle of their first book: *How the Fool Beats Wall Street's Wise Men.*

It's very much an us-versus-them attitude, with "us" being the little guy and "them" being the establishment that includes the Wall Street investment community, stockbrokers, mutual funds, other gurus, and analysts. "We want to help you help yourself make money. This was our intention back in 1993, when we launched *The Motley Fool* as an investment newsletter," the brothers write in their book.

The Internet is an essential part of the Gardners' strategy. It is viewed as a tool of democracy, where the little guy, at little or no cost, has access to the type of information previously available only to professional investors, institutions, and the wealthy.

The Fool likes to take potshots at established institutions; mutual funds are one such institution. In a chapter in their book titled "Maybe You Should Avoid Mutual Funds," the Gardners write:

1. Of the 5,845 funds, only 2,615 have a 3-year track record, and of those 2,615 funds, 80.5 percent of them lost to the S&P 500 return of 7.86 percent annual growth.

2. Only 1,936 funds have been around for 5 years. Of those, 79.9 percent lost to the S&P 500 return of 10.78 percent annual growth.

3. Only 780 of the funds have a 10-year track record. Of those, 87.3 percent lost to the S&P 500 annual return of 13.82 percent.

Nearly 90 percent of all funds that have 10-year records under-perform the market. Good God! Imagine that.

In truth, the Fool's naysaying of mutual funds is not entirely misguided. They are not the first to make the observation that the performances of mutual funds usually do not equal, let alone beat, the market averages. The Gardner brothers do a service to individual investors by stressing this fact.

They point out the virtues of index funds: lower costs and performances that equate with the averages. They like index funds, which is reasonable, but they also believe they have investment strategies that can consistently outperform the market.

Like other gurus, the Gardners stress investing in individual stocks, not mutual funds. And despite their little-guy, smart-ass demeanor, their strategies, such as focusing on Dow stocks and suggesting putting at least some of one's money into an index fund, are fairly conservative.

Here's some advice in an article on the Fool's Web site in March 2001: "Blue chips are as promising for investors today as they were 100 years ago. But now, as then, it's important to look for the leaders. Not all blue chips are equally promising, and investors must be diligent about researching stocks and flexible in owning them." That's "foolish"? Our grandmothers might have given the same investment advice had they been inclined to give advice. Such tattle could easily have come from a broker at Merrill Lynch or Morgan Stanley. The Gardners may dress funny but their thinking often isn't all that different from that of mainstream advisors.

They also recommend investing in small cap stocks—another mainstream strategy. They define small caps as stocks whose capitalization is between $50 million and $500 million, and micro-caps as being below $50 million. The Gardners like small caps because, at least according to some historical data they cite, small caps outperform large caps over the long run. Also in these stocks' favor is the fact that their small size precludes mutual funds and institutions from buying them; they're too small and their stocks are too illiquid. The Fool also claims earnings grow fastest among small companies and with this growth comes a rise in share prices. And small caps are typically closely held by management, says the Fool, giving management a significant financial stake in seeing the stock perform well. The Fool likes companies that are at least 10 percent owned by insiders—which are mainly small cap companies.

The Gardners give pointers in their book about how to read financial statements (shades of Benjamin Graham). They note that the income statement, for example, should indicate profit margins that remain at consistent levels if not actually rise and that research and development is being funded and not being short changed (R&D, remember, is a major variable looked at by one of our other gurus, Ken Fisher). The Gardners want to see from the income statement that the company is paying full income taxes and that the number of shares the company has outstanding isn't growing like a weed; you don't want to see significant increases in the number of shares (it dilutes earnings per share) unless there's a good reason (such as to raise money to launch a new subsidiary).

On the balance sheet, they like to see cash. The Gardners write: "Develop a bias toward stocks backed by cash-generating businesses that have a wad of bills sitting in the bank gathering interest (and ready to be deployed whenever a good opportunity presents itself!)." In addition, they like balance sheets of small cap companies with little or no debt. And they recommend that a company's growth in accounts receivable and inventory approximates sales growth.

Let's now take a close look at how to use The Motley Fool's strategy from its original book, subsequently updated on its Web site.

THE MOTLEY FOOL'S STRATEGY: STEP-BY-STEP

■ Dynacq International Inc. (DYII) is a Houston-based operator of outpatient surgery, X-ray and laboratory facilities, a medical office complex, and an acute care hospital that also provides home infusion services, such as parenteral nutrition (see Figure 5.1).

A second company we use to illustrate the Fool's methodology is Hot Topic Inc. (HOTT), which is based in City of Industry, California, and has almost 300 stores. Hot Topic sells a variety of merchandise—clothing, jewelry, posters, cosmetics—all of which have a music orientation. The company's target market is 12 to 22 year olds (see Figure 5.2).

Profit margin. The Motley Fool's methodology seeks companies with a minimum trailing, 12-month, after-tax profit margin of 7 percent. The companies that pass this criterion have strong positions within their respective industries and offer greater shareholder returns. A true test of the quality of a company is its ability to sustain this margin.

FIGURE 5.1   **DYNACQ INTERNATIONAL INC (DYII)** $16.65 as of 4/18/2001

	Year 1	Year 2
Total Net Income (mil.)	$5.9	$2.7
EPS	$0.41	$0.20
Sales (mil.)	$26.0	$20.3
Avg. PE	11.5	6.9
ROE	40.4%	32.1%
Long-Term Debt-Equity	3%	8%
Dividend	–	–
Payout	0%	0%
Shares Outstanding (mil.)	15.3	12.9

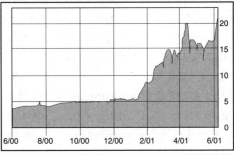

	Year 3	Year 4	Year 5	Year 6	Year 7	Year 8	Year 9	Year 10
Total Net Income (mil.)	$0.9	$(1.1)	$0.6	$0.9	$0.5	$0.9		
EPS	$0.07	$(0.07)	$0.04	$0.07	$0.03	$0.07		
Sales (mil.)	$10.9	$9.8	$7.4	$6.9	$2.6	$3.4		
Avg. PE	8.7	n/a	30.5	25	89.6	n/a		
ROE	15.5%	n/a	9.4%	15.5%	10.4%	29%		
Long-Term Debt-Equity	17%	15%	16%	21%	35%	26%		
Dividend	–	–	–					
Payout	0%	0%	0%					
Shares Outstanding (mil.)	13.1	14.2	14.2	14.2	14.2	13.5		

	Q1	Q2	Q3	Q4	Q5	Q6	Q7	Q8
EPS	$0.17	$0.17	$0.12	$0.13	$0.11	$0.07	$0.21	$0.08
Revenue (mil.)	$9.8	$8.9	$7.5	$7.5	$5.8	$5.2	$6.2	$4.3

	Market Cap (mil.)	TTM Sales (mil.)	Relative Strength	EPS Growth (4-yr. avg.)	Revenue Growth (TTM)	Current Ratio	Insider Buy-Sells (3 months)
DYII	$230.0	$33.7	99	79.0%	69.0%	2.7	0/0
Hospitals Industry	$4,580.0	$3,673.3	81	28.0%	24.0%	2.1	

	PEG	PE	Projected PE	PS	Price-Book	Price-Cash Flow	Free Cash Flow/Share
DYII	0.36	28.2	12.8	6.82	13.5	7.4	0.27
Hospitals Industry	1.15	56.9	34.4	1.99	3.9	15.7	

	Yield	Profit Margin (TTM)	ROE (TTM)	Total Debt-Equity	Long-Term Debt-Equity	Insider Ownership	Institutional Ownership
DYII	0.00%	25.0%	50.0%	47%	2.36%	70.0%	2.1%
Hospitals Industry	0.00%	6.0%	15.0%	117%	n/a		

Recent Balance Sheet Items ($ millions)		Financial Statement Trends			
			Recent 12 mo.	FY1	FY2
Cash	6.2				
Current Assets	16.7	Inventory/Sales	1%	1%	1%
Total Assets	26.7	AR to Sales	34%	32%	41%
Current Liabilities	6.3	R&D to Sales	–	–	–
Long-Term Debt	0.4				
Total Debt	7.95				
Equity	16.92				

FIGURE 5.2	HOT TOPIC INC (HOTT)	$28.00 as of 3/30/2001

Year 1 = FY 2000	Year 1	Year 2
Total Net Income (mil.)	$23.2	$13.5
EPS	$1.09	$0.69
Sales (mil.)	$257.2	$168.9
Avg. PE	15.7	12.1
ROE	23.3%	20.1%
Long-Term Debt-Equity	0%	0%
Dividend	0	0
Payout	0%	0%
Shares Outstanding (mil.)	20.1	19.3

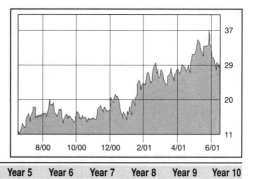

	Year 3	Year 4	Year 5	Year 6	Year 7	Year 8	Year 9	Year 10
Total Net Income (mil.)	$6.0	$4.5	$2.6	$0.4				
EPS	$0.31	$0.23	$0.17	$0.04				
Sales (mil.)	$103.4	$70.5	$43.6	$23.6				
Avg. PE	16.3	24.9	32.4	nc				
ROE	12.3%	10.1%	6.6%	50.0%				
Long-Term Debt-Equity	0%	0%	0%	0				
Dividend	0	0	0	0				
Payout	0%	0%	0%	0%				
Shares Outstanding (mil.)	18.6	19.0	18.4	3.1				

	Q1	Q2	Q3	Q4	Q5	Q6	Q7	Q8
EPS	$0.48	$0.34	$0.145	$0.115	$0.36	$0.22	$0.06	$0.035
Revenue (mil.)	$88,428	$72,203	$51,717	$44,839	$59,920	$47,964	$32,779	$28,286

	Market Cap (mil.)	TTM Sales (mil.)	Relative Strength	EPS Growth (3-yr. avg.)	Revenue Growth (TTM)	Current Ratio	Insider Buy-Sells (3 months)
HOTT	$564	$257.2	91	58%	47.8%	2.6	0/1
Specialty Retail Industry	$2,112	$2,224.9	74	11.1%	8.0%	2.5	

	PEG	PE	Projected PE	PS	Price-Book	Price-Cash Flow	Free Cash Flow/Share
HOTT	0.44	25.7	25.9	2.19	6.8	12.4	0.52
Specialty Retail Industry	2.47	20.3	13.9	1.1	2.3	11.2	

	Yield	Profit Margin (TTM)	ROE (TTM)	Total Debt-Equity	Long-Term Debt-Equity	Insider Ownership	Institutional Ownership
HOTT	0%	9.0%	28.2%	0%	0%	28%	89.5%
Specialty Retail Industry	1.6%	6.4%	15.1%	31.3%	31.3%		

Recent Balance Sheet Items ($ millions)		Financial Statement Trends		
Cash	41.4	Recent 12 mo.	FY1	FY2
Current Assets	73.4	Inventory/Sales	8.2%	9.1%	10.1%
Total Assets	112.4	AR to Sales	0%	0%	0%
Current Liabilities	27.9	R&D to Sales	–	–	–
Long-Term Debt	0.1			
Total Debt	0.2			
Equity	82.3			

■ Dynacq's profit margin, 25 percent, easily passes this criterion. Test results: Pass.

Hot Topic's profit margin is 9 percent, just passing the Fool's test. Test results: Pass.

Profit Margin

1. > 7%   Fail
2. ≦ 7%   Pass

Note: In the Fool's book, this requirement was for 10 percent but was revised on its Web site to 7 percent.

Profit margin consistency.   You want to see profit margins staying the same or even increasing over the past three years. We allow a slight decrease in the second year as long as the dip is within 10 percent of Year 3, and Year 1 has to be greater than Year 3. This is a sign of good management and a healthy and competitive enterprise.

■ Dynacq's profit margin has been consistent or even increasing over the past three years, which has been 22.7 percent (in the most recent year total net income was $5.9 million on sales of $26 million), 13.3 percent (Year 2) and 8.3 percent (Year 3). Test results: Pass—Best case.

Hot Topic's profit margin has been consistent or even increasing over the past three years. It was 9.0 percent in the most recently completed fiscal year, 8.0 percent the prior year, and 5.8 percent three years ago. Test results: Pass—Best case.

Profit Margin Consistency

1. Y1 ≧ Y2 ≧ Y3   Pass—Best case
2. Y1 ≧ Y3 and Y2 ≧ (0.9) × Y3   Pass
3. Anything else   Fail

Relative strength.   The investor must look at the relative strength of the company in question. Companies whose relative strength is 90 or above (that is, the company outperforms 90 percent or more of the market for the past year) are considered attractive. Companies whose prices have been rising more quickly than the market tend to keep rising, says the Fool. The Fool uses the relative strength figure found in *Investor's Business Daily.*

■ Dynacq's relative strength is 99, easily outpacing the Fool's minimum of 90. Test results: Pass.

Hot Topic's relative strength is 91, which is just above the Fool's minimum of 90. Test results: 90.

Relative Strength

1. < 90 Fail
2. ≥ 90 Pass

Sales and EPS growth.   Companies must demonstrate both revenue and net income growth of at least 25 percent in the last quarter (Q1) as compared to the same quarter (Q5) in the prior year. These growth rates identify the dynamic companies you are looking for.

■ The Fool wants to see sales and EPS growth of at least 25 percent, and Dynacq certainly delivers. Its EPS growth from Q5 to Q1 was 242.9 percent and sales growth from Q5 to Q1 was 71.2 percent. Test results: Pass.

Hot Topic also delivers: its EPS growth was 33.3 percent and its sales growth was 17.6 percent. Test results: Pass.

Sales and EPS growth

1. Sales & EPS growth from Q5 to Q1 $< 25\%$ Fail
2. Sales & EPS growth from Q5 to Q1 $\geq 25\%$ Pass

Insider holdings.   Insiders should own at least 10 percent of the company's outstanding stock. A high percentage indicates that the insiders are confident the company will do well and that they have a significant financial stake that motivates them to make sure the company does do well.

Note: Originally, this requirement was 15 percent, but in later years the Fool fine-tuned this to 10 percent.

■ Dynacq is extremely attractive on this score. Insiders own 70 percent of the company, well in excess of the Fool's 10 percent minimum. Test results: Pass.

Hot Topic's "insiders" are shown on many data sheets (including ours) as owning 28.0 percent. Sometimes this reported number includes more than just management; it may include institutions that are long-term holders of 5 percent or more of the stock of the company (because that is the way it is reported to the SEC on a proxy statement, which asks for "beneficial ownership" in the way the SEC defines it). In the case of Hot Topic, it turns out that Driehaus Capital Management owns 10 percent, Pilgrim Baxter & Associates owns 5 percent, and management and board insiders own 13 percent. We are aware of only one place on the Internet to conveniently find this extra information (besides laboriously reading through SEC proxy statements). To find this information, go to <www.multexinvestor.com> and type in the ticker symbol, HOTT, and click "Go." You will be taken to a snapshot for the stock. On the lefthand side, you will find a navigation bar. Scroll down and you will see a link on the navigation bar entitled "Highlights Report." Click on "Highlights Report" and scroll down the page to the bottom of the tables. You will see a section entitled "Equity," which contains this extra information about the breakout of ownership. Because Hot Topic management still owns more than 10 percent, it passes this criterion. Test results: Pass.

Insider Holdings

1. $< 10\%$ Fail
2. $\geqq 10\%$ Pass

Free cash flow from operations.   A positive free cash flow is typically used for internal expansion, acquisitions, dividend payments, and so forth. A company that generates rather than consumes cash is in much better shape to fund such activities on its own rather than needing to borrow funds to do so.

■ Dynacq has a positive free cash flow from operations of $0.27 per share. Test results: Pass.

Hot Topic's free cash flow of $0.52 per share easily meets the Fool's requirement for cash flow to be positive. Test results: Pass.

Cash Flow from Operations

1. Free cash flow per share $\leqq 0$ Fail
2. Free cash flow per share > 0 Pass

Price-earnings growth (PEG).   The Fool ratio is an extremely important aspect of this analysis. It is the price-earnings ratio (using the earnings over the previous 12 months) divided by the company's growth rate. If a company's stock price is $30, its earnings per share is $2, and its estimated growth rate is 20 percent, we have a PE of $24:$2, or 12. We then divide the PE (12) by the estimated future growth rate (20) to arrive at a Fool ratio of 0.60.

Ideally, the Fool prefers to calculate the earnings per share growth rate by basing it on the earnings per share estimated by analysts for the next two to three years. In many cases, particularly with smaller firms, these numbers are not available. In some cases, a long-term growth estimate or a three-year growth estimate will be available and you can use that estimate directly. If estimates are not available, use the three-, four-, or five-year historical EPS growth rate as, in many cases, history is the only basis you have for projecting the future.

If the company has attractive fundamentals and its Fool ratio is 0.5 or less, the shares are looked on favorably. These high-quality companies can often wind up as the biggest winners.

If the company's Fool ratio is between 0.50 and 0.65, the company demonstrates excellence in its fundamentals and has soundly beaten the earnings estimates.

The Fool advises investors to consider holding the shares when the company's Fool ratio is greater than 0.65 and less than 1.00, but initial purchases in this range are unfavorable. The Fool advises considering selling the shares when the company's Fool ratio is between 1.00 and 1.30; and advises considering shorting shares when the company's Fool ratio is greater than 1.30.

■ Dynacq's Fool ratio is 0.36, which is nicely below the Fool's best-case scenario. Test results: Pass.

How we calculated the Fool ratio for Dynacq: We checked the Yahoo! Finance and the Zacks Web sites and found there is no EPS prediction for the next two fiscal years, nor is there a prediction for a five-year growth rate. But there is an estimate for the current fiscal year ending about five months from now in August (the estimate shows 0.65 for the current year versus 0.41 last year—a 58 percent growth rate. There is a PE of 27.5, which gives a Fool ratio of 0.476 (27.5 ÷ 58 = 0.476). If we run this on a historical growth rate, it would of course be even better.

■ Hot Topic's Fool ratio is 0.44, which also fits the Fool's best-case scenario. Test results: Pass.

How we calculated the Fool ratio for Hot Topic: Hot Topic has an estimated EPS of $1.31 for the current year ending in January 2002 and $1.61 for January 2003 versus $0.69 last year, which works out to a compounded growth rate of 52.8 percent per year over two years. (For the compounded two-year rate, take the square root of the increase (1.61/.69 or 2.33), which is 52.8 percent). We note there is a consensus five-year growth rate estimate of 22.5 percent available, but we will use the shorter term two-year compounded rate. The current PE is 25.7, making the Fool ratio 0.49. If the two-year rate hadn't been available, we would have averaged the one-year growth rate of (1.31/.69) of 89 percent with the longer-term rate of 22.5 percent to obtain a rate of 56 percent. If the one-year rate had not been available, we would have used the historical rate.

Price-Earnings Growth (PEG). Also known as the Fool Ratio

1. $\geqq 1.3$	Fail—Worst case
2. > 0.65 and < 1.3	Fail
3. > 0.5 and $\leqq 0.65$	Pass
4. $\leqq 0.5$	Pass—Best case

Cash and cash equivalents.   Good operations generate cash. If a company is a cash generator, it has the ability to pay off debt (if it has any), acquire other companies, or otherwise grow the business, which is why cash is desirable.

There are two ways of determining if a smaller cap company has lots of cash. You can either look at the cash on the balance sheet as a percentage of annual sales or compare the cash per share to the price per share of the business. If either one is above a certain threshold, this company has lots of cash. More specifically:

If cash to sales $\geq$ 20%

or

Cash per share to current price $\geq$ 12.5%

$\rightarrow$ The company has lots of cash.

■ Dynacq is a small company, so we first look for a cash-annual sales ratio of 20 percent or greater. Dynacq shows $26 million of sales for the last fiscal year. On the last reported quarterly balance sheet, it shows $6.2 million of cash on hand, which comes to 23.8 percent (6.2 ÷ 26.0 = 23.8%) and exceeds the Fool's 20 percent minimum. The alternative calculation would have used 15.3 million shares to find $0.41 per share of cash (6.2 ÷ 15.3 = 0.41). With a share price of $14.82, that is a cash per share to current price of only 2.8 percent (.41 ÷ 14.82 = 2.8%). The stock only needs to pass one of the two criteria to pass. Test results: Pass.

Hot Topic is a small company too, so we look for a cash-annual sales ratio of 20 percent or greater. HOTT has $41.4 million of cash on hand, $257.2 million of sales, 20.1 million shares, and a current price per share of $28. This company's cash to sales is 16.1 percent, thus not meeting the Fool's criterion. The alternative test also fails: the cash per share is $2.06 and the cash per share to the current price is 7.4 percent. Test results: Fail.

Determining the sufficiency of cash and cash equivalents of larger market cap companies requires a different analysis. If the company is a large cap—that is, it has a market cap $\geq$ $1.5 billion—and has more than $500 million in cash, we define that as meeting the criterion for having "lots of cash." Notice though (under the heading of Sales on page 123) that the Fools' methodology described in their book is for smaller cap companies with a market cap of less than $500 million, so this extra rule is here to be helpful if you should try to apply the Fools' rules to larger companies (as we sometimes do ourselves).

Cash and Cash Equivalents

1. Cash/ Annual sales $\geq$ 20%	Pass
2. Cash per share/Price per share $\geq$ 12.5%	Pass
3. Cash and marketable securities $\geq$ $500 million	Pass
4. All others	Fail

Growth in inventory vis-à-vis growth in sales. Growth in inventory should approximate growth in sales. If the company is financially oriented or service oriented, this criterion doesn't apply. Obviously, these types of companies have little or no physical inventories.

This methodology indicates a strong belief that companies, especially small ones, should have tight control over inventory. It's a warning sign if a company's inventory relative to sales increases significantly when compared with the previous year. Based on the Fool's examples, we interpret the Fool to mean that up to a 30 percent increase over the increase in sales is allowed but no more. This should be examined both over the last quarter and over the last year.

■ This criterion really doesn't apply to Dynacq because it is a service company with little in the way of inventory. Note, however, that the inventory-sales ratio last year was 0.0 percent (it basically had no inventory) and this year is 1.2 percent. Although the inventory-sales ratio is rising, it is below the maximum of 30 percent that is allowed. But again this is not an important criterion for a service company like Dynacq. Test results: Pass.

This criterion does apply to Hot Topic because it is a retailer and therefore has a significant amount of inventory. The inventory-sales ratio for Hot Topic was 10.1 percent last year, whereas for this year it is 9.1 percent. The inventory-sales ratio is therefore decreasing by 0.9 percent, which fits the Fool's best-case scenario. Test results: Pass.

Growth in Inventory Compared with Growth in Sales in the Last Quarter and the Last Year

1. > 30%	Fail
2. > 0% and ≤ 30%	Pass
3. ≤ 0%	Pass—Best case

Growth in accounts receivable vis-à-vis growth in sales. Growth in accounts receivable (AR) should approximate growth in sales. If the company is financial (or the AR is nonexistent), this criterion is not applied. Financial companies have little or no accounts receivable.

This methodology also wants to make sure that a company's AR does not get significantly out of line with sales, which could indicate a potentially serious problem. Perhaps the product is being stuffed into, and not selling through, the distribution channel, is being sold because of especially advantageous terms, or the company is aggressively booking revenues on longer-term contracts well before the final product is delivered to the customer. It's a warning sign if a company's AR relative to sales increases significantly when compared with the previous year. We interpret the Fool's examples to mean that up to a 30 percent increase over the increase in sales is allowed but no more. This should be examined both over the last quarter and over the last year.

Growth in AR Compared with Growth in Sales in the Last Quarter and the Last Year

1. > 30%   Fail
2. > 0% and ≦ 30%   Pass
3. ≦ 0%   Pass—Best case

Long-term debt-equity ratio (DE).   This criterion doesn't apply to financial companies, but all other companies—the superior companies the Fool is looking for—don't need to borrow money in order to grow.

If the long-term debt-equity ratio is greater than 0 but less than or equal to 5 percent, it is a little higher than the figures this methodology is looking for but is still at an acceptable level. Anything higher than 5 percent is unacceptable.

■ Dynacq's most recent long-term debt-equity ratio of 2 percent is a little higher than the ideal of 0, but it still does not exceed 5 percent. This company has borrowed very little to grow, which is good. Test results: Pass.

Hot Topic's long-term DE ratio is 0.0 percent. It has no debt; can't do better than that. Test results: Pass.

Debt-Equity Ratio (DE)

1. DE > 5%   Fail
2. DE > 0% and DE ≦ 5%   Pass
3. DE is equal to 0   Pass—Best case

R&D-sales ratio. This criterion is not critically important for companies that aren't in the high-tech or medical sectors because they are not as R&D-dependent as companies within these sectors. This criterion is particularly important for high-tech and medical stocks because they are so R&D-dependent.

The R&D-sales ratio should be greater than or equal to the previous year's. That is, it is either maintaining the same levels of R&D expenditures or increasing them, which is a good sign. This allows the company to develop the superior technology and new products that will lead to a competitive advantage or put everyone else out of business.

■ This criterion does not really apply to companies like Dynacq and Hot Topic because they are not dependent on R&D for growth. Test results: Neutral.

R&D-Sales Ratio

1. R&D-sales for Y1 < R&D-sales for Y2   Fail
2. R&D-sales for Y1 ≧ R&D-sales for Y2   Pass

Noncritical Criteria

The following criteria are less important, which means you would place less emphasis on them when using this strategy to make your investment decisions.

Average shares outstanding. Generally, when a small cap company issues more stock, the existing stock becomes diluted and hence devalued by the market. Check to see if the company has issued a significant amount of shares in the last year or if it has been issuing more shares over the past five years. We define a "significant amount" to be 20 percent or more in the last fiscal year or it has increased the shares issued by at least 3 percent in any three of the last five years, implying that the company is frequently increasing its shares (which will dilute future earnings per share if the pattern continues).

Average Shares Outstanding

1. $Y1 \geqq Y2 \times 120\%$ Fail
2. If three or more are true:
   $Y1 \geqq 103\%$ of Y2
   $Y2 \geqq 103\%$ of Y3
   $Y3 \geqq 103\%$ of Y4
   $Y4 \geqq 103\%$ of Y5
   $Y5 \geqq 103\%$ of Y6   Fail
3. Otherwise   Pass

Often, however, there are legitimate reasons for increasing shares, such as an acquisition or a series of acquisitions, so this criterion can still be a pass if you know legitimate reasons to be the case.

■ Dynacq has not been significantly increasing its number of shares outstanding in recent years, which is good. It currently has 15 million shares outstanding, which suggests the company is not taking any measures that will dilute or devalue the stock with regard to its number of shares. Test results: Pass.

Hot Topic has not been significantly increasing its number of shares either. That's good. The company currently has 20 million shares outstanding. As with Dynacq, this suggests Hot Topic is not diluting or devaluing its stock. Test results: Pass.

Sales.   Companies with less than $500 million in sales should be chosen. It is among these small cap stocks that investors can find "an uncut gem," one that institutions won't be able to buy yet. It is companies with $500 million or less in sales that are most likely to double or triple in size in the next few years.

■ Dynacq's sales were $33.7 million based on trailing 12-month sales, which is well below the Fool's cap of $500 million. Test results: Pass.

Hot Topic's sales were $257 million, which is comfortably below the Fool's $500 million limit. Test results: Pass.

Sales

1. Sales > $500 million   Fail
2. Sales $\leqq$ $500 million   Pass

Daily dollar volume (DDV).

Daily dollar volume = Price × Average daily trading volume

In general, mutual and hedge funds do not like to buy more than 1 percent of a company's outstanding shares in a day. More than that can cause the stock price to jump up as a result of strong buying demand. Yet at the same time a fund may need to buy millions of dollars or even tens of millions of dollars of a company's stock for it to be a meaningful percentage of the fund's portfolio. If, for instance, a stock traded only $25 million in a day, the most one fund would like to buy in a day would be $250,000 (1% of $25 million). If a fund were going to acquire a $5 million position, it would take 20 days to do so, and even then chances are that it would drive up the stock price at an estimated 1 percent per day.

The Fool prefers that the DDV be greater than $1 million and less than $25 million because these are the stocks that are liquid but remain relatively undiscovered by institutions.

■ Dynacq's daily dollar volume of $1.2 million fits this test. Test results: Pass.

Hot Topic's daily dollar volume of $14.2 million is also below the Fool's maximum of $25 million. Test results: Pass.

Daily Dollar Volume

1. < $1 million		Fail
2. ≧ $1 million and ≦ $25 million		Pass
3. > $25 million		Fail

Price.   Basically, the Fool prefers low prices because "small numbers multiply more rapidly than large ones" and the potential for big returns expands. The price should be above $7 to eliminate penny stocks and ideally below $20 as most stocks in this price range are undiscovered by the institutions, says the Fool.

■ Dynacq's price on the day this was written was $14.88, which fits nicely in the $7 to $20 range specified by the Fool. Test results: Pass.

Hot Topic's share price is $28. Although the price tops the ideal range, by itself this should not rule out the stock, so we grade it neutral rather than failing it. Test results: Neutral.

Price

1. Price < $7   Fail
2. Price ≧ $7 and price ≦ $20   Pass
3. Price > $20   Neutral

Income tax percentage.   Income tax paid expressed as a percentage of pretax income, either this year or last year, must be greater than 20 percent because a tax rate below 20 percent could mean that the earnings the company reported appear unrealistically inflated as a result of the lower level of income tax paid. That is, the company appears to be more successful than it actually is. However, we have used a sophisticated formula so that the appropriate figures reflect a "normal" tax rate (35 percent). When we notice in any period that the tax rate is less than 35 percent, we recalculate that period's earnings. We start with pretax earning and then treat it as if the company had paid the average 35 percent taxes to get net earnings. This way, we don't give the company credit for a higher profit margin compared with its peers just because of a lower tax rate.

■ Dynacq's paid income tax expressed as a percentage of pretax income this year was 66.1 percent and last year 41.2 percent, both of which are greater than the Fool's minimum acceptable level of 20 percent. This is good. If the tax rate were below 20 percent, the earnings might have been unrealistically inflated as a result. Test result: Pass.

Hot Topic's paid income tax expressed as a percentage of pretax income this year was 52.1 percent and last year 53.1 per share, both of which are greater than 20 percent. Test result: Pass.

Income Tax Percentage

1. Income/Pretax income for Y1 or Y2 < 20%   Recalculate earnings
2. Income/Pretax income for Y1 or Y2 ≧ 20%   Pass

The Fool is attracted initially to a stock because either the amount the company's earnings has increased over the most recent quarter compared with the quarter one year prior is one of the highest—as compared with other stocks whose earnings were announced on that same day (usually in *Investor's Business Daily*)—or because of the Lynch philosophy that you know the company through your work, hobby, shopping, or geography and are impressed with it.

Also, the Fool wants you to know that these small cap stocks can fluctuate by 30 to 50 percent or more in a single quarter and sometimes in a month; and if you are not prepared to sit though that, provided your companies have remained fundamentally sound, you shouldn't be investing in high-growth, small cap companies.

BOTTOM LINE

Dynacq

Tests passed:	Profit margin
	Profit margin consistency
	Relative strength
	Sales and EPS growth
	Insider holdings
	Free cash flow from operations
	Price-earnings growth ratio (PEG)
	Cash-annual sales ratio
	Growth in inventory compared with growth in sales
	Long-term debt-equity ratio (DE)
	Average shares outstanding
	Daily dollar volume
	Price
	Income tax percentage
Tests neutral:	R&D-sales ratio
Score:	100 percent (14 of 14 passed; 1 neutral)

BOTTOM LINE: There is STRONG INTEREST in Dynacq.

Hot Topic

Tests passed:	Profit margin
	Profit margin consistency
	Relative strength
	Sales and EPS growth
	Insider holdings
	Free cash flow from operations
	Price-earnings growth ratio (PEG)
	Growth in inventory compared with growth in sales
	Long-term debt-equity ratio (DE)
	Average shares outstanding
	Daily dollar volume
	Income tax percentage
Tests neutral:	R&D-sales ratio
	Price
Tests failed:	Cash-annual sales ratio
Score:	92 percent (12 of 13 passed; 1 failed; 2 neutral)

BOTTOM LINE: There is STRONG INTEREST in Hot Topic.

THE MOTLEY FOOL'S KEY INVESTING CRITERIA

■ Look for a high and consistent profit margin above 7 percent.

■ Look for a high relative strength above 90.

■ Look at sales and EPS growth compared with last year.

■ Look for a significant amount of insider holdings.

■ Look at cash flow from operations to be positive.

■ Look for a low PEG ratio based on estimated growth rate.

■ Look at cash and cash equivalents. Lots of cash is good.

- Look at changes in the inventory-sales ratio to verify that inventory has not blossomed out of control.

- Look for low or no long-term debt-equity ratio.

- Look for a consistent or increasing R&D-sales ratio.

Noncritical criteria to consider:

- Look for consistent or decreasing average shares outstanding.

- Look for sales that are less than $500 million.

- Look at daily dollar volume between $1 million and $25 million.

- Look at current price between $7 and $20.

- Look at income tax percentage to be approximately 35 percent.

- Look a Fool in the eye. Don't take everything so seriously.

WHICH INVESTORS MIGHT BEST USE **David Dreman?**

RISK: Dreman goes after battered stocks, out-of-favor companies—the stuff other people view as the dregs. These stocks are already beaten down, making any additional significant price drops unlikely (though not impossible). For this reason, his strategies are relatively low risk. Dreman should appeal to those investors who want to buy stocks at a discount and have the personality to go against the conventional wisdom—who are, in fact, contrarians.

TIME HORIZON: Dreman's time horizon is two to eight years; if a company has not turned itself around largely within two years, Dreman bails out.

EFFORT: Following Dreman's strategy involves a relatively small amount of effort.

If there's a personality trait common to the strategists we cover in *The Market Gurus,* it is probably that they are contrarians or at least claim to be. They do things differently. They say they go against the conventional wisdom and by doing so have an edge over most other market watchers who, presumably, follow the herd.

David Dreman has made a career of being a contrarian. He uses the word *contrarian* in the title of his books, including the well-received *Contrarian Investment Strategy: The Psychology of Stock Market Success* written in 1980, *The New Contrarian Investment Strategy* (1982), and his latest, *Contrarian Investment Strategies: The Next Generation* (1998), which we use as the basis of our analysis of his strategy. The jacket of his book even refers to, "the family yacht, *The Contrarian.*"

Dreman really does have a contrarian streak. He seeks out-of-favor stocks that the market undervalues, loads up on them, and unloads them when the market values them at about the same level it values most stocks (price-earnings ratios are a telltale means for Dreman to determine if a company is out of favor or in favor).

WHO IS DAVID DREMAN?

Dreman is a longtime money manager, now chairman of Dreman Value Management, L.L.C. of Jersey City, New Jersey, and director of investment research and money management. Dreman Value Management focuses on the assets of pension, foundation, and endowment funds as well as those of high net worth individuals, according to the company. Dreman founded his first investment firm, Dreman Value Management Inc., in 1977 and was its president until 1989. He was chairman of Dreman Value Management from 1989 to 1995 and of Dreman Value Advisors Inc. from 1995 to 1997. Through a subadvisory agreement with Scudder Kemper Investments Inc., Dreman also manages two mutual funds and two annuity products.

Dreman, 64, is from the Canadian city of Winnipeg. According to an article in *Fortune* (29 January 1990), his father had a seat on the Winnipeg Commodity Exchange for over half a century. It is likely that investing and trading have been abiding interests of Dreman since childhood. In 1965, Dreman moved to New York, where he was an investment advisor and security analyst for more than 20 years. He was director of New York research for Rauscher Pierce Refsnes Securities Corporation, senior investment officer with J&W Seligman, and senior editor with the Value Line Investment Service. He has been a *Forbes* columnist for 18 years.

Dreman's mutual funds are generally highly rated, which gives him the cachet of not only having a strategy, which he popularized via books, but a track record of implementing his ideas and seeing them perform well.

WHAT DREMAN SAYS

More so than perhaps any other guru we discuss in this book, Dreman is a student of psychology, specifically the psychology of markets and investors. In fact, he wrote a book called *Psychology and the Stock Market* (1977). This makes him particularly worth reading because he not only presents a strategy for investing—and one that has worked well for him as witnessed by the performance of his mutual funds—but deals with the issues of trying to motivate investors to use a strategy and not rely on emotion.

Here's an example of Dreman's take on the psychology of most investors: *"It is not enough to have winning methods, we must be able to use them. . . .* Sure, the methods are easy to understand and initiate. But most investors, whether professional or individual [and] even with the best of intentions, *cannot follow through.* There is an enormous but little recognized barrier in the way—investor psychology." (Dreman's emphasis)

Dreman is convinced his contrarian strategy, which we'll discuss in detail below, works. His interest in investor psychology raises the question: Why, if this strategy works so well, doesn't everyone use it? As Dreman puts it, investor psychology "is the reason why most people cannot use these [contrarian] strategies even though they are known to have provided superior results for years."

What is it about investor psychology that prevents investors from using strategies that will help them? One important characteristic of this psychology is that investors overreact to events and, under certain well-defined circumstances, do so predictably and systematically. If a stock is "good," investors consistently overprice it, says Dreman, while underpricing the worst stocks. Not only do investors overvalue the "best" and undervalue the "worst," but they often go to extremes.

Here's an example of how Dreman's information can be used effectively by savvy investors. Surprises are a way of life in the stock market. Surprises are any occurrences that happen in ways the market does not expect, such as unexpectedly good or bad earnings reports, government actions that may help or harm an industry, and the like. Dreman's studies of the market suggest that surprises gen-

erally help stocks that are out of favor with the market (these are the ones contrarians like) and harm stocks that are in favor.

Here's Dreman's take on how you can use surprises profitably in your investment strategy:

- Surprises, as a group, improve the performance of out-of-favor stocks while impairing the performance of favorites.
- Positive surprises result in major appreciation for out-of-favor stocks while having minimal impact on favorites.
- Negative surprises result in major drops in the price of favorites while having virtually no impact on out-of-favor stocks.
- The effect of an earnings surprise continues for an extended period of time.

Dreman's point: Buy out-of-favor stocks because surprises (positive and negative ones) are commonplace. If you own favorites, you'll get clobbered by negative surprises but won't get much upside by positive surprises, whereas if you own out-of-favor stocks, you'll hardly be penalized for negative surprises but will be rewarded handsomely by positive ones.

Dreman, in fact, spends an entire chapter discussing how poorly Wall Street analysts forecast company performances, which makes it very likely that any given stock will experience a surprise and probably sooner rather than later. He claims "there is only a 1 in 130 chance that the analysts' consensus forecast will be within 5 percent for any four consecutive quarters. . . . To put this in perspective, *your odds are ten times greater of being the big winner of the New York State Lottery than of pinpointing earnings five years ahead.*" (Dreman's emphasis)

Getting back to Dreman's premise that people tend to have a bias toward optimism, he cites three reasons for this:

1. People have unrealistic optimism about future events. They think such events will come out better than they realistically are likely to.
2. People view themselves in an unrealistically positive light.

3. People have unrealistic confidence in their ability to control a situation, such as having lots of information that will shield them from surprises in the market, because they have studied everything worth studying and therefore know all that's worth knowing.

An example Dreman gives is the securities analyst who knows that high-flying stocks will drop from the skies faster than a pelican diving for a fish if earnings come in below the Street's expectations. Yet the same analyst will still recommend high flyers because he is confident he knows enough about the stocks he has recommended so there is no chance they will experience negative surprises. That might happen to other analysts, but not to him.

The bottom line for Dreman is that investors should never underestimate the probability that bad things will happen, and when they do they are likely to be worse than ever expected. On the upside, take advantage of the overoptimism and overconfidence of other investors and analysts. Go against the grain. Be a contrarian. As Dreman notes: *"The findings show that companies the market expects the best futures for, as measured by the price/earnings, price-to-cash flow, price-to-book value, and price-to-dividend ratios, have consistently done the worst, while the stocks believed to have the most dismal futures have always done the best."* (Dreman's emphasis)

One of Dreman's "rules" (these he shows in boldface type throughout his book) reads: "Buy solid companies currently out of market favor, as measured by the low price-to-earnings, price-to-cash flow or price-to-book value ratios, or by their high yields."

In a *Fortune* article (22 March 1993), "Where to Invest Now," Dreman is quoted as saying he doesn't just focus on individual companies but, at least with his mutual fund, will focus on individual industries that have characteristics similar to out-of-favor companies. He says: "What makes High-Return [one of his funds] different from most funds is that I can, and will, take big positions in certain sectors. I don't load up on one stock, but I will buy many stocks in the same industry when it looks like an industry is in crisis and trading at ridiculously cheap levels."

As an example, he says that banks "were literally being given away" in 1990, so he bought those and did well with them. This could be a strategy individual investors might pursue: find an industry that is out of favor and buy several of its members. If you do, follow Dreman's overall contrarian strategy, which is looking for the least expensive stocks, defined as those fitting his four contrarian strategies—low price-earnings, low price-book, low price-cash flow, or high yields.

Another important point to remember is that Dreman buys for profit over the relatively longer term—two to three years—and his studies show that it is even profitable to hold as long as eight years. So if you follow this strategy, you need to be prepared to sit with stocks that are out of favor with the market for a couple of years in order to be in the stock when it turns around and makes its move.

Dreman likes to look beyond the stock market to the world at large and see what's happening there. In particular, he especially likes a crisis, which fits neatly with his contrarian streak. He writes: "A market crisis presents an outstanding opportunity to profit, because it lets loose overreaction at its wildest. . . . People no longer examine what a stock is worth; instead, they are fixated by prices cascading ever lower. . . . Further, the event triggering the crisis is always considered to be something entirely new." He goes on to say, "Buy during a panic, don't sell."

Dreman provides a table that charts what he calls "11 major postwar crises." These include the Berlin blockade, Korean War, Kennedy assassination, Gulf of Tonkin crisis, 1979–1980 oil crisis, and 1990 Persian Gulf War. He shows how, one year after all but one (the Berlin Blockade, when the market dropped), the market was up between 22.9 percent and 43.6 percent, except for a 7.2 percent rise after the Gulf of Tonkin crisis. The average gain was 25.8 percent. Two years after the crisis, the average gain was 37.5 percent.

Admittedly, one wonders if Dreman played a little fast and loose in the "crises" he picked. Why include the Kennedy assassination but not the Nixon resignation? Why are 3 of these 11 crises described as "stock market breaks"? And that doesn't even include the 1987 market crash, which is on his list. It seems tautological to talk about how the stock market rebounds from a crisis when the crisis was the stock market itself.

Nevertheless, Dreman's argument is compelling. Bad news often gives the market the jitters, only to have it recover when the bad news turns out not to be as devastating as first feared.

RISK

Dreman in his book discusses risk, which doesn't get the attention from investors it should. Dreman notes, "Of all the evils the investor must face, the devil of risk is perhaps the most treacherous."

Conventional theory holds that investors are risk averse, requiring higher returns for taking on more risk and accepting lower returns when accepting less risk. Risk is conventionally measured by volatility, with more volatility creating greater risk.

Dreman, the contrarian, not surprisingly disagrees with this conventional view of risk. He admits a rational person would want more return for taking on greater risk but questions how rational most people are as decision makers. "It has been known for decades that there is no correlation between risk, as the academics define it, and return. Higher volatility does not give better results, nor lower volatility worse," he writes. Studies have shown, he says, that there is not necessarily any stable long-term relationship between risk and return, and often there is no relationship between the return achieved and the risk taken. Going against conventional wisdom, Dreman states: "Volatility is not risk. Avoid investment advice based on volatility."

Dreman's answer to the question of what is risk is to focus on the risk that inflation presents investors. He writes: "An all-encompassing strain of risk permanently entered the investment environment for the first time after World War II. The virulent new risk is called inflation. Nothing is safe from this virus, although its major victims are savings accounts, T-bills, bonds, and other types of fixed-income investments. . . . While a relatively small number of companies may flounder financially or go under in any normal period, credit risk is far less dangerous than inflation risk."

One of the points Dreman is making is that investors usually use Treasury bills as their benchmark for risk. These are considered risk free, and all other investments go up from there on the risk scale. For Dreman, though, T-bills are in fact highly risky because of their susceptibility to inflation risk. *"Trouble is, the 'risk-free asset' of academic theory is one of the riskiest assets out there over time,"* he writes. (Dreman's emphasis)

He goes on to write: "The major risk is not the short-term stock price volatility that many thousands of academic articles have been written about. Rather it is the possibility of not reaching your long-term investment goal through the growth of your funds in real terms. *To measure monthly or quarterly volatility and call it risk—for investors who have time horizons 5, 10, 15, or even 30 years away— is a completely inappropriate definition."* (Dreman's emphasis)

Dreman says a realistic definition of risk recognizes the potential loss of capital through inflation and taxes, and includes (1) the probability your investment will preserve your capital over your investment time horizon and (2) the probability your investments will outperform alternative investments during the period.

For Dreman, the statistics are unambiguous: No investment over time, based on his view of risk, performs better than stocks. Investors who put some or most of their money into bonds and other investments on the assumption they are lowering their risk are deluding themselves.

Let's now look at how we can implement Dreman's strategies to invest in stocks.

DREMAN'S STRATEGY: STEP-BY-STEP

Market cap.   Medium-sized to large-sized companies (the largest 1,500 companies) should be chosen because they are more in the public eye. Furthermore, the investor is exposed to less risk of accounting gimmickry, and companies of this size have more staying power. At the time of this writing, the minimum market capitalization a company must have to get into the group of the 1,500 largest companies is $963 million.

If market cap $\geq$ \$963 million: Pass

■ One company we use to illustrate Dreman's strategies is The St. Paul Companies Inc. (stock symbol: SPC), an insurance company that has its headquarters in St. Paul, Minnesota. It operates 15 companies and has about 12,000 employees. It also owns 80 percent of John Nuveen Company, which is in the business of asset management and investor services. The St. Paul Companies (see Figure 6.1) has a market cap of \$9.5 billion, thereby easily surpassing Dreman's minimum cap. Test results: Pass.

The other company used to illustrate Dreman's approach is Mack-Cali Realty Corporation (stock symbol: CLI). Based in New Jersey, this is a real estate investment trust (REIT) that owns and manages a variety of types of real estate, including industrial and residential, but primarily owns offices (see Figure 6.2). It has 400 employees and its market cap is \$1.5 billion. Test results: Pass.

Market Cap

1. < \$963 million   Fail
2. $\geq$ \$963 million   Pass

Earnings trend.   Dreman likes to see a rising trend in the reported earnings for the most recent quarters. In other words, the most recent quarter (Q1) should have greater earnings than the previous quarter (Q2).

If EPS Q1 > EPS Q2: Pass

■ St. Paul Companies' earnings per share for the latest quarter was less than for the prior quarter. Test results: Fail.

Mack-Cali, on the other hand, has enjoyed a rising trend in reported earnings for the most recent quarters. Therefore, its test results: Pass.

Earnings Trend

1. EPS Q1 $\leq$ EPS Q2   Fail
2. EPS Q1 > EPS Q2   Pass

| FIGURE 6.1 | SAINT PAUL COMPANIES INC (SPC) | $44.05 as of 3/30/2001 |

	Year 1	Year 2
Total Net Income (mil.)	$1,013.0	$779.0
EPS	$4.32	$3.37
Sales (mil.)	$8,608.0	$7,569.0
Avg. PE	9.1	9.3
ROE	13.8%	13.4%
Long-Term Debt-Equity	23%	23%
Dividend	$1.07	$1.03
Payout	25%	31%
Shares Outstanding (mil.)	218.3	214.9

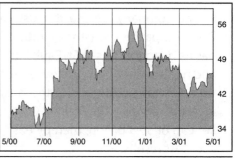

	Year 3	Year 4	Year 5	Year 6	Year 7	Year 8	Year 9	Year 10
Total Net Income (mil.)	$89.3	$773.2	$557.9	$521.2	$442.8	$427.6	$(232.5)	$405.1
EPS	$(0.33)	$4.20	$3.10	$2.84	$2.47	$2.39	$(1.43)	$2.26
Sales (mil.)	$9,108.4	$6,219.3	$5,734.2	$5,409.6	$4,701.3	$4,460.2	$4,498.7	$4,351.7
Avg. PE	n/a	8.5	8.9	9.1	8.4	9	n/a	7.3
ROE	1.3%	15.3%	11.3%	14%	16.2%	14.2%	n/a	16%
Long-Term Debt-Equity	19%	17%	17%	19%	23%	21%	26%	19%
Dividend	$0.99	$0.93	$0.86	$0.79	$0.74	$0.70	$0.68	$0.64
Payout	−300%	22%	28%	28%	30%	29%	−48%	28%
Shares Outstanding (mil.)	228.9	167.5	167	168	168.4	169.2	168	170.1

	Q1	Q2	Q3	Q4	Q5	Q6	Q7	Q8
EPS	$0.82	$0.98	$0.92	$1.51	$0.70	$1.43	$(1.18)	$0.79
Revenue (mil.)	$2,220.0	$2,031.0	$2,105.0	$2,253.0	$1,741.0	$1,856.0	$1,998.0	$2,244.0

	Market Cap (mil.)	TTM Sales (mil.)	Relative Strength	EPS Growth (3-yr. avg.)	Revenue Growth (TTM)	Current Ratio	Insider Buy-Sells (3 months)
SPC	$9,552.0	$8,608.0	80	0.9%	27.5%	n/a	0/2
Property/Casualty Insur.	$37,160	$17,351	62	6.0%	12.1%	n/a	

	PEG	PE	Projected PE	PS	Price-Book	Price-Cash Flow	Free Cash Flow/Share
SPC	3.1	10.4	13.7	1.1	1.3	12.0	−5.1
Property/Casualty Insur.	1.8	17.0	16.7	1.5	2.9	18.4	

	Yield	Profit Margin (TTM)	ROE (TTM)	Total Debt-Equity	Long-Term Debt-Equity	Insider Ownership	Institutional Ownership
SPC	2.5%	12.0%	13.8%	23.0%	23.0%	2%	80.4%
Property/Casualty Insur.	1.2%	10.2%	11.7%	48.0%	32.0%		

Recent Balance Sheet Items ($ millions)		Financial Statement Trends			
Cash	Not Reported		Recent 12 mo.	FY1	FY2
Current Assets	Not Reported	Inventory/Sales	–	–	–
Total Assets	41,075	AR to Sales	–	–	–
Current Liabilities	Not Reported	R&D to Sales	–	–	–
Long-Term Debt	1,647				
Total Debt	1,647				
Equity	7,227				

FIGURE 6.2	MACK CALI REALTY CORP (CLI)	$27.00 as of 3/30/2001

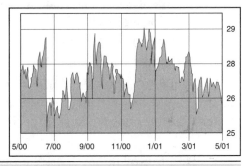

	Year 1	Year 2
Total Net Income (mil.)	$185.3	$119.7
EPS	$3.10	$2.04
Sales (mil.)	$661.5	$553.4
Avg. PE	8.3	13.9
ROE	12.8%	8.3%
Long-Term Debt-Equity	112%	103%
Dividend	$2.35	$2.23
Payout	76%	109%
Shares Outstanding (mil.)	57	58.4

	Year 3	Year 4	Year 5	Year 6	Year 7	Year 8	Year 9	Year 10
Total Net Income (mil.)	$119.0	$5.0	$32.4	$13.6	$3.9			
EPS	$2.11	$0.12	$1.73	$1.22	$0.38			
Sales (mil.)	$493.7	$249.8	$101.2	$62.3	$16.9			
Avg. PE	16	297.4	14.9	15.3	42.4			
ROE	8.4%	0.4%	4.6%	7.3%	3.6%			
Long-Term Debt-Equity	n/a	84%	38%	73%	71%			
Dividend	$2.05	$1.85	$1.73	$1.21	$0.13			
Payout	97%	1542%	100%	99%	34%			
Shares Outstanding (mil.)	57.3	49.9	26.4	15.1	10.5			

	Q1	Q2	Q3	Q4	Q5	Q6	Q7	Q8
EPS	$0.60	$0.34	$1.52	$0.62	$0.62	$0.55	$0.32	$0.55
Revenue (mil.)	$143.1	$153.4	$219.8	$145.2	$142.4	$139.1	$137.0	$134.9

	Market Cap (mil.)	TTM Sales (mil.)	Relative Strength	EPS Growth (3-yr. avg.)	Revenue Growth (TTM)	Current Ratio	Insider Buy-Sells (3 months)
CLI	$1,537	$661.5	66	193%	0.5%	n/a	0/0
REIT - Office Industry	$1,733	$537	68	66.4%	18.0%	n/a	

	PEG	PE	Projected PE	PS	Price-Book	Price-Cash Flow	Free Cash Flow/Share
CLI	0.1	8.7	10.3	2.3	1.0	8.8	−4.56
REIT - Office Industry	1.55	28.1	12.2	3.0	1.1	12.53	

	Yield	Profit Margin (TTM)	ROE (TTM)	Total Debt-Equity	Long-Term Debt-Equity	Insider Ownership	Institutional Ownership
CLI	8.9%	28%	12.8%	112%	112%	4%	86%
REIT - Office Industry	8.34%	22.5%	9.3%	116%	116%		

Recent Balance Sheet Items ($ millions)		Financial Statement Trends			
Cash	Not Reported		**Recent 12 mo.**	FY1	FY2
Current Assets	Not Reported	Inventory/Sales	Not Applicable		
Total Assets	3,677	AR to Sales	Not Applicable		
Current Liabilities	Not Reported	R&D to Sales	Not Applicable		
Long-Term Debt	1,628				
Total Debt	1,628				
Equity	1,453				

EPS growth in the immediate past and future. For non-cyclical companies only, Dreman looks for a higher rate of earnings growth than for the S&P 500 in the immediate past and the likelihood that it will not plummet in the near future. He looks at EPS growth during the past six months.

The company's percent growth in the past six months (i.e., from Q2 to Q1) and its estimated percent growth for this year has to be greater than the same figures, respectively, for the S&P 500.

> If EPS growth 6M > EPS growth S&P 500 6M and
> Est. Y1 growth > S&P 500 Est. Y1 growth
> Then: Pass

Check if the earnings were temporarily depressed. Dreman states that some stock prices are irrationally battered down from a temporary depression in earnings. He sees these occurrences as opportunities for buying good stocks at cheap prices. However, evaluate if the depression in earnings is a temporary feature or the result of long-term weakness in the company.

The first criterion we use to determine this is that the projected EPS growth rate for the next few quarters should be greater than that projected for the same quarters for the S&P 500. It is also desirable if the estimated EPS growth rate for the next year compared with the current year should be greater than that of the S&P 500.

The next criterion is that projected EPS in either of the next two quarters should be greater than the quarter before the earnings dip. Put another way, Dreman wants to see that earnings will more than bounce back quickly and that therefore the dip is projected to not be long term. He uses conservative (low) EPS estimates, if available. One important note in comparing earnings estimates to actual historical earnings: estimates are usually based on fully diluted earnings *before* extraordinary items. That means when you compare estimates with historical earnings, you must be sure you are using the fully diluted historical earnings before the extraordinary items.

> If EPS est. Q1 low > EPS_Q2, then we can safely conclude
> that because the stock appears poised for long-term growth,

the dip in earnings was a temporary phenomenon and
Dreman would consider investing in this stock.

If EPS est. Q2 low $>$ EPS_Q2, then we can safely conclude
that because the stock appears poised for long-term growth,
the dip in earnings was a temporary phenomenon and
Dreman would consider investing in this stock.

Otherwise, if the projected EPS for the next two quarters is not
greater than the EPS in the quarter before the dip, it is possible that
the dip in earnings is part of a long-term sickness in the company,
and hence it would not pass this criterion.

■ Dreman wants to see companies whose EPS growth rate is higher
than the S&P 500 in the immediate past and has a good likelihood
that this trend will continue in the near future. At the time of this
writing, the S&P 500 was down 5.2 percent for the past six months
while St. Paul Companies' EPS fell 19.5 percent. Test results: Fail.
   Mack-Cali's earnings per share was up 76 percent during the past
six months, while the S&P 500's was down 5.2 percent. Future EPS estimates not available. Test results: Pass.

EPS Growth in the Immediate Past and Future

1. EPS growth from Q2 to Q1 and projected growth for this year
   $\leq$ S&P 500 Growth for same time periods   Fail
2. EPS growth from Q2 to Q1 and projected growth for this year
   $>$ S&P 500 Growth for same time periods   Pass

Note: Dreman suggests that cyclical companies are better evaluated using a price-cash flow ratio.

Look for a contrarian indication.   This methodology uses four
separate criteria to determine if a company is a contrarian stock. In
order to eliminate weak companies, we have stipulated that the
stock should pass *at least two of the following four major criteria* in
order to receive some interest.

Price-earnings ratio (PE).   The PE of a company should be in
the bottom 20 percent of the overall market. Dreman conducted stud-

ies from 1970 to 1996 that showed stocks with PEs in the bottom 20 percent of the market had an average annual return of 19 percent versus 15.3 percent for the market. His studies also showed that low PE stocks have higher returns than high PE stocks (they returned 12.3 percent) while exposing the investor to less risk.

If PE < Bottom 20% among PEs: Pass

■ The St. Paul Companies' PE ratio is 10.4, while the bottom 20 percent of the overall market is below 12.9. Test results: Pass.

Again, the market's bottom 20 percent has PE ratios of 12.9 or below, while Mack-Cali comes in comfortably under this at 8.7. Test results: Pass.

Price-Earnings (PE)

1. ≥ Bottom 20%	Fail
2. < Bottom 20%	Pass

Dreman also suggests that when dealing with cyclical companies (airlines, autos, forest products, etc.) that instead of using trailing 12-month earnings, one should use the average earnings of the last five years. Cyclical companies can have seductively low traditional PE ratios just before the industry goes into a recession, whereupon the company might make very little money or even lose money, which then causes the PE to appear to be sky-high or not even calculable. Averaging over five years avoids these problems and gives the investor a more meaningful number to compare.

Price-cash flow ratio (PCF).   The PCF of a company should be in the bottom 20 percent of the overall market. In studies conducted from 1970 to 1996, Dreman showed that stocks, which had PCF ratios in the bottom 20 percent of the market, returned 18 percent versus 15.1 percent for the market. His studies also proved that lower PCF stocks have greater returns than higher PCF stocks, all while incurring less risk.

Dreman defines cash flow as "after-tax earnings, adding back depreciation and other noncash charges. It is a measure of a company's real earnings power, as well as an indicator of its financial viability."

If PCF < Bottom 20% PCF: Pass

■ To be in the bottom 20 percent of the overall market for the PCF ratio, a company must be at or below 6.5; The St. Paul Companies' PCF is 12.0. Test results: Fail.

Mack-Cali comes close to passing this test—its PCF is 8.7—but no cigar. It is still above the market's 6.5, and therefore is not in the bottom 20 percent. Test results: Fail.

Price-Cash Flow Ratio (PCF)

1.	≧ Bottom 20%	Fail
2.	< Bottom 20%	Pass

Price-cash flow ratio is a particularly good measure for finding bargain cyclical companies during a recession, when the traditional PE ratio tends to get very high or not calculable.

Price-book ratio (PB).   The PB value of a company should be in the bottom 20 percent of the overall market. In studies conducted from 1970 to 1996, Dreman showed that stocks with PB ratios in the bottom 20 percent of the market had an average annual return of 18.8 percent versus 15.1 percent for the market. His studies also proved that low PB stocks have greater returns than high PB stocks while incurring less risk.

Book value is the value of a company's common stock less all liabilities and preferred shares, says Dreman.

If PB < Bottom 20% PB: Pass

■ To be in the bottom 20 percent for the price-book ratio, a company's ratio must be below 1.6; The St. Paul Companies' PB is 1.3. Test results: Pass.

Mack-Cali's PB is an anemic 1.1, well below the cutoff point of 1.6. Test results: Pass.

Price-Book Ratio (PB)

1. ≧ Bottom 20%   Fail
2. < Bottom 20%   Pass

Price-dividend ratio (PD).   The PD ratio for a company should be in the bottom 20 percent of the overall market. That is, the yield (the dollar amount of dividends for the last four quarters divided by the current share price) should be in the top 20 percent. Dreman conducted studies from 1970 to 1996 that showed stocks with PD ratios in the bottom 20 percent of the market had an average annual return of 16.1 percent versus 14.9 percent for the market. Dreman cautions about investing on the basis of this criterion, as it is mainly for income-seeking investors, who are better off investing in stocks that pass this criterion rather than investing in bonds. For investors with different objectives, this is a very useful criterion that should be used in conjunction with Dreman's other criteria.

If PD < Bottom 20% PD: Pass

■ The dividend yield at The St. Paul Companies is 2.5 percent versus the market's yield for the top 20 percent of 3.70 percent. Test results: Fail.

The yield for Mack-Cali is 8.9 percent, which exceeds our target of 3.70 percent. Test results: Pass.

Price-Dividend Ratio (PD)

1. ≧ Bottom 20%   Fail
2. < Bottom 20%   Pass

Look at the financial ratios.   This methodology maintains that investors should look for as many healthy financial ratios as possible to ascertain the financial strength of the company. These criteria are detailed below.

Current ratio.   A prospective company must have a strong current ratio. This is the relationship between current assets to current liabilities and is an indicator of a company's ability to pay its current (one year or less) debts. Dreman wants to see a current ratio that is higher than the average of the company's industry or greater than 2. He feels this criterion is a good identifier of financially strong companies.

If $\geq$ avg. industry current ratio or if current ratio $\geq$ 2: Pass

Current Ratio

1. $\geq$ Industry avg. or $\geq$ 2   Pass
2. Otherwise   Fail

Payout ratio.   A good indicator that a company has the ability to raise its dividend is a low payout ratio. If the recent payout ratio is less than its five-to-ten-year historical average, Dreman feels there is a lot of room for the company to increase its dividend. The payout ratio is the percentage of a company's earnings paid out as dividends.

If payout $<$ historical avg. payout: Pass

If payout $>$ 40% and $\leq$ 80% and company is an electric or water utility: Pass. This is low for these types of companies.

■ The payout ratio for The St. Paul Companies is 25.2 percent, while its historical payout ratio has been 28 percent. Test results: Pass.
    Mack-Cali's payout ratio is 75.8 percent, while its historical payout ratio has been 94.1 percent. Test results: Pass.

Payout Ratio

1. $\geq$ Avg. payout   Fail
2. $<$ Avg. payout   Pass

Return on equity (ROE).   The company should have a high ROE, as this helps to ensure there are no structural flaws in the company. Dreman feels the ROE should be greater than the ROE earned from the top one-third of the 1,500 large cap stocks and considers anything over 27 percent to be staggering.

> If company has an ROE that falls within the top one-third
> of ROEs from 1,500 largest stocks: Pass

■ The St. Paul Companies' ROE is 13.8 percent, while the top one-third of ROE from among the top 1,500 large cap stocks is 9.86 percent. That's high enough. Test results: Pass.
    Mack-Cali's ROE is 12.8 percent. Test results: Pass.

Return on Equity (ROE)

1. Top 3rd of all ROEs   Pass
2. ≧ 27%   Pass—Best case
3. All others   Fail

Pretax profit margins.   Dreman looks for pretax profit margins of at least 8 percent and considers anything over 22 percent to be staggering.

■ Dreman wants a pretax profit margin of at least 8 percent, while The St. Paul Companies has a pretax profit margin of 16.9 percent. Test results: Pass.
    Dreman considers any pretax profit margin over 22 percent to be staggering; he should be staggered by Mack-Cali, which has a pretax profit margin of 28 percent.

Pretax Profit Margins

1. < 8%   Fail
2. ≧ 8%   Pass
3. ≧ 22%   Pass—Best case

Yield.   The stock in question should have a high yield that can be maintained or increased. We consider high to be at least 1 percent higher than the yield of the Dow.

> If yield ≧ Dow yield + 1%: Pass

■ The Dow's yield at the time of this writing was 1.65 percent, while The St. Paul Companies' yield just missed our test with a yield of 2.50 percent. Test results: Pass.

On the other hand, Mack-Cali's current yield is a robust 8.90 percent, far exceeding our test of the Dow's yield plus 1 percent. Test results: Pass.

Yield

1. < Dow yield + 1 percentage point   Fail
2. ≧ Dow yield + 1 percentage point   Pass

Debt-equity ratio (DE). The company must have a low debt-equity ratio, which indicates a strong balance sheet. We have determined a low debt-equity ratio to be below 20 percent, although we don't apply this ratio to financial companies such as banks.

If DE = 0: Exceptional, according to Dreman
If DE > 0 but ≦ 20%: Acceptable

Debt-Equity Ratio (DE)

1. > 20%   Fail
2. > 0 but ≦ 20% Pass
3. No debt   Pass—Best case

BOTTOM LINE

The St. Paul Companies

Tests passed: Market cap
Price-earnings ratio
Price-book ratio
Payout ratio
Return on equity
Pretax profit margins
Yield

Tests failed: Earnings trend
EPS growth in the immediate past and future
Price-cash flow ratio

Score: 70 percent (7 tests passed, 3 failed)

BOTTOM LINE: There is NO INTEREST in The St. Paul Companies.

Mack-Cali Realty Corporation

Tests passed: Market cap
                Earnings trend
                EPS growth in the immediate past and future
                Price-earnings ratio
                Price-book ratio
                Payout ratio
                Return on equity
                Pretax profit margins
                Yield

Tests failed: Price-cash flow ratio

Score: 90 percent (9 tests passed, 1 failed)

BOTTOM LINE: There is STRONG INTEREST in Mack-Cali Realty
                  Corporation.

DREMAN'S KEY INVESTING CRITERIA

To use Dreman's approach, you must have a strong contrarian strategy, which means you need the guts to go against what the market is saying. The companies that meet his criteria look, on the surface, like losers or at least frayed around the edges. Their stocks are cheap because the market doesn't think the companies are likely to do well in the future. To use Dreman, you need the self-confidence to say, "You may think this company is a dog, but I think it will turn around within the next couple of years and become a desirable stock. And then you will have to pay me a lot more for my stock than I am paying now to buy it." If you like to run with the herd, stay away from Dreman.

■ Look for the largest cap stocks.

■ Look for an increasing earnings trend.

■ Look at EPS growth in the immediate past and future.

Look for a contrarian indication. This methodology uses four separate criteria to determine if a company is a contrarian stock. To eliminate weak companies, we have stipulated that the stock should pass at least two of the following four major criteria to receive a Some Interest rating.

- Look for a low price-earnings (PE) ratio.

- Look for a low price-cash flow (PCF) ratio.

- Look for a low price-book (PB) ratio.

- Look for a low price-dividends (PD) ratio.

Look at the financial ratios. This methodology maintains that investors should look for as many healthy financial ratios as possible (shown in the following list) to ascertain the financial strength of the company.

- Look for a strong current ratio.

- Look for a low payout ratio.

- Look for solid EPS growth.

- Look for a high return on equity (ROE).

- Look at the pretax profit margins.

- Look for a high yield.

- Look for a low debt-equity (DE) ratio.

CHAPTER 7

MARTIN ZWEIG

WHICH INVESTORS MIGHT BEST USE **Martin Zweig?**

RISK: Moderate or a little below moderate.

TIME HORIZON: Medium to long term.

EFFORT: Fairly low.

NOTE: If you want to buy growth stocks and hold on for a few years, Zweig provides a strategy. In effect, he's an alternative to Peter Lynch for growth stocks. One important difference between them: Zweig is more selective. If you use our Web site, Validea.com, to screen for stocks by guru, you'll find relatively few with Zweig but lots and lots with Lynch.

Martin Zweig has been writing and talking about stock market investing longer than most. In 1971, he began publishing the newsletter *The Zweig Forecast,* which he continued to do for 27 years. The newsletter was ranked number one on a risk-adjusted return over the 15 years that it was monitored by *Hulbert Financial Digest,* which tracks the records of stock market gurus.

Zweig has also been a regular panelist and guest host of the PBS program *Wall $treet Week with Louis Rukeyser* since 1973 and was voted into its Hall of Fame in 1992.

Currently, Zweig is the asset allocation strategist for the Phoenix-Zweig series trust, which are seven retail mutual funds that are part of Phoenix Investment Partners. He is also chairman of two New York Stock Exchange–listed closed-end funds, The Zweig Fund Inc. and The Zweig Total Return Fund Inc.

WHO IS MARTIN ZWEIG?

Zweig, born in 1942, has a BSEcon from the Wharton School of Finance, University of Pennsylvania (1964), and is a member of the Wharton Undergraduate Executive Board. He has an MBA from the University of Miami (1967), where he was recognized as Alumnus of Distinction in 1991. He has a PhD in finance from Michigan State University (1969), which awarded him its Outstanding Alumni Award in 1990.

For 15 years Zweig was a finance professor at such colleges and universities as the University of Miami, Michigan State University, City University of New York, and Iona College. He has written numerous articles on the stock market in *Barron's,* beginning in 1970; he invented the puts-calls ratio and has been published in academic journals. He is the author of two books, including the best-selling *Winning on Wall Street,* which was published in 1986 and which we use for our analysis of his strategy, and the no-longer-in-print *Winning with New IRAs.* He is a trustee of the Museum of American Financial History and a founder of the Penn Club.

Publicity about Zweig reports he is an avid runner, running up to six miles a day, and that he once bought a $52,000 pool table for his home. This is how a story in *Financial World* (reproduced on the Web site streetstories.com) describes Zweig's Manhattan office:

> Marty Zweig's cluttered 30th-floor office overlooking Third Avenue might as well be a day-care center for affluent adults. There's a huge traffic light on the windowsill, fully lit up, a five-foot toothbrush leaning in the corner given to Zweig three years ago by some Drexel colleagues who were amused by his constant brushing and flossing during a road show, a gum ball machine also perched on the windowsill that still charges a penny—if you're

nice, Zweig supplies the change—and a 1950s jukebox that frequently blares during late nights. The collection bug first bit 17 years ago when Zweig bought several old stock certificates, one signed by Commodore Vanderbilt. But now it's gotten a little out of control. Zweig's favorite new toys are two old gas pumps that are almost identical to those he saw daily in the Mobil station across from his childhood home in Cleveland. Zweig found a place in Arizona that was advertising old pumps and he called up, certain they could not be like the ones he remembered, complete with the flying red horse. "He said, 'We have two of them—you want regular or ethyl?'" Zweig says with a laugh. "I said I'll take them both." On the wall across from his desk hangs his high school basketball uniform encased in glass, given to him by an old high school buddy at his surprise 45th birthday party. Zweig still muses, "I don't know how the hell he got it."

An article in the *Wall Street Journal* (29 March 1999) reports that Zweig is a major collector of Hollywood, sports, and rock 'n' roll memorabilia. He's got Buddy Holly's guitar, the gun from *Dirty Harry,* the motorcycle from *Easy Rider,* and Michael Jordan's jersey from his rookie season with the Chicago Bulls. "He even owns the 'sperm' costume from Woody Allen's *Everything You Always Wanted to Know About Sex* movie," reports the *Journal,* which also says Zweig was planning to build a 1950s-style gymnasium in his home to house his sports memorabilia collection.

Zweig got into the newsletter publishing business when he was teaching (remember, Zweig has a PhD in finance) and was offered a position as a consultant to a brokerage firm. There he was asked to write a newsletter for the firm's institutional customers. The firm, however, went out of business before he completed the second issue. He had already written some articles for *Barron's,* and these generated enough interest in Zweig that he was able to continue the newsletter.

He introduced his first mutual fund, The Zweig Fund, in 1986, the year his book *Winning on Wall Street* was published; his second fund, The Zweig Total Return Fund, was introduced in 1988. Zweig sold some of his mutual funds in late 1998 to Phoenix Investment Partners, which manages $50 billion of assets.

ZWEIG'S TAKE ON WALL STREET

According to an interview in *Stocks & Commodities* (January 1994), Zweig, when studying the market, first focuses on monetary conditions. Keep in mind that monetary policy relates to the policies that affect the money supply, such as interest rates, money supply, and margin requirements, and are generally controlled by the Federal Reserve System. Monetary policy is different from fiscal policy, which is generally dictated by Congress and the president, and relates to government spending, including the use of deficits and surpluses, and taxes.

Zweig notes, "We follow short-term, long-term and eurodollar rates. I'm not trying to forecast the rate; what I'm looking at is the trend. . . . The Fed's tools are the discount rate and the reserve requirement rate. When the Fed starts to tighten, the indicator gets negative points; and when the Fed starts to stimulate by lowering those rates, the indicator gets positive points." The "indicator" he refers to is based on what the Fed can overtly do to manage the growth of the economy, particularly the discount rate and the reserve requirement rate.

Among the variables Zweig looks at is the discount rate, which he says is a lagging interest rate indicator with some psychological importance. When the Fed changes the discount rate, it's because it has already moved in the same direction with the federal funds rate, he says. The discount rate helps confirm the Fed's current policy.

Installment debt is another variable Zweig studies. Here he looks for year-to-year changes. If installment debt rises rapidly, consumers are borrowing a lot, which, in turn, can put upward pressure on interest rates. And, he says, in an economic upturn this signifies we're in the latter stages of the upturn, which is negative for stocks. A downturn in the installment debt rate is positive, because that's seen as indicating less pressure on interest rates resulting from less borrowing. This usually happens when the economy is soft and perhaps bottoming out.

Of course, Zweig pays serious attention to interest rates. He has a very strong motto: "Don't fight the Fed." When he sees the Fed starting to tighten the money supply and raise interest rates, that's an indicator a bear market is likely around the next bend. Sentiment indicators, before a bear market, also turn negative, at least as he defines negative. "The longer-term sentiment indicators tend to get pretty negative before the top or around the top—lots of secondaries and stock offerings, lots of public buying, lots of speculation. The market may be overvalued or it may not be. It helps if it is. It's not enough just to have a lot of speculation to stop a market."

In addition to looking at the monetary environment, Zweig focuses on technical indicators in the stock market. Here's how he describes his technical side:

> There are two main sets of models in that area: sentiment and what I would call tape or momentum. A lot of people would call sentiment technical; I don't. I find the sentiment to be the next most important group after the monetary. The monetary is the most important signal because it tests better in the longer run. But I'll be the first to tell you that it's possible to have a stock market in an uptrend with interest rates going up, and you can have a downtrend stock market with interest rates going down."

Sentiment refers to the stock market's optimism or pessimism. One way Zweig measures sentiment is the amount of cash mutual funds hold in relation to their assets. More cash suggests fund managers are keeping cash because fund holders are cashing out (they are viewing the market negatively). The reverse is also true, with less cash being held by mutual funds suggesting a more optimistic view by investors.

Zweig, you should note, is not a stickler for one static model. He says: "We design our models to change and be changed. Models have to evolve. No indicator works forever." An example of an indicator that he used to look at but now considers obsolete is odd lot short sales, which worked for years but today, as a result of programmed trading and other factors, isn't a valuable indicator.

ZWEIG'S MAJOR INDICATORS

Zweig looks at a number of indicators that figure prominently in his strategy. This discussion is based on his book *Winning on Wall Street*. These indicators include the *prime rate,* which is the interest rate banks charge their best customers, such as major corporations. Most rates banks charge on other types of loans are based on this prime rate. According to Zweig, one advantage of the prime is that it doesn't change frequently; he estimates about once a month. Also, the prime lags other interest rates, such as the federal funds rate or the yields on CDs. This lag is a virtue, says Zweig, because changes in interest rates generally lead changes in the stock market. The result: If you follow the prime, which moves a little behind other interest rates, you can often mark the point when stocks finally begin to respond to the changes in the rates.

Zweig's rule for the prime rate: 8 percent or above is a relatively high interest rate and below 8 percent is relatively low. Even small declines in rates below 8 percent are therefore enough to be a boost to stocks, but if rates are above 8 percent, larger drops in the interest rates are needed for a bullish signal.

Zweig advises buying if there's an initial cut in the prime rate when the prime's peak was less than 8 percent (meaning it never topped 8 percent because of the cut). If the prime's peak reaches 8 percent or higher, for a buy signal you need either two cuts in the prime or a full 1 percent cut.

Any initial hike in the prime if the prime's low is 8 percent or above is a sell signal. If the prime's low is less than 8 percent, you get a sell signal with the second of two hikes or a full 1 percent jump in the rate.

Unlike the other gurus we discuss, Zweig is not either totally in the market or out of it when he gets a sell or buy signal. Instead, he lightens up his portfolio a bit as he gets one or more sell signals. He removes some money from the table but generally not by selling shares. Rather, he makes brilliant use of stock index futures. If he wants to lighten up, he will sell one or more futures contracts, which is calculated to be the equivalent of taking, say, 5 percent of his portfolio off the table by executing just one trade. Futures contracts once traded in very big sizes (i.e., $250,000 apiece) so this wasn't applicable to most retail investors' portfolios ($250,000 represents 5 percent of a $5,000,000 portfolio). But now the futures exchanges offer "mini" contracts at one-fifth or one-tenth this price, making this technique feasible for a larger number of investors.

We touched briefly above on the indicator that uses *the Federal Reserve's discount rate and reserve requirements.* An increase in either the discount rate or reserve requirements is bearish. Decreases are bullish. The reasoning behind this is that rising interest rates are generally negative for stock prices, whereas falling interest rates generally help stock prices.

The *installment debt* indicator is another Zweig favorite. Zweig summarizes this indicator in these words: "A buy signal is given when the year-to-year change in installment debt has been falling and drops to under 9 percent. A sell signal comes when the year-to-year change has been rising and hits 9 percent or more. That's it."

Zweig takes the above three indicators—the prime rate, the Fed's discount rate and reserve requirements, and installment debt—and combines them into what he calls his Monetary Model. He then adds to this his Four-Percent Model Indicator, which measures market momentum and gives a buy signal when the weekly close of the Value Line Geometric Index increases 4 percentage points or more from any weekly close since the previous signal. And a sell signal is given when the index drops 4 percentage points from any weekly close since the previous buy signal. This is what he uses to stay in sync with the trend of the stock market. A favorite Zweig motto is: "The trend in your friend." This may shift only a few times a year.

Every so often, Zweig's rule of "Don't fight the Fed" is in conflict with "Don't fight the tape (the trend is your friend)." We wondered how this conflict should be resolved. The answer was found in his June 1992 newsletter, which said, "The tape takes precedence over the Fed." Zweig then comes to a grand finale with his Super

Model, which combines the Monetary Model and the Four-Percent Model Indicator. We discuss his approach in more detail below.

Before getting into the step-by-step discussion of Zweig's strategy, every investor should consider a comment he made in the *Stocks & Commodities* interview: "I would say that each person should dig deep into themselves to figure out what makes them comfortable. You've got to have a system or method that you're comfortable with. I could never be a fully invested manager. Warren Buffett's done it for years and has made more money than anybody. But *I* could never do it. . . . You have to have a system . . . and once you have it, stick to what you can do. Don't try to be something you're not."

ZWEIG'S STRATEGY FOR EVALUATING A STOCK: STEP-BY-STEP

■ One company we use to illustrate Zweig's strategy is Linear Technology Corporation (stock symbol: LLTC) based in Milpitas, California. It makes a variety of linear integrated circuits used in electronics. (See Figure 7.1.)

The second company we use as an illustration is Capital One Financial Corporation (stock symbol: COF). Based in Falls Church, Virginia, Capital One is one of the top ten credit card issuers in the country issuing both Visa and MasterCard products. (See Figure 7.2.)

PE ratio.   The PE of a company must be greater than 5. Zweig wants companies that are able to command a multiple of at least 5 to eliminate weak companies. This is an important distinction of Zweig's. No other strategy we discuss sets a minimum on PE. Zweig does because he finds, in a practical sense, a very low PE indicates a weak company. But the PE should never be more than three times the market's current PE; any higher and the stock is considered much too risky. And in absolute terms, never buy a stock whose PE is greater than 43, no matter what the market PE is.

■ Linear's PE is 35.7, while the current market's PE is 28. Test results: Pass.

Capital One's PE is 24.8. Test results: Pass.

FIGURE 7.1   **LINEAR TECHNOLOGY CORP. (LLTC)** $41.06 as of 3/30/2001

	Year 1	Year 2
Total Net Income (mil.)	$287.9	$194.3
EPS	$0.88	$0.61
Sales (mil.)	$705.9	$506.7
Avg. PE	58.2	35.9
ROE	21.8%	21.4%
Long-Term Debt-Equity	0%	0%
Dividend	$0.15	$0.08
Payout	17%	7.6%
Shares Outstanding (mil.)	315.2	307.5

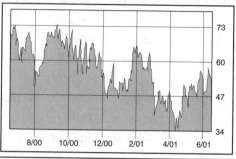

	Year 3	Year 4	Year 5	Year 6	Year 7	Year 8	Year 9	Year 10
Total Net Income (mil.)	$180.9	$134.4	$134.0	$84.7	$56.8	$36.4	$25.0	$16.9
EPS	$0.57	$0.43	$0.43	$0.28	$0.19	$0.13	$0.09	0.06
Sales (mil.)	$484.8	$379.3	$377.8	$265.0	$200.5	$150.9	$119.4	$94.2
Avg. PE	28.6	22.9	21.9	23.3	25.6	22.9	21.5	17.6
ROE	23.9%	22.8%	30.4%	27.5%	25.4%	22.4%	20.2%	18.8%
Long-Term Debt-Equity	0%	0%	0%	0%	0%	0%	0.01%	0.07%
Dividend	$0.06	$0.05	$0.04					
Payout	9.5%	11.6%	10.7%					
Shares Outstanding (mil.)	307.3	303.8	298.6	294.3	290.5	285.4	280.1	267.0

	Q1	Q2	Q3	Q4	Q5	Q6	Q7	Q8
EPS	$0.34	$0.31	$0.27	$0.23	$0.20	$0.18	$0.17	$0.16
Revenue (mil.)	$258.4	$232.1	$211.0	$185.1	$162.3	$147.5	$140.5	$130.1

	Market Cap (mil.)	TTM Sales (mil.)	Relative Strength	EPS Growth (3-yr. avg.)	Revenue Growth (3-yr. avg.)	Current Ratio	Insider Buy-Sells (3 months)
LLTC	$12,942	$886.7	47	26.6%	23.0%	6.1	0/10
Specialized Semiconductor	$5,543	$971.4	38	61.3%	53.0%	4.5	

	PEG	PE	Projected PE	PS	Price-Book	Price-Cash Flow	Free Cash Flow/Share
LLTC	1.34	35.7	29.5	14.59	8.49	35.6	$1.06
Specialized Semiconductor	0.83	31.6	30.6	8.32		39.0	

	Yield	Profit Margin (TTM)	ROE (TTM)	Total Debt-Equity	Long-Term Debt-Equity	Insider Ownership	Institutional Ownership
LLTC	0.3%	43%	25.0%	0%	0%	35%	86%
Specialized Semiconductor	0.03%	27%	26.5%	11.4%	11.4%		

Recent Balance Sheet Items ($ millions)		Financial Statement Trends			
			Recent 12 mo.	FY1	FY2
Cash	301.1				
Current Assets	1,522.0	Inventory/Sales	2.5%	3.1%	3.0%
Total Assets	1,792.1	AR to Sales	11.4%	10.2%	12.2%
Current Liabilities	251.6	R&D to Sales	8.8%	7.7%	9.1%
Long-Term Debt	0				
Total Debt	0				
Equity	1524.0				

| **FIGURE 7.2** | **CAPITAL ONE FINANCIAL CP (COF)** | **$55.50 as of 3/30/2001** |

	Year 1	Year 2
Total Net Income (mil.)	$496.6	$363.1
EPS	$2.24	$1.72
Sales (mil.)	$5,424.3	$3,965.9
Avg. PE	23.5	27.9
ROE	23.9%	24.0%
Long-Term Debt-Equity	2.06%	2.56%
Dividend	$0.11	$0.11
Payout	6.4%	8.3%
Shares Outstanding (mil.)	197.4	199.7

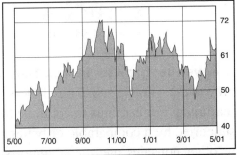

	Year 3	Year 4	Year 5	Year 6	Year 7	Year 8	Year 9	Year 10
Total Net Income (mil.)	$275.2	$189.4	$155.3	$126.5	$95.2		(only 7 Years Avail.)	
EPS	$1.32	$0.93	$0.77	$0.64	$0.48			
Sales (mil.)	$2,599.8	$1,787.1	$1,423.9	$1,010.4	$655.6			
Avg. PE	22.8	15.2	12.7	11.7	10.6			
ROE	21.7%	21.2%	21.0%	21.1%	20.1%			
Long-Term Debt-Equity	3.02%	4.18%	5.39%	4.16%	0.11%			
Dividend	$0.11	$0.11	$0.11	n/a	n/a			
Payout	11.8%	14.3%	12.5%	0%	n/a			
Shares Outstanding (mil.)	197.2	196.3	98.9	198.7	198.4			

	Q1	Q2	Q3	Q4	Q5	Q6	Q7	Q8
EPS	$0.66	$0.61	$0.58	$0.54	$0.51	$0.47	$0.45	$0.41
Revenue (mil.)	$649,873	$706,235	$631,713	$536,507	$515,447	$450,604	$412,036	$377,773

	Market Cap (mil.)	TTM Sales (mil.)	Relative Strength	EPS Growth (3-yr. avg.)	Revenue Growth (3-yr. avg.)	Current Ratio	Insider Buy-Sells (3 months)
COF	$10,930	$5,424.3	73	30.4%	42.8%	n/a	0/8
Credit Service Industry	$19,423	$9,780	77	24.0%	20.4%		

	PEG	PE	Projected PE	PS	Price-Book	Price-Cash Flow	Free Cash Flow/Share
COF	0.82	24.8	19.1	2.02	6.2	31.4	$4.51
Credit Service Industry		17.7	13.8	2.84		18.2	

	Yield	Profit Margin (TTM)	ROE (TTM)	Total Debt-Equity	Long-Term Debt-Equity	Insider Ownership	Institutional Ownership
COF	0.2%	8.7%	26.5%	n/a	206%	8%	69.2%
Credit Service Industry	1.74%	18.1%	22.9%		343%		

Recent Balance Sheet Items ($ millions)		**Financial Statement Trends**			
Cash	74.5		**Recent 12 mo.**	**FY1**	**FY2**
Current Assets	Not Applicable	Inventory/Sales		Not Applicable	
Total Assets	18,889	AR to Sales		Not Applicable	
Current Liabilities	Not Applicable	R&D to Sales		Not Applicable	
Long-Term Debt	4,050				
Total Debt	6,976				
Equity	1,962				

Price-Earnings Ratio

1. < 5 or > 43 — Fail
2. $> 3 \times$ Market PE — Fail
3. $> 5, < 43,$ and $\leqq 3 \times$ Market PE — Pass

Revenue growth in relation to EPS growth. Revenue growth must not be substantially less than earnings growth. Zweig's reasoning: For earnings to continue to grow over time, they must be supported by a comparable or better sales growth rate. Cost cutting or other nonsales measures cannot sustain earnings growth in the long term. Our interpretation of "substantially less" is 85 percent of the growth rate of sales, although we also feel this can be relaxed somewhat when sales are growing at more than 30 percent. Ideally, these growth rates would be compared over a three-year period. Figures 7.3 and 7.5 present the quarterly revenue of Linear and Capital One, respectively, for 12 most recent quarters. Figures 7.4 and 7.6 show the EPS for each company, respectively, during the same period.

FIGURE 7.3	LLTC QUARTERLY REVENUE			
Quarters	**1998**	**1999**	**2000**	**2001**
SEP	$109,802	$116,032	$147,531	$232,141
DEC	117,004	120,020	162,294	258,450
MAR	125,982	130,093	185,075	
JUN	132,011	140,524	211,017	
Totals	**484,799**	**506,669**	**705,917**	**$490,591**

Note: Units in thousands of U.S. dollars

FIGURE 7.4	LLTC QUARTERLY EARNINGS PER SHARE			
Quarters	**1998**	**1999**	**2000**	**2001**
SEP	$0.128	$0.140	$0.180	$0.310
DEC	0.138	0.148	0.200	0.340
MAR	0.148	0.160	0.230	
JUN	0.155	0.170	0.270	
Totals	**0.569**	**0.618**	**0.880**	**$0.650**

Source: Market Guide, March 2001   **Note:** Units in U.S. dollars

| FIGURE 7.5 | COF QUARTERLY REVENUE | | | |

COF QUARTERLY REVENUE

Quarters	1997	1998	1999	2000
MAR	$168,594	$258,042	$353,071	$515,447
JUN	166,870	271,438	377,773	536,507
SEP	178,970	283,109	412,036	631,713
DEC	203,551	298,947	450,604	706,235
Totals	**717,985**	**1,111,536**	**1,593,484**	**$2,389,902**

Note: Units in thousands of U.S. dollars

FIGURE 7.6   COF QUARTERLY EARNINGS PER SHARE

Quarters	1997	1998	1999	2000
MAR	$0.210	$0.320	$0.390	$0.510
JUN	0.193	0.320	0.410	0.540
SEP	0.243	0.333	0.450	0.580
DEC	0.287	0.340	0.470	0.610
Totals	**0.933**	**1.313**	**1.720**	**$2.240**

Note: Units in U.S. dollars

■ Linear's revenue growth is 23 percent, which is not substantially less than its earnings growth rate of 26.6 percent. Test results: Pass.

Capital One's revenue growth is 42.8 percent, while it's earnings growth rate is 30.4 percent. Test results: Pass.

Revenue Growth in Relation to EPS Growth

1. Revenue growth $\geq$ 30% per annum   Pass
2. Revenue growth $<$ 85% of EPS growth   Fail
3. Revenue growth $\geq$ 85% of EPS growth   Pass

Sales growth. Another important issue regarding sales growth is that the rate of quarterly sales growth must be rising. To evaluate this, look at the change from the quarter one year ago (Q5) to the most recently reported quarter (Q1). Then look at the quarter previous to the quarter one year ago (Q6) and compare it with the previous quarter of the current year (Q2). Once you've done that, compare the two. The percentage change in sales growth from Q5 to Q1 must be greater than the percentage sales growth that occurred between Q6 and Q2. In other words, sales growth is accelerating. Notice that, like O'Neil, Zweig doesn't compare acceleration between sequential quarters here. He always compares a quarter to the same quarter a year earlier to eliminate seasonality. It is rare to find more than 4 quarters of sales or earnings history on the Web, but one place to find 12 quarters' worth is at <www.multexinvestor.com>. While looking at a ticker quote on that site, select the "Highlights Report" from the navigation bar on the lefthand side.

■ Linear's previous quarter's rate of sales growth was 57.4 percent, while its most recent was 59.3 percent. Test results: Pass. (This is based on quarterly earnings from the most recently completed quarter, Q1, to six quarters ago, or Q6.)
  Capital One's comparable figures are 31.3 percent and 38.2 percent. Test results: Pass.

Sales Growth

1. Growth from Q5 to Q1 < Growth from Q6 to Q2	Fail
2. Growth from Q5 to Q1 ≧ Growth from Q6 to Q2	Pass

EARNINGS STABILITY

Zweig also examines the earnings numbers of a company from various angles. Three of these angles are stability in the trend of earnings, earnings accelerations, and earnings persistance.

Trend of Earnings

The four tests are as follows:

1. Current quarterly earnings. The first of these four criteria is that the current EPS be positive (> 0).

■ Linear's EPS is 34 cents. Test results: Pass.
  Capital One's EPS is 66 cents. Test results: Pass.

Current Quarterly Earnings

1. Q1 EPS ≦ 0	Fail
2. Q1 EPS > 0	Pass

2. Quarterly earnings one year ago.   The EPS for the quarter one year ago must be positive (> 0).

■ Linear's EPS for this quarter last year was 20 cents. Test results: Pass. Capital One's EPS for this quarter last year was 51 cents. Test results: Pass.

Quarterly Earnings One Year Ago
1. Q5 EPS ≦ 0   Fail
2. Q5 EPS > 0   Pass

3. Positive earnings growth for current quarter.   This tests to see if the current quarters' (Q5 to Q1) EPS growth rate is positive. The growth rate of the current quarter's earnings compared to the same quarter a year ago must also be positive.

■ Linear's growth rate was 70.0 percent. Test results: Pass. Capital One's growth rate was 32.6 percent. Test results: Pass.

Positive Earnings Growth in Current Quarter
1. Growth from Q5 to Q1 ≦ 0   Fail
2. Growth from Q5 to Q1 > 0   Pass

4. Earnings growth for past several quarters.   Compare the earnings growth rate of the past four quarters with the long-term EPS growth rate. Earnings growth in each of the past four quarters should be at least half of the long-term EPS growth rate. A stock should not be considered if it posted one or more quarters of skimpy earnings, which we interpret as less than half of the historical growth rate.

■ Half of the long-term EPS growth rate for Linear is 13.3 percent. This is less than the growth rates for the three previous quarters, which were 43.8 percent, 58.8 percent, and 72.2 percent. Test results: Pass. For Capital One, half of its long-term EPS growth rate is 15.2 percent. This is less than the growth rates for the three previous quarters, which were 45.7 percent, 38.5 percent, and 41.5 percent. Test results: Pass.

Earnings Growth in Past Several Quarters

1. Growth Q8 to Q4, Q7 to Q3, Q6 to Q2,
   and Q5 to Q1 $\geq$ 50% of historical growth   Pass
2. All others   Fail

Earnings Acceleration

EPS growth for current quarter compared with prior three quarters.   Look at the percentage growth rate of the current quarter's earnings compared with the same quarter one year ago. If this is greater than the percentage growth rate of the prior three quarters' earnings (averaged together) compared with the same three quarters one year ago, then the stock passes the test, as it is showing earnings acceleration. Otherwise, the company fails this criterion, with one exception. The exception: If the growth rate in earnings between the current quarter and the same quarter one year ago is greater than 30 percent, then the stock passes.

■ For Linear, its growth rate for the prior three quarters' earnings was 58.8 percent, which is less than the current quarter earnings growth of 70.0 percent. Test results: Pass.

For Capital One, if the growth rate for the prior three quarters' earnings of 41.7 percent (versus the same three quarters a year earlier) is greater than the growth rate of the current quarter earnings of 32.6 percent (versus the same quarter one year ago), then the stock fails because it implies a recent earnings deceleration, with one exception: If the growth rate in earnings between the current quarter and the same quarter one year ago is greater than 30 percent, then the stock would pass. The growth rate over this period for Capital One is 32.6 percent. Test results: Pass.

**EPS Growth in Current Quarter Compared with
Previous Three Quarters**

1. Percentage growth Q5 to Q1 $\geq$
   Avg. percentage growth from
   Q8 to Q4, Q7 to Q3, Q6 to Q2   Pass—Best case
2. Growth Q5 to Q1 $\geq$ 30%   Pass
3. All others   Fail

EPS growth for current quarter compared with historical growth. The EPS growth rate for the current quarter must be greater than or equal to the historical growth rate. That is, growth from Q5 to Q1 exceeds the historical rate.

■ Linear: The EPS growth rate for the current quarter is 70 percent, while the historical rate over the prior three years is 26.6 percent. Test results: Pass.

Capital One: EPS growth rate for the current quarter is 32.6 percent and the historical rate is 30.4 percent. Test results: Pass.

EPS Growth Rate in Current Quarter Compared with Historical Growth Rate

1. EPS growth from Q5 to Q1 $\leq$ Historical Growth	Fail
2. EPS growth from Q5 to Q1 > Historical Growth	Pass

Earnings Persistence

Earnings persistence. Companies must show persistent yearly earnings growth. To fulfill this requirement, a company's earnings must increase each year for five years. This is annual EPS growth before extraordinary items for the previous five years. We'll allow one year of flat earnings if all the other years are increasing.

■ Linear shows persistent earnings growth: $0.43, $0.43, $0.57, $0.61, and $0.88. Test results: Pass.

Capital One demonstrates persistent earnings growth: $0.77, $0.93, $1.32, $1.72, and $2.24. Test results: Pass.

Earnings Persistence

1. Y1 > Y2 > Y3 > Y4 > Y5; one year of flat earnings is allowed	Pass
2. All others	Fail

Long-term EPS growth. One final earnings test is required: the long-term earnings growth rate must be at least 15 percent per year, with anything over 30 percent exceptional.

Long-Term EPS Growth

1. EPS growth < 15%   Fail
2. EPS growth ≧ 15%   Pass
3. EPS growth ≧ 30%   Pass—Best case

■ Linear's long-term growth rate of 26.6 percent per year over three years beats Zweig's 15 percent minimum. Test results: Pass.

Capital One's long-term growth rate of 30.4 percent fits into Zweig's best-case criterion. Test results: Pass.

Total debt-equity ratio (DE).   A company must not have a high level of debt, a criterion not applied to financial companies however. A high level of total debt resulting from high interest expenses can have a very negative effect on earnings if business turns even moderately down. If a company does have a high level, an investor may want to avoid the stock altogether. Zweig notices that DE varies considerably by industry and, unlike other gurus, compares a company's DE with its industry average, not to an absolute number, to determine if a company has a high level of debt.

If DE is < industry average: Pass

■ Linear's DE is 0.0 percent compared with its industry's 11.4 percent. Test results: Pass.

Capital One is a financial company, so this criterion isn't applied.

Total Debt-Equity (DE)

1. DE ≧ Industry average   Fail
2. DE < Industry average   Pass

Insider transactions.   This factor adds to a stock's attractiveness if the number of insider buy transactions is three or more during a three-month period, while insider sell transactions are zero.

Three or more insider sell transactions within three months and zero insider buy transactions are a sell signal that decrease a stock's attractiveness. Zweig, unlike Lynch, considers insider selling for any reason to be undesirable, whereas Lynch believes that insider selling happens often for acceptable reasons, and therefore no importance can be attached to it. Both believe that insider buying is a very good sign.

You can find reported insider transactions at several places on the Internet. One place is <www.marketguide.com>. On that site, enter a ticker symbol and then click on the link on the left-hand side for "Insider Trading." Here is an example of what you might see for an insider buy signal run on April 9, 2001:

PNTE Insider Trading Activity

Filer's Name	Title	Trade Date	Trade Type	Shares Traded	Price Range	Shares Held
Mead, D. Richard Jr	DIR	02/12/01	Buy	8,000	$10.63	22,179
Thomson, Parker D.	DIR	02/12/01	Buy	5,000	$10.63	17,734
Elias, Steven A.	DIR	02/12/01	Buy	3,000	$10.63	11,343
Mcginn, Timothy M.	DIR	02/12/01	Buy	3,135	$10.63	34,103
Massry, Morris	DIR	02/12/01	Buy	8,000	$10.63	180,271

Insider Transactions

1. Insider sell transaction = 0 and
   Buy transactions ≧ 3   Pass
2. Insider buy transaction = 0 and   Fail—Worst case
   Sell transactions ≧ 3   (counts as failing two criteria)
3. All others   Fail

■ Looking at the table of insider transactions in the last three months prior to April 9, 2001, LLTC had ten insider sales in the last three months, and no buys. Test results: Fail—Worst case (counts as failing two criteria).

LLTC Insider Trading Activity

Filer's Name	Title	Trade Date	Trade Type	Shares Traded	Price Range	Shares Held
McCarthy, Leo T.	DIR	02/27/01	Sell	5,000	$46.89	28,000
McCarthy, Leo T.	DIR	02/27/01	Option	5,000	$ 5.41	184,400
Chantalat, V. Paul	OFF	02/08/01 to 02/08/01	Sell	20,000	$58.06–$62.00	0
Chantalat, V. Paul	OFF	02/08/01 to 02/08/01	Option	20,000	$ 1.44	549,000
Lee, David S.	DIR	01/31/01	Option	20,000	$14.63–$15.06	76,000

Lee, David S.	DIR	01/31/01	Sell	20,000	$64.00	*0*
Dobkin, Robert C.	OFF	01/25/01	Option	10,000	$ 4.06	*1,300,000*
Dobkin, Robert C.	OFF	01/25/01	Sell	10,000	$62.25	*708,212*
Moley, Richard M.	DIR	01/24/01	Option	64,000	$14.63– $15.06	*52,000*
Moley, Richard M.	DIR	01/24/01	Sell	64,000	$62.85	*0*
Zapf, Hans J.	OFF	01/23/01	Sell	5,000	$65.00	*50,000*
McCarthy, Leo T.	DIR	01/23/01	Sell	4,000	$65.00	*28,000*
McCarthy, Leo T.	DIR	01/23/01	Option	4,000	$ 5.41	*189,400*
Cox, Timothy D	OFF	01/23/01	Option	42,000	$ 6.19– $12.97	*169,000*
Cox, Timothy D	VP	01/23/01	Sell	42,000	$64.50	*0*
Davies, Clive B.	PR	01/23/01 to 01/23/01	Option	22,000	$ 6.19	*838,000*
Davies, Clive B.	PR	01/23/01 to 01/23/01	Sell	22,000	$65.00	*636,256*
Dinardo, Louis	OFF	01/19/01	Option	14,000	$ 8.91– $47.25	*0*
Dinardo, Louis	OFF	01/19/01	Sell	14,000	$63.31	*0*

■ COF had eight insider sales in the last three months and no buys. Test results: Fail—Worst case (counts as failing two criteria).

COF Insider Trading Activity

Filer's Name	Title	Trade Date	Trade Type	Shares Traded	Price Range	Shares Held
Schnall, Peter A.	OFF	02/08/01	Sell	20,000	$62.86	*6,527*
Schnall, Peter A.	OFF	02/07/01	Option	15,893	$12.52– $16.25	*63,603*
Morris, Nigel W.	PR	01/30/01	Option	670,000	$ 5.33	*261,608*
Morris, Nigel W.	PR	01/30/01	Sell	670,000	$65.00	*1,781*
Fairbank, Richard D.	CB	01/30/01	Sell	1,114,262	$65.00	*573,289*
Fairbank, Richard D.	CB	01/29/01	Option	1,305,000	$ 5.33	*1,028,027*
Connelly, Marjorie M.	OFF	01/29/01	Sell	3,160	$66.00	*26,732*
Liberson, Dennis H.	OFF	01/26/01	Sell	40,000	$65.30	*94,699*
Connelly, Marjorie M.	OFF	01/25/01	Option	7,600	$12.52	*6*
Liberson, Dennis H.	OFF	01/25/01	Option	109,784	$13.58– $15.49	*898*
Willey, David M.	EX VP	01/25/01	Option	20,997	$16.25	*21,663*
Willey, David M.	EX VP	01/25/01	Option	72,968	$16.25	*24,469*

Willey, David M.	EX VP	01/25/01	Sell	20,997	$64.51	*8,153*
Willey, David M.	EX VP	01/25/01	Sell	72,968	$64.51–$67.25	*50,877*
Finneran, John G. Jr	EX VP	01/24/01	Option	305,400	$12.52–$16.25	*3*
Finneran, John G. Jr	EX VP	01/24/01 to 01/24/01	Sell	305,400	$64.50–$66.65	*27,051*

BOTTOM LINE

Linear Technology Corporation

Tests passed: Price-earnings ratio
Revenue growth in relation to EPS growth
Sales growth
Current quarterly earnings
Quarterly earnings one year ago
Positive earnings growth in current quarter
Earnings growth for past several quarters
EPS growth in current quarter compared with previous three quarters
EPS growth in current quarter compared with historical growth
Earnings persistence
Long-term EPS growth
Total debt-equity ratio

Tests failed: Insider trading (showed sell signal)

Score: 86 percent (12 of 14 passed; insider signal counts as two criteria)

BOTTOM LINE: There is SOME INTEREST in Linear Technology. (Note: Assuming no more sell transactions reported by May 9th, the score will jump to 93 percent and the interest level will jump to STRONG.)

Capital One Financial Corporation

Tests passed: Price-earnings ratio
Revenue growth in relation to EPS growth
Sales growth

Current quarterly earnings
Quarterly earnings one year ago
Positive earnings growth in current quarter
Earnings growth for past several quarters
EPS growth in current quarter compared with previous three quarters
EPS growth in current quarter compared with historical growth
Earnings persistence
Long-term EPS growth

Tests failed: Insider trading (showed sell signal)

Score: 86 percent (12 of 14 passed; insider signal counts as two criteria)

BOTTOM LINE: There is SOME INTEREST in Capital One Financial Corporation (Note: Assuming no more sell transactions reported by May 9th, the score will jump to 93% and the interest level will jump to STRONG.)

ZWEIG'S INVESTING CRITERIA

- Look at the PE ratio.

- Look at revenue growth in relation to EPS growth.

- Look at sales growth.

- Look at current quarterly earnings.

- Look at quarterly earnings one year ago.

- Look for positive earnings growth in the current quarter.

- Look at earnings growth in the past several quarters.

- Compare EPS growth in the current quarter with the prior three quarters.

- Compare EPS growth in the current quarter with historical growth.

- Look for earnings persistence.

- Look at the long-term EPS growth rate.

- Look for no debt or a low debt-equity ratio compared to its industry.

- Look at insider transactions.

- Look at the economy, especially the actions of the Fed. More than most gurus, Zweig, who has a PhD in finance, is a student of the overall economy.

CHAPTER 8

KENNETH L. FISHER

RISK: Using Fisher's original methodology entails a moderate amount of risk because a key component of his approach, the price-sales ratio, goes in and out of favor over time.

TIME HORIZON: Expect to hold for a long time but not indefinitely—typically five to ten years.

EFFORT: Relatively low.

The Bush family has shown how, in politics, a son can follow in the old man's footsteps with both making it to the top. George and George W., one-time oilmen who left the oil business to enter politics, eventually made it all the way to the White House. The comparable family in investment advising is, arguably, the Fisher clan, with Phillip A., the patriarch, and his youngest son, Ken, both making their mark with stock market investors. In fact, Ken has a son who, when in his teens, wrote a book about investing for teenagers. Perhaps the dynasty will continue.

Phil Fisher wrote the highly influential investment books *Common Stocks and Uncommon Profits* (1958) and *Conservative Investors Sleep Well* (1975). He was a father of growth-stock investing, and his strategy involved evaluating management, company policies, and products without getting too involved with financial analysis or other quantitative techniques. It can be said that he was instrumental in making investing a national pastime: *Common Stocks and Uncom-*

mon Profits was the first investment book to make it to the *New York Times* list of best-sellers. So impressed was the young Warren Buffett by this book that he traveled to California to meet Fisher and learn his strategies firsthand. Phil Fisher's writings are still read by investors, and it is not much of a stretch to refer to *Common Stocks and Uncommon Profits* as a "bible" of growth-stock investing.

WHO IS KENNETH L. FISHER?

Closely following in his father's footsteps is Kenneth Lawrence Fisher. Born on November 29, 1950, Fisher has been married to Sherrilynn since 1970, and they have three grown sons. He is a graduate of California State University, Humbolt (now Humbolt State University). It's been reported that Ken Fisher was the only person his father professionally trained. Initially, the younger Fisher wanted a career in forestry but family pressure hooked him into the family business. He ended up with some of both worlds.

First, he started working with his father. In an article in *Millionaire* magazine, Fisher is quoted as saying about his working relationship with the senior Fisher: "It was something I figured out was not going to work very well. When I started with him, he was already 65 years old and, in that regard, was very habitual. At that point in time, he was not interested in changing very much . . . and I am very much of a rebel."

In 1973, Ken Fisher separated from his father professionally and created his own investment company, Fisher Investments Inc., located in Woodside, California, next to a lush forest preserve that is in splendid isolation from the financial world. He has conveniently placed his business and his home in the forest he learned to love as a youngster. Fisher's collection of logging history is the largest non-institutionally-owned library of its kind.

Fisher Investments is a money management firm whose target markets include high net worth individuals, smaller pension funds, and the large pension funds of such organizations as state and airline pension funds. Fisher's company has a workforce of 250.

The rebelliousness of Fisher is seen in the isolated location of his business empire and his attitude toward the investment community. He is quoted in *Millionaire* magazine as follows:

In the financial world, people have a tremendous tendency to think all the same things that everyone else thinks. It's actually very hard to build a corporate culture in the middle of an urban environment where people can, so freely, if you will, get their thoughts contaminated by all the people around them. So by having most of the firm [Fisher Investments] up here, we more easily establish a corporate identity and a corporate culture unique to us—which you can only get with the separation from a typical downtown firm.

Today, Fisher's name is perhaps as well known for his writings as for his investment strategies. Since 1984, he's been a columnist for *Forbes,* where he writes a column on portfolio strategy. His column is now the sixth longest running in the 83-year history of the magazine. In addition, he has authored or coauthored numerous other articles for such publications as *Financial Analysts Journal, Journal of Portfolio Management,* and *Research.*

His first book, *Super Stocks,* which came out in 1984 and is the basis for our analysis of Fisher's strategy, has been a best-seller and, though 17 years old, remains in print. His other books include *The Wall Street Waltz* (1987) and *100 Minds That Made the Market* (1993). He is reportedly working on a book that will cover how he looks at stocks today.

PRICE-SALES RATIO

In his book *Super Stocks,* Fisher made the price-sales ratio (PSR) popular. It is similar to the price-earnings ratio, except that sales are used in place of earnings. PSR, writes Fisher in *Super Stocks,* "is the total market value of a company divided by the last 12 months' corporate sales." To calculate the total value of a company, or its total capitalization, you simply multiply its stock price by the company's total number of shares. It is, in a sense, what you would pay for the company if you wanted to buy the company in its entirety.

If a company's stock is trading at $20 and it has 10 million shares outstanding, its market value or market cap is $20×10 million or $200 million. If its sales last year were $250 million, its PSR is 0.80 ($200 million/$250 million = 0.80). However, if its sales are but $100 million, its PSR is 2.0 ($200 million/$100 million = 2.0).

Here is what Fisher writes in his book about the PSR: "Why should one consider Price Sales Ratios at all? Because they measure popularity relative to business size. Price Sales Ratios are of value because the sales portion of the relationship is inherently more stable than most other variables in the corporate world."

His point: Earnings can be highly volatile, including the earnings of good companies, while sales rarely decline for top-flight businesses. They may be flat, but they generally tend to be less volatile than earnings. Earnings, however, can be moved quickly and dramatically by a wide variety of variables that do not necessarily portend that the company will perform well, such as changes in accounting procedures or in the amount of research and development the company engages in. Wall Street focuses on earnings and abandons companies with earnings troubles, which is why Fisher likes to look at sales. A company with troubled earnings but strong sales is a company Fisher may well want to own.

Fisher's thinking: If a company has a low PSR, even a slight improvement in its margins can produce a big gain in earnings. But companies with high PSRs don't have this leverage.

He goes on to note: "By itself, a PSR shows how much the stock market is willing to pay for a dollar of a company's sales—what the financial community, de facto, thinks of the company—its popularity. A company's worth to a private buyer should be a function of the volume of future sales and average future profit margins—how much future business it will have and how much money it will make doing that business."

He then concludes: "What is the bottom line? To buy stocks successfully, you need to price them based on causes, not results. The causes are business conditions—products with a cost structure allowing for sales. The results flow from there—profits, profit margins, and finally earnings per share." He also doesn't like looking at per-share numbers because he thinks it is important to focus on the overall business, including its size.

Fisher lists three rules regarding PSRs:

Rule 1: Avoid stocks with PSRs greater than 1.5, and never buy those with a PSR in excess of 3. In this case, you are paying $3 for every $1 of sales. He admits stocks with such high PSRs can increase in price but only based on hype, not anything of substance.

Rule 2: Aggressively look for stocks with PSRs of 0.75 or less. Such a PSR means you are paying 75 cents or less for every $1 of sales. These are the stocks you want, and you should hold onto them for a long time, he says.

Rule 3: Once you've bought a stock with a desirable PSR (0.75 or less), sell it when the PSR reaches 3.00 (if you don't want to take much risk) or hold it even longer, to 6.00 or higher, if you are really a risk taker.

Fisher's research indicates the following about PSRs:

- Big companies tend to have lower PSRs than smaller companies (lower PSRs are better).
- Pleasant surprises come mostly from stocks with PSRs of less than 1.
- Disappointments come from stocks with the highest PSRs just prior to reporting the poor results.

The PSR was a new and different concept when Fisher introduced the world to it, but it was only part of what Fisher then advocated. He never suggested simply buying stocks that met quantitative screens. Instead, he advocated combining quantitative screens with qualitative fundamental research to make stock selections. A material part of his book *Super Stocks* was devoted to explaining how to look at a company qualitatively and how to do qualitative research. The point is that small cap value stocks have a potential big hole:

when in trouble, they can fall through the bottom and disappear. Therefore, you can't just screen these stocks but must also do a qualitative analysis to protect against this and be confident the stocks will get over their current troubles. Otherwise, you may put your money in a company that never gets out of trouble, and you'll lose most or all of your investment.

Since the publication of *Super Stocks,* Fisher has refined his PSR strategy to include debt. He found that a low PSR wasn't enough; the company has to be financially solid and not mortgaged to the hilt. He likes companies with current assets at least double current liabilities and total equity at least half of total assets.

STYLE ROTATION STRATEGY

Super Stocks came out ages ago by today's historical standards. It was written in the early 1980s, and since then a lot has happened in terms of the stock market, a lot has happened in terms of investment strategies, and a lot has happened in terms of Fisher's view of how to invest in stocks. He hasn't been sitting around looking at his beloved redwoods; he's been thinking about the best strategies for investing and one of the ways he has updated his approach is with his emphasis on *style.*

Investors, says Fisher, need to focus on style and to rotate their investment holdings to match the popular style of the time. In "Against the Odds," a paper self-published in December 1995, Fisher writes: "Success in the institutional investment business depends on style— what's in and what's out. When a firm's style is 'in,' they are often perceived as the sharpest managers around. When the firm's style is 'out,' they are often perceived as incapable of managing money. Ironically, both interpretations will apply to the same firm over time."

In an article in *Research* (June 1999), Fisher wrote: "Folks think stock-picking is the most important investment skill. Wrong! In most years, financial failure or success is simply a matter of style."

An article in *Wealth Management* (May 1998) sums up Fisher's approach this way:

Fisher Investments contend that portfolio returns depend on three main factors:

1. asset allocation—the division of assets between stocks, bonds and cash;
2. style selection—the selection of equities according to market capitalization and valuation; and
3. stock picking—which adds value within each style category.

Of these three factors, style selection is the single most important factor influencing portfolio returns. According to Fisher Investments, a dollar invested in the best investment style each year will substantially outperform a dollar invested in the best asset class.

Fisher identifies six styles: big cap value, midcap value, small cap value, big cap growth, midcap growth, and small cap growth. Fisher really, though, discusses big and small caps (both value and growth) but doesn't say much about midcaps.

Fisher looks at the top 2,500 market cap stocks listed by Standard & Poor's Compustat Services, which, when Fisher wrote his paper in 1995, included a total of 6,841 companies. Big cap companies, says Fisher, are the top 250 of those in the database, which represented 3.3 percent of the total number of companies but 62 percent of the total market value. The midcap companies are the next 750 companies, which comprise 10 percent of companies and 24.4 percent of the market's value. The final group he looks at is the next 1,500 companies, which represent 19.9 percent of the companies and have 9.9 percent of the market's value. The rest of the companies, over 4,000, are about 67 percent of the total number of companies but have only 3.8 percent of the market's value.

He divides each of the big cap, midcap, and small cap categories into two segments—value and growth—giving him a total of six segments or styles Fisher determines whether a company is a value or growth investment via a proprietary valuation measure he calls "rank," which combines four traditional valuation measures on an equal-weighted basis. The four measures are price-earnings ratio, price-book ratio, price-sales ratio, and dividend yield.

Generally, big growth companies like Microsoft and Intel have strong balance sheets, own the leading share of their market, and, rather than pay dividends, reinvest their earnings to propel the company's growth. Big value companies, such as Citigroup and General Motors, are typically well established, operate in economically sensitive areas, and usually pay a dividend. They are expected to remain industry titans, says Fisher, but are not viewed as having exciting future growth potential. The differences between midsized and small growth and value companies are similar to the differences between large growth and value companies except that they operate on a smaller scale.

According to Fisher, there is a large spread between styles that win and styles that lose. Also, the best four styles at any given time usually outperform the market. It all sounds simple: pick the right style at the right time and you make off like a bandit. True, but nearly impossible to achieve, a shortcoming that Fisher recognizes. His solution is to avoid the two worst styles. By avoiding the two worst styles (which would seem easier to achieve than picking the single best style and avoiding the remaining five worst styles), he earns a return significantly above the market's overall return.

Fisher studied the period of January 1976 to June 1995. He found that from January 1976 to September 1978, small value was the leading style, which produced an annualized return of 42.69 percent. This beat the loser, big growth, by 37.84 percent. The spread of the best four styles over the worst two was 23.25 percent. While the returns of the best four styles were 9.59 percent less than the performance of the single best style—small value, which increased 42.69 percent—they still outperformed the S&P 500 by 23.41 percent.

This is a critical illustration of Fisher's thinking about style: By not trying to find the single best style (which in the period mentioned above was small value and represented only 17 percent of the market) but rather by trying to find the best four styles (which represented 67 percent of the market) and avoiding the two worst styles, the investor will still earn a healthy return and outpace the market, while avoiding the higher risk of trying to perfectly time the buying and selling of a very small segment, namely, the single best style.

From January 1976 to September 1978, the best four styles were small value, small growth, midvalue, and midgrowth.

The next cycle went from October 1978 to December 1981, with Fisher now comparing the styles to the returns of the Wilshire 5000, a broader measure than the S&P 500. In this cycle, the single best style was small growth, followed by midgrowth, small value, and midvalue. There were additional cycles between January 1982 and November 1983; December 1983 and December 1988; January 1989 and November 1991; December 1991 and November 1993; and December 1993 and December 1995.

The bottom line for the entire period studied (January 1976 to June 1995) was:

The annualized return for the best four styles	17.79%
Annualized market return (Wilshire 5000)	14.64%
Premium of best four over the market	3.15%

Fisher notes:

The implications of style rotation's potential are clear. While the best results come from always picking the best style, this strategy is the most aggressive and risky. You might want to call it the Go Big–Go Home strategy. If you're constantly right, you'll go big to the bank. If you miss a couple of times, you'll go home with subpar returns.

Style rotation shows there is a better way. By avoiding the two worst styles and owning the rest, you still obtain very good results which, on average, beat the market by 3.15 percent over the full time period.

To choose between the best styles, Fisher says look at the yield curve spread—the difference between long-term and short-term interest rates. These help you determine whether to buy growth or value stocks. To make a pick, Fisher created a rule he calls the "–1% & –3% Rule." When the yield curve spread moves from a more negative number through minus 1 percent, buy growth. When this happens, says Fisher, the spread will likely shrink until it is either flat or inverted. This prohibits lending and punishes value companies. Hold growth until the spread widens to minus 3 percent and spends at least two consecutive months below minus 2.25 percent, then sell growth and buy value. At minus 3 percent, the spread won't widen much. Instead, writes Fisher, it will shrink again, loosening credit and favoring value.

To choose between big and small cap cycles, Fisher looks overseas. The group of major industrialized countries that get together to talk about trade and economics is called the Group of Seven or G-7. In addition to the United States, it includes Canada, France, Germany, Italy, Japan, and the United Kingdom. Not counting the United States, Fisher calls them the G-6.

When the United States is growing faster than the G-6, small cap shares do better than big cap, and when the G-6 countries' growth is outpacing that of the United States, large cap companies are the better performers.

In his paper, Fisher writes: "Big cap companies derive more revenue and earnings from foreign sources than their small cap brethren. As a company grows and matures, it eventually hits the domestic market limits. With its size and resources, it can afford to look overseas for higher growth potential." He says that foreign revenues as percent of sales is 33.7 percent for big cap companies versus 11.1 percent for small cap companies.

The result is that big cap companies benefit more from overseas growth than small cap ones. If the G-6 is growing faster than the United States, it's the big cap companies that are taking the greatest advantage of this. And when the United States is growing faster, the advantage of the big cap companies is minimized and the small cap companies can take full advantage of domestic growth.

Discerning what is hot and what is not involves more than looking at yield curve spreads. You have to look at what the market favors or, in Fisher's words, "what is your neighbor doing?" First, you want to know what's hot among investors. To determine that, track where institutional money is flowing. He mentions a consulting firm, Eager & Associates, which was merged into William Mercer Associates—<www.wmmercer.com>—which does this tracking. Alternatively, *Investor's Business Daily* also has a daily chart showing the four-month performance trend of big versus small cap and value versus growth funds. Barra Associates—<www.barra.com/research/summary_returns.asp>—shows returns of these styles over periods from one month to ten years of the S&P 500. These are the closest sources publicly available to show you what institutions have been buying over a specific historical period. Once you determine where institutions are placing their money—in growth or value—do the opposite. Says Fisher in his paper: "Whatever is hot by definition has already made its run. To be successful, one must avoid hot areas and invest in other parts of the market."

Fisher in his style analysis has one additional variable, namely, the standard deviation from the mean. He notes: "If you assume capitalism is efficient, and no single style can outperform in the long run, then there must be band widths containing the potential gains of any style over time." When value outperforms by over 1 standard deviation from the mean, then Fisher believes it is time to consider investing in growth stocks. When growth reaches 2 standard deviations from the mean, it is time to consider value stocks.

Here's Fisher's explanation of how he calculates this: "We take a standard style series like the S&P Barra Value & Growth Indexes and determine the average yearly performance differences for any given month back to 1975. After determining the standard deviation of these differences over the whole period, we normalize the series by subtracting the mean difference from the difference at a specific time and then dividing by the standard deviation."

Also, when big caps get to be approximately 1.6 standard deviations from the mean, buy small caps. In this case, he substitutes the Barra Indexes with the S&P 500 for big caps and Ibbotson's small cap return series for small caps. When you use this signal with those of yield curve spread and institutional cash flows, you can predict style changes, he suggests.

In an article he authored in *Research* (June 1999), "Investing With Style," Fisher goes a step further and talks about the fact that many companies that investors think are "big" really aren't.

At the end of 1998, Fisher notes, the average capitalization of the S&P 500 was over $87 billion. But—and this will surprise many—of the 500 stocks in the S&P-500 index, only 35 were larger than the average, including Microsoft, Proctor & Gamble, and Coca-Cola. That left 465 of the 500 smaller than average, including such household names as Campbell Soup ($26.6 billion), Colgate-Palmolive ($21.8 billion), J. C. Penney ($15.1 billion), and Delta Air Lines ($7.5 billion). Fisher's point: Most of the S&P 500 stocks move closer to the moves of the Russell 2000 stocks (average capitalization: $770 million) than to the S&P because they are, in fact, closer in size to the Russell index with its generally smaller companies. That's why in a year like 1998, most larger-company stocks can lag the S&P 500. Just 33 huge stocks provided more than 75 percent of the S&P 500's 1998 performance gain, which was a very strong, 28.5 percent.

The stocks bigger than the market are almost all growth stocks, says Fisher, explaining why value investors lagged badly that year. Generally, Fisher likes larger companies but recognizes that no style works all the time. In the *Research* article, he writes: "A rule of thumb is that big stocks lead in the last two-thirds of a bull market and throughout a bear. Small stocks beat big ones in about the first third of a bull market, and by a mile. So after a bear market, shift to small stocks, and not necessarily tiny ones; remember, $10 billion-sized stocks act very close to the Russell 2000, without the risks and illiquidity [of smaller stocks]."

FISHER TODAY

Fisher has not written a book explaining his strategies since *Super Stocks* appeared in 1984. He has written, of course, many articles and columns but has not put his thoughts in one place nor written a comprehensive model of his current thinking. In our portrayal of Fisher's strategies, we rely heavily on *Super Stocks,* which we believe still has a lot of validity. Also, the book remains in print and is, in fact, available for purchase directly from Fisher's Web site. So we don't feel we are misrepresenting him by covering his approach as described in this book. However, we do want to cover some of his more recent thinking, so we spoke with him personally, and report a general outline of how he looks at investment strategies today. He was not specific enough to provide a step-by-step approach to analysis, yet his thoughts are provocative and worth considering.

Today, Fisher seems to be saying he is proud of his work in *Super Stocks* and with price-sales ratios but adds he is proud in much the same way he is proud of a report he did in the third grade on Guatemala. He now says: "It was a good report back then, but I've completely evolved into something else since then. Every year I learn a bit more about the market and apply it to stay one step ahead of the market. Back then, I was a value investor. I'm not any longer—I believe that believing in just growth or value or large cap or small cap is inherently wrong and anticapitalistic."

He feels that the price-sales ratio (PSR) is now priced into the market, so just focusing on that strategy won't earn you excess returns, and you can get walloped when value and the PSR are out of style. The trick now is to have the tools to tell you when value is in style and to have more tools to tell you when, during the period, value is in style, if PSR is the best value strategy to follow or whether to place more emphasis on other value styles, such as low price-earnings or price-book ratios.

Part of Fisher's evolution over the past couple of decades has been in developing and "morphing" these tools. He focuses especially on using tools or proving investment hypotheses that arouse disbelief in the average person or fly in the face of common knowledge. As an example, he likes to take on the widely accepted wisdom that a market with a high PE is very risky, noting that when you present something to people in terms of height, they naturally think of falling and getting hurt. Maybe they would be better off if they thought in terms of the probability of the ground coming up to hit them in the face while standing on the top of the ladder. That's the type of contrarian thinking Fisher is now engaging in.

He tested out the belief about high PE markets and found that the accepted wisdom was false: high PE markets are *not* riskier than low PE markets because the environment is conducive to positive earnings surprises. Yet nobody believes it. And that makes it a sure bet for Fisher. This is his contrarian streak at work, much like his belief that when you've identified a hot area based on where institutional money is flowing, do the opposite. In fact, the more his readers write in to vehemently reject his research, the more and more certain he is that his strategy is likely to be a winner—and not just any winning strategy but one that is robust and likely to persist for a long time!

Another example of his contrarian views is market timing, which, he notes, is widely viewed as a strategy that doesn't work. But on a recent *Forbes* cruise, he stood up in a panel session and identified himself as a market timer (again, his contrarian nature). He admits, though, that market timing often does not work, and it usually does only if you have something the market doesn't know, something big and powerful that you know is right but other people don't see.

Yet if you look at the fact that Fisher uses tools to tell you when to emphasize value versus growth, small cap versus large cap, as in the styles we discussed above, you can correctly say that he frequently uses timing or at least follows some subrotations within the market.

Where Fisher thinks many investors go wrong is in collecting stocks according to their biases or types they like (i.e., growth, emerging, size, country, technology, etc.). He recommends that in the long term you become a "benchmark agnostic," whereby your choice of a benchmark doesn't make a difference—you go for what will get you to the bench with the lowest volatility. This view is related to our earlier discussion about the fact that most big cap companies aren't all that big and investing in these "small" big caps can provide many of the benefits of investing in small caps while minimizing the risks.

Finally, Fisher believes that today humans know only a small amount about how capital markets function compared with what could eventually be known. We are early in our understanding of financial markets, and steady progress can be made over the years in learning new bits and pieces that add to society's knowledge of markets. And as we progress, we gain a slight edge against competitors.

Fisher sees his firm, which in 2001 managed more than $7 billion, as striving not to be like traditional Wall Street firms but like an early Intel or Wal-Mart, trying to be different to create change that eventually helps society. This goal combines Fisher's qualities as rebel, innovator, contrarian, and lover of capitalism. When we spoke to him, he stressed his sense that everything he did 5, 10, and 15 years ago is now basically obsolete, and his goal is to learn new things that no one knows yet over the next several years to make obsolete everything he is doing now.

In recent years, Fisher's research has evolved toward pioneering portions of behavioral finance theory, and he stresses the intersection of core finance theory with behavioralism. In core finance theory, you cannot achieve excess returns trying to make decisions based on the same information everyone else has. The market is a discounter of all known information. Anyone who tries to outguess markets based on the same information others have will get lucky sometimes but more often will be unlucky, and overall he will do worse than if he had done nothing at all.

To achieve excess returns, according to finance theory, you have to know something other people don't, which isn't easy. For most people it may not be possible. Hence, Fisher aims today to keep doing fundamental capital markets research that lets him learn incremental features about how markets work that others don't and can't understand yet. In the process, he learns and knows something others don't, and that allows him to make excess returns consistent with finance theory. He would tell you that while he is proud of what he did in the past, he manages money differently now and in the future hopes to be managing money differently than the way he does today. Although Fisher isn't critical of the stock examples we use below, he points out that he doesn't own those stocks, wouldn't own them today, and yet might well have owned them 10 or 15 years ago. That means if Fisher is successful in his attempts to continually change and adapt, we may well be able to revisit him some years from now and write a different chapter about him and his evolution.

FISHER'S STRATEGY: STEP-BY-STEP

■ One of the companies we use to illustrate Fisher's strategy is Chicago Rivet & Machine Company, which is based in Naperville, Illinois, and is listed on the American Stock Exchange (stock symbol: CVR). Chicago Rivet makes rivets and rivet-working equipment used in the appliance and automobile industries. (See Figure 8.1.)

FIGURE 8.1	**CHICAGO RIVET & MACHINE (CVR)**	$19.75 as of 3/22/2001

	Year 1	Year 2
Total Net Income (mil.)	$2.7	$3.5
EPS	$2.60	$3.00
Sales (mil.)	$45.4	$49.1
Avg. PE	7.6	7.9
ROE	12.6%	14.6%
Long-Term Debt-Equity	16%	6%
Dividend	$1.07	$1.07
Payout	41%	36%
Shares Outstanding (mil.)	0.967	1

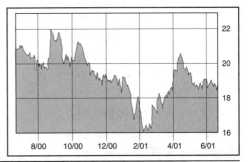

	Year 3	Year 4	Year 5	Year 6	Year 7	Year 8	Year 9	Year 10
Total Net Income (mil.)	$3.4	$3.9	$1.9	$2.2	$1.9	$1.4	$1.0	$0.8
EPS	$2.90	$3.30	$1.66	$1.91	$1.63	$1.19	$0.81	$0.63
Sales (mil.)	$44.9	$44.5	$22.5	$23.7	$23.0	$20.4	$15.8	$15.3
Avg. PE	12.2	8.4	9.9	7.9	9.2	11.2	14.9	17
ROE	15.5%	19%	10.7%	13%	12.1%	9.5%	7.1%	5.8%
Long-Term Debt-Equity	15%	24%	40%	0%	0%	0%	0%	0%
Dividend	$1.12	$0.91	$0.90	$0.88	$0.78	$0.65	$0.60	$0.68
Payout	39%	28%	54%	46%	48%	55%	74%	108%
Shares Outstanding (mil.)	1.2	1.2	1.2	1.2	1.2	1.2	1.2	1.2

	Q1	Q2	Q3	Q4	Q5	Q6	Q7	Q8
EPS	$0.58	$0.28	$0.89	$0.81	$0.87	$0.42	$1.00	$0.82
Revenue (mil.)	$10.3	$10.3	$12.4	$12.4	$11.9	$11.7	$12.9	$12.9

	Market Cap (mil.)	TTM Sales (mil.)	Relative Strength	EPS Growth (3-yr. avg.)	Revenue Growth (TTM)	Current Ratio	Insider Buy-Sells (3 months)
CVR	$20.0	$45.4	57	−7.6%	−13.5%	3.3	0/0
Small Tools & Accessories	$1,071.9	$1,425.1	73	16.7%	4.9%	3.0	

	PEG	PE	Projected PE	PS	Price-Book	Price-Cash Flow	Free Cash Flow/Share
CVR	0.36	7.70	250.0	0.43	0.91	3.90	$1.65
Small Tools & Accessories	1.20	13.63	10.64	0.82	2.09	6.99	

	Yield	Profit Margin (TTM)	ROE (TTM)	Total Debt-Equity	Long-Term Debt-Equity	Insider Ownership	Institutional Ownership
CVR	3.6%	5.9%	12.6%	18%	18%	16%	10.1%
Small Tools & Accessories	2.0%	6.4%	17.0%	44%	44%		

Recent Balance Sheet Items ($ millions)		**Financial Statement Trends**			
			Recent 12 mo.	FY1	FY2
Cash	2.3				
Current Assets	16.8	Inventory/Sales	16%	15%	15%
Total Assets	31.2	AR to Sales	11%	10%	15%
Current Liabilities	4.8	R&D to Sales	0%	0%	0%
Long-Term Debt	3.4				
Total Debt	5.2				
Equity	21.5				

The second company we use as an example is Hansen Natural Corporation, of Corona, California (stock symbol: HANS). The company is a drink manufacturer that makes a line of natural sodas, fruit juices, smoothies, and "functional" drinks designed to provide people with energy, stamina, and stress relief. Its products are distributed primarily in the western part of the country. (See Figure 8.2.)

Price-sales ratio (PSR).   The prospective company should have a low PSR ratio. For companies with very large market caps, buy if their PSR is 0.4 or less and sell when their PSR reaches between 2 and 3.

For noncyclical and technology stocks:

$$\text{If PSR} \leqq 0.75$$

Fisher says to aggressively seek noncyclical companies with PSRs of less than 0.75. Noncyclical (nonsmokestack) companies with PSRs below 0.75 are tremendous values and should be sought.

$$\text{If PSR is between } >0.75 \text{ and } \leqq 1.5$$

Fisher says companies with PSRs falling between 0.75 and 1.5 are good values.

$$\text{If PSR is between } >1.5 \text{ and } \leqq 3.0$$

If PSR is in this range, Fisher says to hold the stock but not buy more. Noncyclical companies with PSRs greater than 1.5 and less than 3.0 should not be purchased. If you are currently holding such a stock, keep holding it.

$$\text{If PSR} >3$$

Fisher says never buy a stock when it reaches a PSR this high. If you own it, sell, unless you are willing to take on additional risk; it all depends on your aversion or willingness to assume additional risk. If you are willing to take on more risk, consider holding the stock until the PSR ratio reaches 6.

FIGURE 8.2	HANSEN NATURAL CORP (HANS)	$3.38 as of 3/22/2001

	Year 1	Year 2
Total Net Income (mil.)	$3.9	$4.5
EPS	$0.38	$0.43
Sales (mil.)	$79.7	$72.3
Avg. PE	12.3	10.5
ROE	17.6%	24.2%
Long-Term Debt-Equity	44%	5%
Dividend	–	–
Payout	0%	0%
Shares Outstanding (mil.)	9.7	10

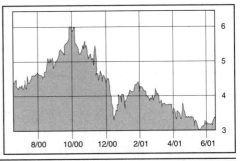

	Year 3	Year 4	Year 5	Year 6	Year 7	Year 8	Year 9	Year 10
Total Net Income (mil.)	$3.6	$1.3	$0.4	$(1.3)	$(1.4)	$0.6	–	–
EPS	$0.34	$0.13	$0.04	$(0.15)	$(0.15)	$0.07	–	–
Sales (mil.)	$53.9	$43.1	$35.6	$34.0	$28.8	$23.7	$9.6	$0.4
Avg. PE	12.2	14.1	41.4	n/a	n/a	48.2	n/a	n/a
ROE	25.9%	13%	4.5%	n/a	n/a	5.7%	0%	0%
Long-Term Debt-Equity	9%	34%	0%	48%	41%	37%	50%	0%
Dividend	–	–	–	–	–	–	–	–
Payout	0%	0%	0%	0%	0%	0%	0%	0%
Shares Outstanding (mil.)	9.9	9.1	9.1	9.1	9.1	8.8	7.6	7.2

	Q1	Q2	Q3	Q4	Q5	Q6	Q7	Q8
EPS	$0.02	$0.13	$0.16	$0.07	$0.08	$0.14	$0.09	$0.06
Revenue (mil.)	$22.7	$22.7	$16.0	$17.4	$20.5	$19.1	$15.2	$12.1

	Market Cap (mil.)	TTM Sales (mil.)	Relative Strength	EPS Growth (3-yr. avg.)	Revenue Growth (TTM)	Current Ratio	Insider Buy-Sells (3 months)
HANS	$34.0	$79.7	48	43%	5.8%	2.7	0/1
Beverages-Soft Drinks	$21,214.7	$7,905.7	68	15.9%	10.3%	1.3	

	PEG	PE	Projected PE	PS	Price-Book	Price-Cash Flow	Free Cash Flow/Share
HANS	0.07	8.90	8.67	0.42	1.54	10.50	$0.10
Beverages-Soft Drinks	2.94	26.96	20.91	1.82	7.16	16.05	

	Yield	Profit Margin (TTM)	ROE (TTM)	Total Debt-Equity	Long-Term Debt-Equity	Insider Ownership	Institutional Ownership
HANS	0.0%	5%	17.8%	40%	40%	44%	8.9%
Beverages-Soft Drinks	1.2%	7.9%	17.3%	92%	92%		

Recent Balance Sheet Items ($ millions)		Financial Statement Trends			
Cash	0.1		Recent 12 mo.	FY1	FY2
Current Assets	19.3	Inventory/Sales	14%	14%	14%
Total Assets	38.7	AR to Sales	12%	12%	7%
Current Liabilities	5.7	R&D to Sales	0%	0%	0%
Long-Term Debt	9.7				
Total Debt	10.0				
Equity	22.1				

For cyclicals:

If PSR ≦ 0.4

Fisher says to aggressively seek cyclical companies with PSRs equal to or less than 0.4. These are tremendous values and should be sought.

If PSR is between >0.4 and ≦ 0.8

Stocks within this range are considered good values for cyclical industries.

If PSR > 0.8

Fisher says cyclical companies with PSRs greater than 0.8 are poor values and should not be purchased. If you own any, consider selling them.

■ Chicago Rivet is a noncyclical whose price-sales ratio is 0.43 based on trailing 12-month sales. Fisher considers a PSR of less than 0.75 a tremendous value, and CVR meets this best-case scenario. Test results: Pass.

Like Chicago Rivet, Hansen is a noncyclical with a PSR of 0.42, again meeting Fisher's best-case scenario. Test results: Pass.

Price-Sales Ratio (PSR) for Noncyclical and Technology Stocks

1. > 3	Fail
2. > 1.5 and ≦ 3.0	Pass—OK
3. > 0.75 and ≦ 1.50	Pass
4. ≦ 0.75	Pass—Best case

Price-Sales Ratio (PSR) for Cyclicals

1. > 0.8	Fail
2. > 0.4 and ≦ 0.8	Pass
3. ≦ 0.4	Pass—Best case

Total debt-equity ratio (DE).   This variable does not apply to financial companies. For other companies, less debt equals less risk, according to this methodology.

DE ratio = 0 is exceptional, thus passing the test.

A DE ratio between >0 and ≦ 0.4 means the DE ratio is less than 40 percent. Fisher approves of a DE ratio of this size because he believes that less debt translates into less risk.

If the DE > 40%, the ratio is too high and fails the test.

■ Chicago Rivet's debt-equity ratio is a modest 18 percent, less than half the maximum Fisher is willing to accept. Test results: Pass.
Hansen's DE is 40 percent, which just squeaks by Fisher's maximum of 40 percent. Test results: Pass.

Total Debt-Equity Ratio (DE)
1. > 40%   Fail
2. ≦ 40%   Pass

Price-research ratio (PRR).   Companies in the technology and medical sectors should be looked at differently from other companies because of their need for research. For companies in these industries, Fisher likes to look at the PRR ratio. However, if the company is neither a technology nor medical company, do not put much emphasis on this particular variable.

$$PRR = Market\ cap/RD12M$$
(research and development over the past 12 months)

$$PRR < 5$$

To Fisher, technology and medical companies with PRRs below 5 are rare and should be purchased. Usually, these companies are snapped up by larger companies because they are very undervalued.

$$PRR\ between \geqq 5\ and \leqq 10$$

To Fisher, companies with PRRs between 5 and 10 are bargains and should be purchased. Fisher would actively pursue such stocks.

$$PRR\ between >10\ and \leqq 15$$

To Fisher, companies with PRRs between 10 and 15 are borderline. Fisher advises investors to actively seek those between 5 and 10. PRR indicates how much a market values a company's R&D.

PRR >15

To Fisher, companies with PRRs greater than 15 should never be purchased because they either spend too little on R&D or are extremely overvalued.

Price-Research Ratio (PRR)

1.	> 15%	Fail
2.	> 10 and ≦ 15%	Pass—OK
3.	≧ 5% and ≦ 10%	Pass
4.	< 5%	Pass—Best case

■ Chicago Rivet is neither a technology nor medical company and therefore this criterion does not apply.

Likewise, Hansen is not a technology company nor a medical one, thus making this criterion largely irrelevant when analyzing the company.

Preliminary grade: Because both Chicago Rivet and Hansen pass all of Fisher's tests to this point, his preliminary grade for both is: SOME INTEREST.

But are they *Super Stocks?* It turns out the answer is no for Chicago Rivet and yes for Hansen.

Four additional criteria require passing results for a stock to be considered a "Super Stock." To be a Super Stock, Fisher requires an even lower PSR than the criterion above.

Price-sales ratio (PS) for Super Stocks

For noncyclical and technology stocks:

Fisher says to aggressively seek noncyclical companies with PS ratios less than 0.75.

For cyclical stocks:

$$\text{If} \leq 0.4$$

Fisher says to aggressively seek cyclical companies with PS ratios less than 0.4. Cyclical companies with price-sales ratios below 0.4 are tremendous values.

■ Chicago Rivet's PS ratio of 0.43 is very strong (less than 0.75). Test results: Pass.
    Hansen's PS ratio of 0.42 is likewise very strong. Test results: Pass.

Price-Sales Ratio (PS) for Noncyclical and Technology Super Stocks
1. > 0.75 Fail
2. ≤ 0.75 Pass

Price-Sales Ratio (PS) for Cyclical Super Stocks
1. > 0.4 Fail
2. ≤ 0.4 Pass

Inflation-adjusted EPS growth.   To be a Super Stock, a company needs to have an inflation-adjusted long-term EPS growth rate greater than 15 percent.

$$\text{If (EPS growth rate} - \text{Inflation rate)} \geq 15\%: \text{Pass}$$

Inflation-Adjusted EPS Growth
1. $< 15\%$ Fail
2. $\geq 15\%$ Pass

■ Chicago Rivet's long-term EPS growth rate was −7.6 percent, and inflation is currently running about 2% for an inflation-adjusted growth rate of −9.6%, badly failing Fisher's 15 percent minimum. Test results: Fail.
    Hansen's results are stronger than those of Chicago Rivet's. Hansen's inflation-adjusted EPS growth rate is a strong 45 percent. Test results: Pass.

Free cash flow per share.   To be a Super Stock, a company needs positive free cash flow or for a company currently operating with a negative free cash flow, it should have enough cash available to sustain three years of negative free cash flow. This is based on the premise that companies that run out of cash will soon be out of business.

If > 0: Pass

■ Chicago Rivet has a positive amount of free cash flow per share of $1.65. Test results: Pass.

Hansen's free cash flow per share comes in at 10 cents. Test results: Pass.

Free Cash Flow per Share

1. If free cash flow per share $\leq$ 0   Fail
2. > 0   Pass

Three-year average net profit margin.   To be a Super Stock, a company needs to have an average net profit margin of 5 percent or greater over a three-year period.

If this margin $\geq$ 5%: Pass

■ Net profit margin is found by dividing the total net income for the year by sales for the year. For the last three years this came to 5.9 percent, 7.1 percent, and 7.6 percent, which averages to 6.7 percent. Chicago Rivet's average net profit margin of 6.7 percent exceeds Fisher's minimum of 5 percent. Test results: Pass.

Hansen's net profit margin for each of the last three years was 5.0 percent, 6.2 percent, and 6.7 percent. Therefore, Hansen's average net profit margin is 6.0 percent, which is above Fisher's minimum of 5 percent. Test results: Pass.

Three-Year Average Net Profit Margin

1. < 5%   Fail
2. $\geq$ 5%   Pass

BOTTOM LINE

Chicago Rivet

Tests passed:	Price-sales ratio
	Total debt-equity ratio
	Price-sales ratio for Super Stocks
	Free cash flow per share
	Three-year average net profit margin
Tests failed:	Inflation-adjusted EPS growth
Tests neutral:	Price-research ratio
Score:	83 percent (5 of 6 passed; 1 neutral)

BOTTOM LINE: There is SOME INTEREST in Chicago Rivet.

Hansen Natural

Tests passed:	Price-sales ratio
	Total debt-equity ratio
	Price-sales for Super Stocks
	Inflation-adjusted EPS growth
	Free cash flow per share
	Three-year average net profit margin
Tests neutral:	Price-research ratio
Score:	100 percent (6 of 6 passed; 1 neutral)

BOTTOM LINE: There is STRONG INTEREST in Hansen Natural.

FISHER'S KEY INVESTING CRITERIA

■ Look for a low price-sales ratio.

■ Look for a low debt-equity ratio.

■ Look at the price-research ratio.

If the company passes all of these criteria, Fisher has some interest. He would then continue testing to see if the company was a Super Stock.

Is the Company a Super Stock?

- Look for a low price-sales ratio under .75 for Super Stocks.

- Look at the inflation-adjusted EPS growth rate greater than 15 percent.

- Look at free cash flow per share to be positive.

- Look at the three-year average net profit margin to be greater than 5 percent.

If the company passes all of the Super Stock criteria, Fisher has a significant interest in the stock. The most important variable here is the price-sales ratio.

CHAPTER 9

JAMES O'SHAUGHNESSY

WHICH INVESTORS MIGHT BEST USE **James O'Shaughnessy?**

RISK: Moderate.

TIME HORIZON: To get the full benefit of O'Shaughnessy's approach, you need to use his strategy for a number of years through a full cycle of the market. But he rebalances his portfolio at the beginning of each year, so in that respect his time horizon is one year.

EFFORT: Lots of paperwork, but not much research. In fact, if you use his Netfolio.com Web site to buy and sell, much of the effort is eliminated as the Web site does the work.

NOTE: To get the statistical properties his studies were based on, you need to invest in a sizable number of stocks—25 to 50. Thus, O'Shaughnessy is perhaps better suited to the larger investor.

James P. O'Shaughnessy made his name as the author of *What Works on Wall Street: A Guide to the Best-Performing Investment Strategies of All Time* (McGraw-Hill, 1996). The book is based on his testing Standard & Poor's huge Compustat database. "This is the *first* [O'Shaughnessy's emphasis] time the historical S&P Compustat data have been released in their entirety to an outside researcher. *What Works on Wall Street* includes 43 years of results for Wall Street's most popular investment strategies," writes O'Shaughnessy in his book.

O'Shaughnessy started his own mutual funds and sold them during spring 2000 to Hennessey, <www.hennessey-funds.com>. Afterwards, he started an innovative Web site, Netfolio.com, that allowed investors, in effect, to create their own personalized mutual funds. It has since ceased operations.

The performance of his funds, both under his management and for about a year after he sold them (the investment strategy of the funds remains the same under the new management), has been quite good. His growth fund (now called Hennessey Cornerstone Growth), from inception on November 1, 1996, to March 31, 2001, had an annualized average rate of return of 17.1 percent, which is better than the performance of the S&P 500 and the average fund in its category.

O'Shaughnessy's value fund (now called Hennessey Cornerstone Value) hasn't done quite so well (not surprising, as value investing generally hasn't done well the past few years), but it has beat its benchmark funds and the S&P 500 from 1998 to the first quarter of 2001.

WHO IS JAMES O'SHAUGHNESSY?

Born and raised in Saint Paul, Minnesota, he studied international economics and business diplomacy at the School of Foreign Service of Georgetown University and has a degree in economics from the University of Minnesota. O'Shaughnessy lives in Greenwich, Connecticut, with his wife and three children.

According to Netfolio, O'Shaughnessy became the first person to hold a patent on an investment strategy with a November 2, 1999, issuance of United States Patent number 5,978,778 entitled *Automated Strategies For Investment Management.*

O'SHAUGHNESSY'S GENERAL APPROACH TO INVESTING

O'Shaughnessy was interviewed by Chris Farrell on Farrell's public television program *Right on the Money!,* which was taped in September 2000 and aired on various PBS stations in early 2001. He made some important points on this program.

One was—and it is a good one—that investors need a strategy they consistently follow. Never pick stocks based on what you read in the newspaper or hear touted on television or by your brother-in-law. Says O'Shaughnessy: "Never, never [buy a stock] on a whim. On Wall Street, an ounce of emotion equals a pound of facts, and you don't want your emotions making your decisions for you. Never buy what cousin Vinnie tells you to. Never buy something because you like the sound of the story. Buy it based on the underlying strategy that says now's the time to own this stock."

He goes on to note: "If you have an underlying strategy for picking stocks, you can do very well with stocks. But if you follow a hit-and-miss, gotta hunch, bet-a-bunch-type approach, you're probably not going to do very well if you go on a stock-by-stock basis."

This point is, of course, consistent with our book, *The Market Gurus*. We believe all investors should have a strategy that is right for them, and we have presented nine different strategies, describing them in detail so that readers have enough information to choose—and implement—a strategy that fits their needs. One could even argue that it is more important to *have* a strategy than the strategy one uses. Even a mediocre strategy that an investor sticks with through a whole market cycle, especially including the grim years when the media is writing articles making a persuasive case that the strategy is dead, can be more profitable than the investing done by someone without any strategy at all.

O'Shaughnessy is also a firm believer in the buy-and-hold approach to investing. You buy a good investment and hold on to it for the long term. He backs up this opinion with a University of California study done by Terry O'Deane that found an inverse correlation between how much you trade and your total return. Says O'Shaughnessy: "It's irrefutable. The more you trade, the less well you do. Have a strategy and then let that strategy work."

He notes: "You've gotta buy stocks based on the idea that you can hold them to stick with [your] strategy over long periods of time. If you're not, you're gambling. And you know if you want to gamble . . . go to Vegas. You'll have more fun."

O'Shaughnessy, unlike other buy-and-hold strategists, such as Warren Buffett, doesn't generally hold stocks for years and years.

He usually holds for a year and then "rebalances" his portfolio. By doing so, he keeps his investments in tune with his strategies and answers the question, When do I sell? He sells at the beginning of each year when he rebalances his portfolio. "If you don't clean your garage out once a year, it's going to fill up with a lot of junk. The same is true of your portfolio," he says.

In *What Works on Wall Street*, O'Shaughnessy notes there are two primary approaches to investing in the stock market—active and passive—and that most investors use the active approach, which he believes is doomed to fail. Using an analysis by Morningstar, the Chicago-based company that tracks the mutual fund industry, he says that during the years 1991 to 1995, among actively managed funds with at least a ten-year track record, between 16 percent (in year 1992) and 26 percent (in year 1994) of the funds beat the S&P 500. That means that during this five-year period the best year found only 26 percent of fund managers beating the market.

However, O'Shaughnessy believes research can identify strategies that can consistently produce higher-than-average returns, and of course he has identified those strategies.

Dow 10

The Dow 10, also known as the Dogs of the Dow, is a simple strategy that O'Shaughnessy has promoted (though he didn't invent it). It consists of investing an equal amount of money in the 10 stocks of the Down Jones Industrial Average (DJIA) that have the highest dividend yields; the DJIA has a total of 30 stocks. At the end of 12 months, you rebalance the portfolio by selling those 10 stocks, which are no longer among the 10 highest yielding Dow stocks, and replacing them with those that are. The yield is the expected dividend payments for the year ahead divided by the stock's price.

There are several advantages to using this strategy. In an article in the *Washington Post* (11 January 1998), O'Shaughnessy is quoted as saying he tested this strategy going back to 1952 and found it produced an average annual return of 17 percent compared with 13.8 percent for the Standard & Poor's 500-stock index.

In the seven years prior to the *Post* article's publication in 1998, the Dow 10 returned 24.8 percent compared with 21.4 percent for the full Dow and 20.5 percent for the S&P. In fact, notes the article, the Dow 10 has beaten the full Dow in 20 of the past 27 years.

If a company has good profits but is out of favor with the market, it may be a bargain, and this would be reflected in its yield. A low stock price and a strong dividend produce a high yield. That, in theory, is why this strategy works.

As with most things in life, simple things are not always as simple as they may appear at first blush. Sometimes, a high yield is not the sign of a stock that's a bargain but of a company that's in some trouble. In *What Works on Wall Street,* O'Shaughnessy reported that when one invested in the 50 highest yielding stocks each year, the returns were *lower* than returns of the market as a whole and with higher risk. Presumably, the reason is that many of these stocks had low prices because the companies were poor performers. In other words, the low stock prices were justified and were not examples of bargain stocks.

But by sticking to companies that make up the Dow Jones Industrial Average, one largely eliminates the chances of investing in a struggling company whose stock has been justifiably battered. The companies that make up the Dow are generally large, sound businesses with long track records of success. The likelihood of their falling apart is considerably less than the likelihood of high-yielding companies in general falling apart. A high-yielding Dow stock, therefore, is more likely to be a bargain than a dog.

STRATEGIES FROM
WHAT WORKS ON WALL STREET

In the 1996 best-seller *What Works on Wall Street,* O'Shaughnessy back-tested 44 years of stock market data from the comprehensive Standard & Poor's Compustat database to find out which strategies work and which don't. To the surprise of many, he concluded that price-earnings ratios aren't the best indicator of a stock's value and that small company stocks, contrary to popular wisdom, don't as a group have an edge on large company stocks.

Based on his research, O'Shaughnessy developed two key investment strategies: "Cornerstone Growth" and "Cornerstone Value," which he used in his Cornerstone mutual funds that have since been sold. Cornerstone Growth favors companies with a market capitalization of at least $150 million and a price-sales ratio below 1.5. To avoid outright dogs, the strategy also looks for companies with persistent earnings growth and shares that have been among the market's best performers over the prior 12 months. This strategy makes sense for value-oriented growth investors who have the patience and personality to stick with a purely quantitative investment approach.

Cornerstone Value looks for large companies with strong sales and cash flows, and from those meeting that profile (as measured by four relevant criteria), it selects the 50 with the highest dividend yield. The strategy is appropriate for income-oriented investors.

One of O'Shaughnessy's most notable findings is that of all the analysis ratios one can use, the price-sales ratio is the best and the one most likely to point to future winners. Also, a company that's a winner tends to continue winning, while losers tend to continue along their path. That's why he is a fan of using relative strength. He also says combining growth and value strategies is a good way to go. O'Shaughnessy likes mixing and matching a number of variables when analyzing stocks, rather than relying on but one. He even says: "Using several factors dramatically improves long-term performance." An example would be to invest in "All Stocks" with the best appreciation from last year and with low price-earnings multiples.

Another of his favorites is better-known companies; for example, though not a big proponent of price-earnings ratios, he thinks they have some value if you are willing to stick to better-known companies with low price-earnings ratios. He also claims "you can do four times as well as the S&P 500 by concentrating on large, well-known stocks with high dividend yields." Along the same line, he downplays the widely publicized strategy of buying small capitalization (and therefore little-known) stocks by saying those who make money using small cap strategies do so because they invest in companies too small for most investors (market cap of less than $25 million). They are too small because they lack trading liquidity.

In some ways, O'Shaughnessy downplays a stock's recent history; for example, keep away from stocks currently in favor, judged by those with high price-earnings ratios. And, what happened last year in terms of a company's profit growth says nothing about how well it will do in the future. However, O'Shaughnessy does say companies that performed poorly last year should not be bought today; a recent poor performance doesn't mean they are about to turn around.

In his book, which is filled with tables and statistics, O'Shaughnessy has identified a number of interesting results. Before we mention them, we need to briefly describe his major variables. The universe of the stocks he studied came from Standard & Poor's Compustat Active and Research Database from 1950 to 1994. He divides the stocks of interest into two categories, which he calls "All Stocks" and "Large Stocks." He defines All Stocks as "those with market capitalizations in excess of a deflated $150 million." The $150 million threshold he wrote about was in 1996 dollars. In inflation-adjusted dollars as of late 2001, the equivalent is about $170 million. Stocks meeting this criterion at that time represented about 37 percent of the stocks traded on the major U.S. exchanges.

Why the $150 million cutoff? Writes O'Shaughnessy: "I chose the $150 million value after consulting a trader at a large Wall Street brokerage who felt it was the minimum necessary if he was investing $100 million in 50 stocks in 1995. I use this figure to avoid tiny stocks and focus only on those stocks that a professional investor could buy without running into liquidity problems."

The second group of stocks to which he refers repeatedly includes larger, better-known companies he calls "Large Stocks." His definition of Large Stocks is "those with a market capitalization greater than the Compustat database average." In late 2001, a stock had to have a market value of at least $1.9 billion to qualify, and these stocks represented only about 11 percent of the market. O'Shaughnessy's analysis includes a basket of 50 stocks (such as the 50 lowest price-book value stocks among "All Stocks") and are rebalanced annually to maintain their desired characteristic, such as having the lowest price-book ratios.

O'Shaughnessy finds that All Stocks generally outperform Large Stocks. He is also in favor of companies with low price-book value ratios and finds that All Stocks with low price-book value ratios— here he's again combining variables—do better than comparable Large Stocks. Another positive sign is when a company has low price-cash flow ratios. These companies tend to do better than those with such high ratios. Pay attention to price-sales ratios (PSRs). Among All Stocks, the best performing are those with low PSRs. Likewise, among Large Stocks, you will do better by focusing on those with low PSRs.

The adage that higher risk equals higher rewards doesn't always hold true for O'Shaughnessy. He warns his readers to pay attention to risk. Among the risks he says go unrewarded are high price-earnings, price-book value, price-cash flow, and price-sales ratios.

Let's now discuss how you can use O'Shaughnessy's strategy.

O'SHAUGHNESSY'S CORNERSTONE GROWTH STRATEGY: STEP-BY-STEP

■ NVR Inc. (stock symbol: NVR) is a residential builder that operates mainly along the East Coast from its headquarters in McLean, Virginia. (See Figure 9.1.) The stock trades on the American Stock Exchange.

AdvancePCS Inc. (stock symbol: ADVP) provides management services for health plans, which have a total membership of 75 million, about 25 percent of all the people in the country. (See Figure 9.2.) Headquarters for AdvancePCS is in Irving, Texas.

Market cap.   The first requirement of the Cornerstone Growth Strategy is that the company have a market capitalization of at least $150 million. This requirement screens out companies too illiquid for most investors but still provides enough leeway to include small growth companies.

■ NVR's market cap is $1.4 billion, far in excess of O'Shaughnessy's $150 million minimum. Test results: Pass.

FIGURE 9.1	NVR INC (NVR)	$167.75 as of 4/10/2001

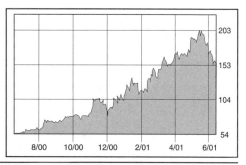

	Year 1	Year 2
Total Net Income (mil.)	$158.2	$108.9
EPS	$14.98	$9.01
Sales (mil.)	$2,317.2	$2,006.6
Avg. PE	5.7	5.3
ROE	63.9%	54.3%
Long-Term Debt-Equity	49%	76%
Dividend	–	–
Payout	0%	0%
Shares Outstanding (mil.)		

	Year 3	Year 4	Year 5	Year 6	Year 7	Year 8	Year 9	Year 10
Total Net Income (mil.)	$66.1	$28.9	$25.8	$16.4	$9.0			
EPS	$4.97	$2.18	$1.70	$1.06	$0.53			
Sales (mil.)	$1,559.8	$1,154.0	$1,069.9	$869.1	$846.0			
Avg. PE	7.2	9.5	6.5	8	15.4			
ROE	39.9%	20%	17%	11.2%	7.4%			
Long-Term Debt-Equity	93%	97%	133%	219%	232%			
Dividend	–	–	–	–	–			
Payout	0%	0%	0%	0%	0%			
Shares Outstanding (mil.)								

	Q1	Q2	Q3	Q4	Q5	Q6	Q7	Q8
EPS	$4.95	$3.97	$3.37	$2.72	$2.19	$2.52	$2.26	$2.02
Revenue (mil.)	$630.0	$617.7	$558.5	$490.6	$561.3	$523.6	$509.0	$446.5

	Market Cap (mil.)	TTM Sales (mil.)	Relative Strength	EPS Growth (3-yr. avg.)	Revenue Growth (TTM)	Current Ratio	Insider Buy-Sells (3 months)
NVR	$1,404.0	$2,317.2	98	90%	12.2%	1.2	0/4
Residential Construction	$1,410.5	$3,108.9	90	45.678%	29.623%	3.9	

	PEG	PE	Projected PE	PS	Price-Book	Price-Cash Flow
NVR	0.13	11.20	9.7	0.61	5.67	6.00
Residential Construction	0.23	8.42	7.5	0.582		6.7

	Yield	Profit Margin (TTM)	ROE (TTM)	Total Debt-Equity	Long-Term Debt-Equity	Insider Ownership	Institutional Ownership
NVR	0%	6.8%	63.9%	49%	49%	15%	55.2%
Residential Construction	1%	0.7%	29.9%	108%	108%		

Recent Balance Sheet Items ($ millions)		Financial Statement Trends			
Cash	137.7		Recent 12 mo.	FY1	FY2
Current Assets	479.1	Inventory/Sales	14%	14%	16%
Total Assets	841.3	AR to Sales	0.3%	0.3%	0.1%
Current Liabilities	420.1	R&D to Sales	0%	0%	0%
Long-Term Debt	841.3				
Total Debt	173.7				
Equity	247.5				

| FIGURE 9.2 | ADVANCEPCS INC (ADVP) | $54 as of 4/10/2001 |

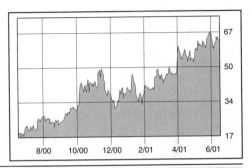

	Year 1	Year 2
Total Net Income (mil.)	$20.6	$12.7
EPS	$0.85	$0.55
Sales (mil.)	$1,968.4	$774.8
Avg. PE	27	38.5
ROE	20.7%	18.4%
Long-Term Debt-Equity	50%	72%
Dividend	–	–
Payout	0%	0%
Shares Outstanding (mil.)		

	Year 3	Year 4	Year 5	Year 6	Year 7	Year 8	Year 9	Year 10
Total Net Income (mil.)	$7.9	$3.1	n/a					
EPS	$0.35	$0.18	$0.03					
Sales (mil.)	$476.7	251.6	125.3					
Avg. PE	36.9	45.8	n/a					
ROE	15.6%	7.3%	n/a					
Long-Term Debt-Equity	0%	0%	n/a					
Dividend	–	–	–					
Payout	0%	0%	0%					
Shares Outstanding (mil.)								

	Q1	Q2	Q3	Q4	Q5	Q6	Q7	Q8
EPS	$0.16	$0.22	$0.25	$0.24	$0.22	$0.21	$0.19	$0.15
Revenue (mil.)	$2,916.5	$619.7	$594.3	$564.0	$553.4	$434.7	$416.3	$229.2

	Market Cap (mil.)	TTM Sales (mil.)	Relative Strength	EPS Growth (3-yr. avg.)	Revenue Growth (TTM)	Current Ratio	Insider Buy-Sells (3 months)
ADVP	$1,617.0	$4,694.5	99	68%	427%	0.8	0/2
Specialized Health Services	$2,186.6	$2,553.9	86	–5%	62%	2.21	

	PEG	PE	Projected PE	PS	Price-Book	Price-Cash Flow
ADVP	0.9	62.1	65.9	0.3	4.1	24.3
Specialized Health Services	0.9	35.6	23.9	1.6		35.6

	Yield	Profit Margin (TTM)	ROE (TTM)	Total Debt-Equity	Long-Term Debt-Equity	Insider Ownership	Institutional Ownership
ADVP	0.0%	50%	6.3%	203%	203%	23%	63%
Specialized Health Services	0.1%	5%	11.8%	86%	86%		

Recent Balance Sheet Items ($ millions)		Financial Statement Trends			
			Recent 12 mo.	FY1	FY2
Cash	141.4				
Current Assets	1,203.2	Inventory/Sales	1%	0%	1%
Total Assets	3,142.6	AR to Sales	22%	10%	14%
Current Liabilities	1,548.5	R&D to Sales	0%	0%	0%
Long-Term Debt	798.6				
Total Debt	810.0				
Equity	393.9				

AdvancePCS, with its market cap of $1.6 billion, is also well beyond O'Shaughnessy's minimum. Test results: Pass.

Market Cap

1. < $150 million   Fail
2. ≧ $150 million   Pass

EPS persistence. The Cornerstone Growth methodology requires looking for companies that show persistent earnings growth without regard to magnitude. To fulfill this requirement, a company's earnings per share before extraordinary items must increase each year for a five-year period. We look at the current EPS before extraordinary items.

If EPS Y1 > EPS Y2 > EPS Y3 > EPS Y4 > EPS Y5: Pass

■ NVR's earnings per share for the last five years (from earliest to the most recent fiscal year) were: $1.70, $2.18, $4.97, $9.01, and $14.98. Its EPS has grown every year. Test results: Pass.

AdvancePCS's earnings per share for the last five years (from earliest to the most recent fiscal year) were: $0.03, $0.18, $0.35, $0.55, and $0.85. Its EPS has increased each year. Test results: Pass.

EPS Persistence

1. EPS Y1 > EPS Y2 > EPS Y3 > EPS Y4 > EPS Y5   Pass
2. All others   Fail

Price-sales ratio (PS). The price-sales ratio should be below 1.5:1.0. This value criterion, coupled with the growth criterion, identifies growth stocks that are still cheap to buy.

■ NVR's price-sales ratio is 0.6, well below O'Shaughnessy's goal of below 1.5. Test results: Pass.

AdvancePCS has a PS even lower than NVR's: 0.3. Test results: Pass.

Price-Sales Ratio (PS)

1. > 1.5   Fail
2. ≦ 1.5   Pass

Relative strength (RS). O'Shaughnessy looks for companies within the top 50 in the market with respect to relative strength ranking. This final criterion for the Cornerstone Growth Strategy requires the relative strength of the company to be among the top 50 of the stocks screened using the previous criteria. This gives you the opportunity to buy the growth stocks you are searching for just as the market is embracing them.

If the stock passes this criterion and the other three criteria, it passes overall.

If the stock is in the top 50 but misses even one of the other criteria, it would fail overall.

If the stock fails this criterion, it would fail, no matter that it passed the other three.

■ NVR's relative strength is 98, placing it in the top 50 of the stocks screened using the other criteria. Test results: Pass.

AdvancePCS's relative strength is 99, which is in the top 50. Test results: Pass.

Top 50 Companies Ranked by Relative Strength

1. In top 50 of the stocks screened using the other criteria	Pass
2. Not in top 50	Fail

BOTTOM LINE

Using Cornerstone Growth Strategy

NVR

Tests passed:	Market cap
	Earnings per share persistence
	Price-sales ratio
	Relative strength
Tests failed:	None
Score:	100 percent

BOTTOM LINE: There is STRONG INTEREST in NVR.

AdvancePCS

Tests passed:	Market cap
	Earnings per share persistence
	Price-sales ratio
	Relative strength
Test failed:	None
Score:	100 percent

BOTTOM LINE: There is STRONG INTEREST in AdvancePCS.

O'SHAUGHNESSY'S CORNERSTONE VALUE STRATEGY

■ General Motors Corporation (stock symbol: GM) is among the world's best-known companies. (See Figure 9.3.) Detroit-based, General Motors is the world's largest automaker. Its car lines include Buick, Cadillac, Chevrolet, Pontiac, Saab, Saturn, Opel, and Vauxhall as well as Oldsmobile (which is being discontinued). It also makes GMC trucks and has a variety of nonautomotive businesses in addition to minority holdings in other automakers, including Fuji Heavy Industries (Subaru) and Fiat Auto (Alfa Romeo, Fiat).

E.I. duPont de Nemours (commonly called DuPont) is the largest U.S. chemical company. (See Figure 9.4.) Its products include Lycra, Dacron, herbicides, pesticides, Kevlar, seeds, and food ingredients. Based in Wilmington, Delaware, DuPont's stock symbol is: DD.

Market cap.   The Cornerstone Value strategy requires looking for large, well-known companies whose market cap is greater than $1 billion. O'Shaughnessy thinks it's useless to apply a PE screen for stocks with market caps less than $1 billion.

The Cornerstone Value Strategy does not include utility stocks because these stocks would dominate the list that the methodology requires looking for as a result of their typically high yields.

■ General Motors' market cap of $28.4 billion far exceeds O'Shaughnessy's minimum of $150 million. Test results: Pass.

DuPont's market cap is even higher: $42.4 billion. Test results: Pass.

FIGURE 9.3   GENERAL MOTORS CORP (GM) $51.85 as of 3/30/2001

	Year 1	Year 2
Total Net Income (mil.)	$4,452	$5,576
EPS	$6.68	$7.12
Sales (mil.)	$184,632	$176,558
Avg. PE	10.7	9.6
ROE	14.8%	29.1%
Long-Term Debt-Equity	472%	628%
Dividend	$2.00	$1.68
Payout	29.9%	23.6%
Shares Outstanding (mil.)	548.2	619.4

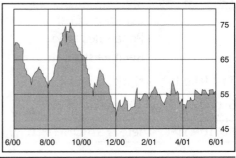

	Year 3	Year 4	Year 5	Year 6	Year 7	Year 8	Year 9	Year 10
Total Net Income (mil.)	$2,956	$6,698	$4,953	$6,932	$5,658	$2,466	$–2,621	$–4,992
EPS	$3.48	$7.18	$5.02	$5.89	$3.90	$1.41	$–4.05	$–7.39
Sales (mil.)	$161,315	$166,445	$158,015	$163,861	$150,591	$133,622	$128,533	$119,753
Avg. PE	14.8	7.2	8.7	6.4	10.9	26.4	NE	NE
ROE	19.7%	38.3%	21.2%	29.7%	44.1%	44.1%	NE	NE
Long-Term Debt-Equity	351%	24%	163%	157%	292%	611%	667%	284%
Dividend	$1.26	$1.68	$1.32	$0.93	$0.66	$0.66	$1.17	$1.32
Payout	36.2%	23.4%	26.3%	15.8%	16.9%	46.8%	NE	NE
Shares Outstanding (mil.)	785.4	831.5	907.2	902.9	904.5	863.4	847.5	744.6

	Q1	Q2	Q3	Q4	Q5	Q6	Q7	Q8
EPS	$–0.69	$1.55	$2.93	$2.79	$1.56	$1.11	$2.46	$2.55
Revenue (mil.)	$46,431	$42,690	$48,743	$44,471	$53,124	$40,473	$42,832	$40,129

	Market Cap (mil.)	TTM Sales (mil.)	Relative Strength	EPS Growth (3-yr. avg.)	Revenue Growth (TTM)	Current Ratio	Insider Buy-Sells (3 months)
GM	$28,441	$184,632	41	–2.25%	–12.8%	3.3	0/5
Major Auto Mfgs.	$41,805	$100,376	54	–7.3%	–3.2%	2.1	

	PEG	PE	Projected PE	PS	Price-Book	Price-Cash Flow	Free Cash Flow/Share
GM	NE	7.8	15.8	0.4	2.45	4.1	$6.14
Major Auto Mfgs.	2.0	19.7	17.0	0.48	1.65	4.6	

	Yield	Profit Margin (TTM)	ROE (TTM)	Total Debt-Equity	Long-Term Debt-Equity	Insider Ownership	Institutional Ownership
GM	3.9%	2.4%	14.8%	472%	472%	1%	57.1%
Major Auto Mfgs.	3.1%	0.7%	9.3%	233%	233%		

Recent Balance Sheet Items ($ millions)		Financial Statement Trends			
Cash	10,284		Recent 12 mo.	FY1	FY2
Current Assets	208,920	Inventory/Sales	5.9%	5.9%	6.0%
Total Assets	303,100	AR to Sales	73.1%	73.1%	69.2%
Current Liabilities	63,156	R&D to Sales	–	–	–
Long-Term Debt	142,447				
Total Debt	144,655				
Equity	30,175				

Market Cap
1. < $1 billion   Fail
2. ≧ $1 billion   Pass

Cash flow per share.   O'Shaughnessy seeks companies whose cash flow per share exceeds the average cash flow per share for the market. The second criterion of the Cornerstone Value Strategy requires that the company exhibit strong cash flows. Companies with strong cash flows are typically the value-oriented investments that this strategy looks for. The company's cash flow per share must be greater than the mean of the market cash flow per share.

If cash flow per share > Market average of
cash flow per share: Pass

■ The mean of the market's cash flow per share is $1.29, while GM's cash flow per share is $7.23. Test results: Pass.
   DuPont's cash flow per share of $1.48 is just above the market's $1.29. Test results: Pass.

Cash Flow per Share
1. > Market Avg.   Pass
2. ≦ Market Avg.   Fail

Shares outstanding.   O'Shaughnessy seeks companies whose outstanding shares exceed the market's average of outstanding shares. Those using this particular strategy therefore look for companies whose total number of outstanding shares exceed the market average. These are the better known and heavily traded companies.

If shares outstanding > Market average
of shares outstanding: Pass

■ The market's average total number of shares outstanding is 91 million; GM has 1.4 billion. Test results: Pass.
   DuPont has 1 billion shares outstanding. Test results: Pass.

FIGURE 9.4   **DUPONT E I DE NEMOURS CO (DD)** $40.70 as of 3/30/2001

	Year 1	Year 2
Total Net Income (mil.)	$2,314	$219
EPS	$2.19	$0.19
Sales (mil.)	$28,268	$26,918
Avg. PE	25.6	336.5
ROE	17.7%	60.8%
Long-Term Debt-Equity	51%	52%
Dividend	$1.40	$1.40
Payout	64%	20%
Shares Outstanding (mil.)	1,043	1,052

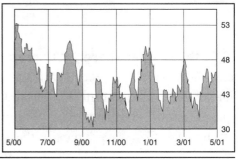

	Year 3	Year 4	Year 5	Year 6	Year 7	Year 8	Year 9	Year 10
Total Net Income (mil.)	$1,648	$2,405	$3,636	$3,293	$2,727	$566	$975	$1,403
EPS	$1.43	$2.08	$3.18	$2.77	$1.98	$0.41	$0.72	$1.04
Sales (mil.)	$24,767	$24,767	$39,730	$38,349	$36,508	$34,042	$33,145	$34,692
Avg. PE	47.6	27.9	13.3	11.3	14.0	60.0	34.2	19.9
ROE	34.1%	21.8%	34.7%	40.2%	21.7%	5.1%	8.5%	8.5%
Long-Term Debt-Equity	33%	54%	49%	69%	51%	59%	62%	39%
Dividend	$1.37	$1.23	$1.12	$1.02	$0.91	$0.88	$0.87	$0.84
Payout	34%	59%	35%	37%	46%	215%	121%	81%
Shares Outstanding (mil.)	1,126	1,153	1,127	1,158	1,362	1,355	1,350	1,342

	Q1	Q2	Q3	Q4	Q5	Q6	Q7	Q8
EPS	$0.25	$0.53	$0.65	$0.76	−$1.36	$7.15	$0.80	$0.58
Revenue (mil.)	$6,316	$6,445	$7,914	$7,593	$7,140	$6,481	$6,994	$6,295

	Market Cap (mil.)	TTM Sales (mil.)	Relative Strength	EPS Growth (3-yr. avg.)	Revenue Growth (TTM)	Current Ratio	Insider Buy-Sells (3 months)
DD	$42,438	$28,268	49	1.7%	−11.5%	1.3	0/2
Chemicals-Major Diversifd	$12,801	$11,572	63	−11.0%	38%	1.36	

	PEG	PE	Projected PE	PS	Price-Book	Price-Cash Flow	Free Cash Flow/Share
DD	3.6	18.6	17.2	1.5	3.25	12.1	1.57
Chemicals-Major Diversifd	4.8	17.4	15.4	1.27	2.89	30.5	

	Yield	Profit Margin (TTM)	ROE (TTM)	Total Debt-Equity	Long-Term Debt-Equity	Insider Ownership	Institutional Ownership
DD	3.4%	8.2%	17.7%	74%	51%	2%	52.2%
Chemicals-Major Diversifd	2.9%	7.7%	20.1%	103%	76%		

Recent Balance Sheet Items ($ millions)		Financial Statement Trends			
Cash	1,540		Recent 12 mo.	FY1	FY2
Current Assets	11,656	Inventory/Sales	16.5%	16.5%	18.8%
Total Assets	39,426	AR to Sales	16.1%	16.1%	19.8%
Current Liabilities	9,255	R&D to Sales	6.3%	5.7%	4.9%
Long-Term Debt	6,658				
Total Debt	9,875				
Equity	13,299				

Shares Outstanding

1. > Market Avg.   Pass
2. ≦ Market Avg.   Fail

Trailing 12-month sales. O'Shaughnessy seeks companies whose trailing 12-month sales per share exceed the market's average trailing 12-month sales per share. A company's trailing 12-month sales per share is required to be 1.5 times greater than the mean of the market's trailing 12-month sales per share.

If sales > 1.5 × Market average of sales (TTM): Pass

■ GM's trailing 12-month sales of $184.6 billion is far more than O'Shaughnessy's minimum of 1.5 times greater than the mean of the market's, which is $1.8 billion. Test results: Pass.

DuPont's trailing 12-month sales came to $28.3 billion. Test results: Pass.

Trailing 12-Months Sales

1. > Market Avg.   Pass
2. ≦ Market Avg.   Fail

Dividends. The final step in the Cornerstone Value strategy is to select the 50 companies from the group of market leaders (those passing the previous four criteria) that have the highest dividend yield. Under his value method, O'Shaughnessy looks for the top 50 dividend payers.

If the company is among the 50 companies with the highest dividend yield, then the stock passes.

■ GM's dividend yield of 3.9 percent puts the company among the top 50 dividend payers passing the previous four criteria. Test results: Pass.

DuPont's 3.4 percent dividend yield also puts it among the top 50 dividend payers passing the previous four criteria. Test results: Pass.

Dividends

1. In top 50 passing the previous criteria   Pass
2. Not in top 50   Fail

BOTTOM LINE

Using Cornerstone Value Strategy

General Motors

Tests passed: Market cap
                 Cash flow per share
                 Shares outstanding
                 Trailing 12-month sales
                 Dividends

Tests failed: None

Score: 100 percent (5 of 5 passed)

BOTTOM LINE: There is STRONG INTEREST in General Motors.

DuPont

Tests passed: Market cap
                 Cash flow per share
                 Shares outstanding
                 Trailing 12-months sales
                 Dividends

Tests failed: None

Score: 100 percent (5 of 5 passed)

BOTTOM LINE: There is STRONG INTEREST in DuPont.

O'SHAUGHNESSY'S GROWTH-INVESTING CRITERIA

- Look at the market cap.

- Look for EPS persistence.

- Look for a low price-sales ratio (PS).

- Look for a high relative strength (RS).

In order for O'Shaughnessy to have any interest at all, the stock has to pass all of these criteria. With this methodology, it is an all-or-none type of thing. There is no "some" level of interest.

O'SHAUGHNESSY'S VALUE-INVESTING CRITERIA

- Look at the market cap.

- Look at cash flow per share.

- Look at shares outstanding.

- Look at trailing 12-month sales.

- Look at the dividends.

In order for O'Shaughnessy to have any interest at all, the stock has to pass all of these criteria. With this methodology, it is an all-or-none type of thing. Again, there is no "some" level of interest.

CHAPTER 10 THE FAMOUS RATIOS

E veryone talks about the price-earnings ratio (PE)—the most frequently mentioned financial ratio. But how do the experts apply a PE in making a decision about a stock? What is a high PE or a low PE? Did you know some experts don't use this ratio at all or only apply it to companies above a certain size. What subtleties do the experts use in applying this and other ratios? Here, for the first time that we are aware of, is a comparison between experts showing how they apply the PE and other famous ratios.

PRICE-EARNINGS RATIO (PE)

Peter Lynch
Types of stocks: growth. Investment time horizon: one–ten years

For companies with sales greater than $1 billion, Lynch likes to see the PE remaining below 40. Companies this large could have a difficult time maintaining a growth rate high enough to support a PE above this threshold, which is why Lynch has this limit. The limit, however, does not apply to smaller companies.

If a company's PE < 40, it passes this test.

If sales < $1 billion, this limit doesn't apply.

To calculate, use the most recent stock price per share and use the TTM (trailing 12 months) earnings per share. Use the earnings before extraordinary items. If earnings are negative or 0, the ratio is not used.

Benjamin Graham
Types of stocks: long-term value. Investment time horizon: two–three years

The PE must be "moderate," which Graham defines as not greater than 15, which will give you the defensive types of stocks that are searched for under this strategy.

If a company's PE < 15, then it passes this test.

Martin Zweig
Types of stocks: growth. Investment time horizon: one–five years

The PE of a company must be greater than 5 to eliminate weak companies, according to Zweig, but to minimize risk, not more than three times the current market PE and never greater than 43.

If a company's PE > 5 but < 3 times the market's PE (based on the S&P) and always < 43, then it passes this test.

David Dreman
Types of stocks: value. Investment time horizon: two–eight years

The PE of a company should be in the bottom 20 percent of the overall market. Dreman defines the market as the 1,700 largest stocks (which at the current time means having a market cap of at least $800 million) because these generally have considerable financial strength and therefore carry less risk than smaller stocks. In studies conducted from 1970 to 1996, Dreman showed that low PE stocks had an average annual return of 19 percent versus 15.3 percent for the market. His studies also proved that low PE stocks have greater returns than high PE stocks (they returned 12.3 percent), all while taking on less risk.

If a company's PE ≦ Bottom 20% of the largest 1,700 market cap stocks, then it passes this test.

James O'Shaughnessy
Types of stocks: value and growth. Investment time horizon: one year and then he recalculates his portfolio, but investors need to follow his strategy for at least five years.

For stocks with a market cap under $1 billion, a low PE is insignificant and should not be used to value these smaller companies. A group of stocks selected on this basis alone returned about 13.5 percent per year in past tests. A stock should have one of the lowest 50 PEs among the stocks with a market cap over $1 billion. Or stated in O'Shaughnessy's terms, the stock should have one of the 50 highest earnings-price ratios (EP). O'Shaughnessy uses EP because it avoids ever having to divide a number by 0 or by a very small number, such as when earnings are 0 or almost 0, which would drive the PE sky-high and distort averages based on this number.

William O'Neil
Types of stocks: fast growth. Investment time horizon: three months to one year

O'Neil maintains that earnings growth is far more important than the price-earnings ratio. During their significant growth periods, many of the leading performance stocks increased their PEs from an average of 20 to 30 (before their big increase) to 45 to 70 or more. If you were not willing to pay an average of 20 to 30 times earnings for growth stocks during the 33-year period through 1985, you automatically eliminated most of the best investments available.

Price-Earnings Ratio (PE)

Guru	General Rule
Lynch	Applies only if sales $\geqq$ $1 billion, then PE $<$ 40
Graham	PE $<$ 15
Zweig	PE $>$ 5 but $<$ 3 $\times$ PE of S&P (or $<$ 43)
Dreman	If market cap $>$ $0.8 billion, then PE $\leqq$ Bottom 20% of market
O'Shaughnessy	Market cap $>$ $1 billion, PE lowest 50 in market

Gurus Who Do Not Use the Price-Earnings Ratio

Buffett
Fisher
The Motley Fool
O'Neil

PRICE-EARNINGS GROWTH (PEG)

Peter Lynch

The investor should examine the PE relative to the growth rate for a company, as this is a quick way of determining the fairness of the price. Divide the PE by the historical EPS growth rate.

PEG:

$\leqq$ 0.5 is an excellent buy.

> 0.5 and $\leqq$ 0.999 makes it attractive.

> 0.999 and $\leqq$ 1.5 is considered OK.

> 1.5 and $\leqq$ 1.8 is fairly unattractive but still somewhat acceptable.

> 1.8 makes it a poor buy.

The Motley Fool

The Fool ratio (price-earnings growth or PEG) is an extremely important aspect of the Fool's analysis, as it determines if a stock is reasonably priced. Divide the PE by the projected EPS growth rate over the next two to three years, if available. If not, use shorter-term growth rate projections or a historical growth rate.

PEG:

< 0 bad—means earnings are negative

≥ 0 and ≤ 0.5. If the company has attractive fundamentals and its Fool ratio is 0.5 or less, the shares should be purchased. These high-quality companies often wind up as the biggest winners.

> 0.5 and ≤ 0.65. If the company's Fool ratio is between 0.50 and 0.65, the company demonstrates excellence in its fundamentals and has soundly beat earnings estimates. Only then should you consider purchasing the stock.

> 0.65 and ≤ 1.0. Consider holding the shares when the company's Fool ratio is greater than 0.65, but initial purchases are not advisable in this range.

> 1.00 and ≤ 1.30. Consider selling the shares when the company's Fool ratio is between 1.00 and 1.30. This is considered high, so if you are holding the stock, you should consider selling it.

> 1.30 and ≤ 1.70. Consider shorting shares when the company's Fool ratio is greater than 1.30.

> 1.70; the Fool ratio is excessively high. It would be very risky to buy shares in this range.

Price-Earnings Growth Ratio (PEG)

Guru	General Rule
Lynch (PE divided by the historical EPS growth rate)	≤ 1.8 (but ≤ 1.0 is more attractive)
The Motley Fool (PE divided by projected EPS growth rate)	≤ 0.65

Gurus Who Do Not Use the PEG

Buffett
Dreman
Fisher
Graham
O'Neil
O'Shaughnessy
Zweig

PRICE-SALES RATIO (PS)

Kenneth L. Fisher

Noncyclical or technology companies:

PS: $\leqq$ 0.75. Noncyclical (nonsmokestack) companies with price-sales ratios below 0.75 are tremendous values and should be sought.

> 0.75 and $\leqq$ 1.5. Noncyclical (nonsmokestack) companies with price-sales ratios between .75 and 1.50 are good values and are considered attractive.

> 1.5 and < 3.0. Noncyclical companies with price-sales ratios greater than 1.5 and less than 3.0 should not be purchased. If you are currently holding such stocks, the PSR is OK, but if you are thinking about purchasing any, the stocks would fail this methodology's first test.

> 3. Noncyclical stocks with price-sales ratios >3 should never be purchased; however, they can be held depending on the investor's risk aversion. If you are currently holding such stocks, think about selling if risk bothers you. If risk does not overly bother you, hold until the PS approaches 6.

Cyclical (smokestack) companies:

$\leqq$ 0.4. Cyclical companies with price-sales ratios below 0.4 are tremendous values and should be sought. They would be considered extremely attractive.

> 0.4 and $\leqq$ 0.8. Smokestack (cyclical) companies with a price-sales ratio between 0.4 and 0.8 represent good values, according to this methodology.

> 0.8. Smokestack (cyclical) companies with price-sales ratios greater than 0.8 are considered very unattractive and should be sold, according to this methodology.

James O'Shaughnessy

Using one factor alone—that is, a company with one of the lowest 50 PSs in the market—you would see one of the best stocks you could choose. Selecting a portfolio of such stocks resulted in a compound return of 16 percent per year with a Sharpe ratio of 52 (which is very good) based on historical tests that O'Shaughnessy ran.

Guru	Price-Sales Ratio (PS) General Rule
Fisher	$\leq$ 1.5 for noncyclicals; $\leq$ 0.8 for cyclicals
O'Shaughnessy	Lowest 50 in market (for stocks with market cap > $150 million)

Gurus Who Do Not Use the Price-Sales Ratio

Buffett
Dreman
Graham
Lynch
The Motley Fool
O'Neil
Zweig

YIELD

David Dreman

The company in question should have a yield that is high and can be maintained or increased. We consider high to be at least 1 percent higher than the average yield on the Dow Jones 30 industrials.

James O'Shaughnessy

He's interested if a company's yield is one of the top 50 (for non-utility stocks) and its market cap is more than $1 billion. Investing in these stocks using this one factor resulted in a compound return of about 13 percent per year with the largest loss of 16.5 percent (for a single year) based on past studies. This is less riskier than the market. Remember, though, that any one stock in this category could have an unusually high risk of default. Yields can be quite high before a dividend is cut at some weaker companies, so you need to own a large number (at least 50) of these stocks to get this overall safety and return.

This methodology mentions nothing about applying a high-yield strategy to utility stocks (electric, water, gas), so use another strategy to evaluate these types of stocks.

Peter Lynch

He only applies this to slow growers (e.g., large companies growing less than 10 percent per year). He wants the yield to be at least that of the S&P 500 or 3 percent, whichever is higher.

	Yield
Guru	**General Rule**
Dreman	$\geqq$ Dow yield + 1%
O'Shaughnessy	Mkt cap $\geqq$ $1 billion; yield one of top 50 in market; only nonutility stocks
Lynch	For slow growers > S&P 500 yield and > 3%
Graham	Wants dividends to have been paid each year for at least 20 years

Gurus Who Do Not Use Yield as a Criterion

Buffett
Fisher
The Motley Fool
O'Neil
Zweig

DEBT-EQUITY RATIO (DE)

This ratio is not applied to financial companies, where it is usually not found.

Peter Lynch

This ratio is one quick way to determine the financial strength of a company. For total debt-equity ratio:

0%, exceptionally low

> 0 and $< 10\%$: the ratio is excellent

$\geq 10\%$ and $< 30\%$: DE is acceptable

$\geq 30\%$ and $< 50\%$: normal

$> 50\%$ and $< 80\%$: mediocre

$\geq 80\%$: may be bad depending on the industry; if the company is in communications services or utilities, this is normal. Otherwise, it is bad.

Benjamin Graham

Long-term debt must not exceed net current assets (current assets less current liabilities). Companies that meet this criterion display an attribute of a financially secure organization. Long-term debt has to be less than current assets minus current liabilities. Another way of saying this is that a company's cash plus inventory must be high enough to cover its entire short-term and long-term debt, which is quite a stringent criterion.

David Dreman

The company must have a low total debt-equity ratio, which indicates a strong balance sheet. The ratio should not be greater than 20 percent.

Kenneth L. Fisher

Less debt equals less risk according to Fisher's methodology. Total DE should be less than or equal to 40 percent.

The Motley Fool

The superior companies that you are looking for don't need to borrow money in order to grow. The ratio of long-term debt to equity should be 0, but up to 5 percent is allowed.

Warren Buffett

Buffett wants to see that long-term debt can be repaid with no more than two years of a company's net earnings.

Debt-Equity Ratio (DE)

Guru	General Rule
Lynch	Total DE < 80%, although exceptions made for utilities and phone companies
Graham	Long-term DE < Net current assets
Dreman	Total DE $\leqq$ 20%
Fisher	Total DE $\leqq$ 40%
The Motley Fool	Long-term DE $\leqq$ 5%
Buffett	Long-term debt < 2× last year's earnings
O'Neil	Long-term debt $\leqq$ 2% or long-term debt declining each year over past 3 years
Zweig	Total DE < industry average

Gurus Who Do Not Use the Debt-Equity Ratio

O'Shaughnessy

EPS GROWTH

Peter Lynch—Fast Growers

For growth companies, Lynch prefers companies with a track record of growing between 20 to 50 percent per year (20 to 25 percent is ideal) for the past two to five years. This allows the company enough time to establish if it has a winning formula for growing.

Annualized EPS growth rate:

$\geq$ 15% and $<$ 20%: this rate considered OK.

$\geq$ 20% and $\leq$ 25%: this rate considered very good as it is large but small enough to sustain.

$>$ 25% and $\leq$ 35%: this EPS growth rate is acceptable.

$>$ 35% and $\leq$ 50%: this would cause some concern. Higher growth rates are hard to sustain over long periods of time.

$>$ 50%: this rate causes concern. Higher growth rates are hard to sustain over long periods of time. A company with an EPS growth rate this high has further to fall if its EPS growth rate comes down.

Benjamin Graham

Companies must increase their EPS by at least 30 percent over a ten-year period. When you have data for just five years, you can adjust this requirement to a 15 percent gain over the five-year period. This gives you companies that are financially secure and have proven themselves over time. Graham averages the beginning and ending three years to eliminate distortions caused by bad years. This is not a very stringent requirement, but just make sure there is some growth bias in the company.

Martin Zweig

The long-term earnings growth rate must be at least 15 percent per year.

David Dreman

Dreman's strategy likes those companies whose growth rate is greater than that of the S&P 500.

EPS growth > SP 500 EPS growth estimated for 5 years

James O'Shaughnessy

O'Shaughnessy believes you should not make investment decisions based on this variable or at least not heavily weight its value.

Kenneth L. Fisher

This criterion is used to identify a perfect "Super Stock." Super Stock companies should be able to increase their future EPS at a long-term rate averaging approximately 15 to 20 percent per year more than the rate of inflation, which can be funded without requiring long-term debt. That is,

EPS growth − Inflation rate should be $\geq$ 15%.

The Motley Fool

Companies must demonstrate both revenue and net income growth of at least 25 percent when compared with the previous year. These growth rates give you the dynamic companies you are looking for. Compare Q5 to Q1 growth:

$$EPQ\_Q5 \; / \; EPS\_Q1 \geqq 25\%$$

William O'Neil

O'Neil's methodology relies on looking for average five-year (or three-year) annual earnings growth above 18 percent but higher than 25 percent is preferable. The higher the better.

	EPS Growth
Guru	**General Rule**
Lynch	$\geqq$ 20% and $\leqq$ 50%
Graham	$\geqq$ 15% (total) over a 5-year period
Zweig	$\geqq$ 15%
Dreman	> S&P 5-year estimated EPS growth
Fisher	(EPS growth rate – Inflation rate) $\geqq$ 15%
The Motley Fool	$\geqq$ 25%
O'Neil	$\geqq$ 18%

Gurus Who Do Not Use EPS Growth as a Criterion

Buffett
O'Shaughnessy

REVENUE GROWTH

Martin Zweig

Revenue growth must not be substantially less than earnings growth. For earnings to continue to grow over time, they must be supported by a comparable or better sales growth rate and not just by cost cutting or other nonsales measures. Revenue growth must be greather than or equal to ($0.85 \times$ EPS growth).

The Motley Fool

Companies must demonstrate both revenue and net income growth of at least 25 percent when compared with the previous year. These growth rates give you the dynamic companies that you are looking for. Compare Q5 to Q1 growth.

Guru	Revenue Growth General Rule
Zweig	$\geq (0.85 \times$ EPS growth)
The Motley Fool	$\geq 25\%$ and EPS growth $\geq 25\%$

Gurus Who Do Not Use Revenue Growth

Buffett
Dreman
Fisher
Graham
Lynch
O'Neil
O'Shaughnessy

CASH AND CASH EQUIVALENTS

The Motley Fool

The Fool wants to see cash as high as possible. If the cash-sales ratio is greater than or equal to 20 percent, or the cash per share-current price ratio is greater than or equal to 12.5 percent, the company has lots of cash—and that's good.

Peter Lynch

Though not a requirement, Lynch likes to see a lot of net cash per share. He defines net cash as cash and marketable securities less long-term debt. 30 percent net cash good, 40 percent attractive, and 50 percent net cash—mortgage your house.

Gurus Who Do Not Use Cash and Cash Equivalents

Buffett
Dreman
Fisher
Graham
O'Neil
O'Shaughnessy
Zweig

FREE CASH FLOW

Peter Lynch

The ratio of free cash flow per share-price, though not a requirement, is considered a bonus if it is high. A positive cash flow (the higher the better) separates a wonderfully reliable investment from a shaky one. A terrific ratio (which is rare) would be above 35 percent. Companies that rely heavily on capital spending are not looked on favorably.

Kenneth L. Fisher

Look for companies with a positive free cash flow per share. However, if a company is running a negative free cash flow, it needs to have cash on hand to cover three years of expected negative free cash flow.

The Motley Fool

Look for companies with a positive free cash flow per share. A positive cash flow is typically used for internal expansion, acquisitions, dividend payments, and the like. A company that generates rather than consumes cash is in much better shape to fund such activities on its own rather than needing to borrow funds.

Free Cash Flow

Guru	General Rule
Lynch	Cash per share-Current price $\geq$ 35%; not a requirement
Fisher	Free cash per share > 0
The Motley Fool	Free cash per share > 0

Gurus Who Do Not Use Free Cash Flow

Buffett
Dreman
Graham
O'Neil
O'Shaughnessy
Zweig

RELATIVE STRENGTH

James O'Shaughnessy

High relative strength can help any of the other strategies. The final criterion for O'Shaughnessy's Cornerstone Growth Strategy, which returned 18.2 percent annually between 1954 and 1994, requires that the relative strength of the company be among the top 50 of the stocks screened. This provides the opportunity to buy growth stocks just as the market is embracing them.

The Motley Fool

The investor must look at the relative strength of the company in question. Companies whose relative strength is 90 or above (that is, the company outperforms 90 percent or more of the market for the past year) are considered attractive. Companies whose prices have been rising much more quickly than the market tend to keep rising.

William O'Neil

Relative strength is one of the most important criteria in O'Neil's methodology. It compares a security's price performance with that of all the other stocks in the market over the same one-year period. Stocks with relative strengths above 80 are acceptable, but the hottest prospects have strengths over 90. These companies are likely to be the best merchandise over the next several months, as stocks that have been outperforming continue to outperform the broad market.

	Relative Strength (RS)
Guru	**General Rule**
O'Shaughnessy	One of top 50 RS of any screen of companies that you are looking at
The Motley Fool	≧ 90
O'Neil	≧ 80

Gurus Who Do Not Use Relative Strength

Buffett
Dreman
Fisher
Graham
Lynch
Zweig

RETURN ON EQUITY (ROE)

Warren Buffett

Buffett requires at least 15 percent ROE. This return should have been made consistently over the past ten years and needs to be predictably above this for the foreseeable future.

William O'Neil

O'Neil wants to see at least 17 percent.

David Dreman

Dreman wants to see ROE as the top one-third of stocks from among the top 1,500 stocks as measured by capitalization. Currently, that ROE is about 10 percent.

Gurus Who Do Not Use Return on Equity

Fisher
Graham
Lynch
The Motley Fool
O'Shaughnessy
Zweig

CONCLUSION

W e have designed *The Market Gurus* to be an introduction to stock market investing; a source of information about the investors we profile that would be of interest to even the most seasoned Wall Street watchers; and a practical guide to investing.

Within its pages are easy-to-understand, step-by-step breakdowns of the gurus' investment strategies. We don't think it an exaggeration to say this is the first book to isolate the essential pieces of great investment strategies in such a practical, simple way. We hope you have enjoyed reading our book and have gotten from it a broad exposure to some of the savviest thinking you can find on Wall Street today.

In a sense, this book is a complement to our Web site Validea.com. Our site provides a wealth of statistics and real-time data about virtually all widely traded public companies. But it's hard to put on a Web site detailed information about the history and philosophy of some of the greatest stock market thinkers of all time, as we have done in *The Market Gurus*. Validea.com has a wonderful amount of detail but by its very nature can't really provide a broad, panoramic view of investing in general and our nine gurus in particular. Cyberspace has its limitations.

On the other hand, it's impossible to have in one book timely information—financial, market, and economic—that changes day by day, even minute by minute. All investors need such information, but only the Internet is capable of collecting it and widely disseminating it in real time.

Now that you have finished *The Market Gurus,* we invite you to visit Validea.com. Use the book and Web site together. Think of them as you would a stock price and its earnings per share—you need them both to gain a complete picture.

INDEX

THE MARKET GURUS

FOR SPECIAL DISCOUNTS on 20 or more copies of *The Market Gurus: Stock Investing Strategies You Can Use from Wall Street's Best,* please call Dearborn Trade Special Sales at 800-621-9621, extension 4455.